# Environmental Mediation

AF705328

Environmental mediation continues to develop and evolve in different jurisdictions across the world in order to prevent potential environmental conflicts or to resolve the conflicts while avoiding the inherent drawbacks of an adjudicated solution. This book takes a comparative approach to explore the legal framework of environmental mediation with a focus on the judicial, administrative and private procedures and the criteria for accrediting mediators in a range of jurisdictions across the world. It also examines practical considerations for environmental mediators while analyzing the effectiveness of different mediation processes.

**Catherine Choquette** is a full professor of law at the University of Sherbrooke where she teaches at the School of Law and at the School of Environment. She holds a doctorate in law from the University of Chicago and a master's in biology from McGill University. She is a lawyer called to the bar of the Province of Quebec and a member of the Quebec Institute for Mediation and Arbitration.

**Véronique Fraser** is an assistant professor of law at the University of Sherbrooke where she teaches in the Master in Dispute Prevention and Resolution. She holds a doctorate in law from the University of Ottawa, a master's in transnational law and common law from the University of Sherbrooke and a master's of laws in dispute resolution from Pepperdine University School of Law. She is a lawyer called to the bars of the provinces of Quebec and Ontario and an accredited mediator by the Quebec Institute for Mediation and Arbitration.

## Routledge Research in International Environmental Law

www.routledge.com/Routledge-Research-in-International-Environmental-Law/book-series/INTENVLAW

**Common Pools of Genetic Resources**
Equity and Innovation in International Biodiversity Law
*Edited by Evanson Chege Kamau and Gerd Winter*

**International Climate Change Law and Policy**
Cultural Legitimacy in Adaption and Mitigation
*Edited by Thoko Kaime*

**International Liability Regime for Biodiversity Damage**
The Nagoya-Kuala Lumpur Supplementary Protocol
*Edited by Akiho Shibata*

**The Precautionary Principle in Marine Environmental Law**
With Special Reference to High Risk Vessels
*Bénédicte Sage-Fuller*

**International Environmental Law and Distributive Justice**
The Equitable Distribution of CDM Projects under the Kyoto Protocol
*Tomilola Akanle Eni-Ibukun*

**Environmental Governance in Europe and Asia**
A Comparative Study of Institutional and Legislative Frameworks
*Jona Razzaque*

**Climate Change, Forests and REDD**
Lessons for Institutional Design
*Edited by Joyeeta Gupta, Nicolien van der Grijp and Onno Kuik*

**International Environmental Law and the Conservation of Coral Reefs**
*Edward J. Goodwin*

**Environmental Mediation**
An International Survey
*Edited by Catherine Choquette and Véronique Fraser*

# Environmental Mediation

## An International Survey

**Edited by**
**Catherine Choquette**
**and Véronique Fraser**

Routledge
Taylor & Francis Group
LONDON AND NEW YORK

First published 2018 by Routledge

2 Park Square, Milton Park, Abingdon, Oxfordshire OX14 4RN
52 Vanderbilt Avenue, New York, NY 10017

*Routledge is an imprint of the Taylor & Francis Group, an informa business*

First issued in paperback 2019

Copyright © 2018 selection and editorial matter, Catherine Choquette and Véronique Fraser; individual chapters, the contributors

The right of Catherine Choquette and Véronique Fraser to be identified as the authors of the editorial material, and of the authors for their individual chapters, has been asserted in accordance with sections 77 and 78 of the Copyright, Designs and Patents Act 1988.

All rights reserved. No part of this book may be reprinted or reproduced or utilised in any form or by any electronic, mechanical, or other means, now known or hereafter invented, including photocopying and recording, or in any information storage or retrieval system, without permission in writing from the publishers.

Notice:
Product or corporate names may be trademarks or registered trademarks, and are used only for identification and explanation without intent to infringe.

*British Library Cataloguing-in-Publication Data*
A catalogue record for this book is available from the British Library

*Library of Congress Cataloging-in-Publication Data*
A catalog record for this book has been requested

ISBN: 978-1-138-04808-9 (hbk)
ISBN: 978-0-367-88872-5 (pbk)

Typeset in Galliard
by Apex CoVantage, LLC

# Contents

# Contributors

**Philippe Barret** is a specialized mediator in territorial dialogue and environmental conflict resolution. Agricultural engineer, Philippe Barret has been working for 30 years within DialTer and Geyser, two structures he cofounded and that are situated in southern France. After having coordinated projects in the ecological engineering and rural development domains, he turned to mediation and environmental concertation. For about 15 years, he has been a mediator on diverse subjects: watercourse management, biodiversity conservation, impacts of industrial activities, etc. He performs numerous trainings, in France and abroad, and published several papers and books, the last one being : *Guide pratique du dialogue territorial : concertation et médiation pour l'environnement et le développement local.*

**Antonia Bousbaine**, a secondary school teacher in geography, has two master's degrees: one in history and geography from the University of Valenciennes (renewal of city/countryside links) and the other in geography from the University of Brussels (agricultural transformations around Charleroi). Her Ph.D. research at the University of Liège focuses on city/countryside relationships and the role of agriculture in the construction of these new territories in Wallonia, where the Walloon Code of Agriculture aims to preserve agricultural land in a region where recently there have been substantial losses of farmland. Her main research objectives focus on governance leading to the development of plans and initiatives through a co-construction process. Her Ph.D. thesis thus aims to contribute to a governance process involving all legitimate interests and their representative actors to create a more sustainable management of agricultural land.

**Anne Browning-Aiken** is a professor at the University of Arizona, USA. She received her Ph.D. in cultural anthropology at the University of Arizona and has worked with communities in Latin America and North America (Southwestern United States) over issues of natural resource governance and policy under the aegis of the Udall Center for Studies in Public Policy at the University of Arizona, the UNESCO HELP and International Hydrology Program, and a Fulbright research grant to Universidade Federal da Santa Catrina in Brazil. In addition, she is a trained facilitator whose main interest lies in supporting the efforts of both drought-ridden areas and communities with multiple environmental issues in the process of finding solutions to natural resource issues with multi-level governmental and non-governmental actors or participants.

**Christopher Bryant** received his doctorate in 1970 at the London School of Economics and Political Science, London. He was progressively Assistant, Associate and Full Professor in Geography at the University of Waterloo (1970–1990), then Full Professor in Geography at the Université de Montréal (1990–2014) and is now Adjunct Professor in Geography at the Université de Montréal and in the School of Environmental Design and Rural Planning, University of Guelph. He is one of the international leaders in research on urban/periurban agricultures (Canada and Western Europe) and a recognized leader in the domain of adaptation of human activities (especially agriculture) to climate change and variability in local and community development, and in strategic planning for local and regional development for and by citizens. Most of his research is in the context of sustainable development and deals with the dynamic of actors.

**Catherine Choquette** holds a doctorate in law from the University of Chicago and a master's in biology from McGill University. She is a full professor of law at the Université de Sherbrooke (Canada), a member of the Quebec Bar and of the Quebec Institute for Mediation and Arbitration (IMAQ). Since 2009, she has been the director of the *Groupe de recherche sur les strategies et les acteurs de la gouvernance environnementale* (SAGE) ('Research Group on Strategies and Actors in Environmental Governance') and the co-director of the *Centre de recherche sur la régulation et le droit de la gouvernance* (CrRDG) ('Regulation and Law of Governance Research Center') since 2016. Her main research interests are in environmental law, ecological analysis of law, governance and environmental mediation.

**Daniel José da Silva** is a professor at the University Federal of Santa Catarina (UFSC), Florianopolis, Brazil, with a Ph.D. that combines both philosophy of the natural environment and the technical aspects of hydrology and wastewater planning. He has spent most of his career working with GITHDRO at the UFSC to support the implementation of Brazilian environmental policies in the state of Santa Catarina with the support of his graduate and undergraduate students, other scientific departments at UFSC and Brazilian government and industrial grants.

**Kars J. de Graaf** is an associate professor and holds the Chair in Public Law and Sustainability in the Department of Constitutional Law, Administrative Law and Public Administration at the University of Groningen, the Netherlands. He received his Ph.D. in 2004 for a thesis concerning the substantive possibilities and procedural consequences of amicable dispute settlement during administrative court procedures. His research and publications focus on the general administrative law and environmental law. He is the managing editor of the *Review of European Administrative Law*, member of the board of both the Dutch Association for Administrative Law and the Dutch Association for Environmental Law, and he is an honorary judge at a district court.

**Haifeng Deng** is an associate professor at Tsinghua University, School of Law. He currently serves as the vice director of the Center for Environmental, Natural Resource and Energy Law, Tsinghua University and the director of the Legal Affair Office, Tsinghua University. He earned his LL.B. LL.M. and PhD at Heilongjiang University and Tsinghua University Law School, respectively. His research interests include environmental law and international energy law. Dr. Deng has memberships in the major environmental law organizations such as the Chinese Society of Environment and Resources Law (Standing Director). He has published many books and articles on environmental protection and climate change issues, such as China's role and contribution in the global governance of climate change (*Journal of World Energy Law and Business*, Volume 8, Issue 6, 2015).

**José Antonio Silvestre Fernandes Neto** works in the Oswaldo Cruz Foundation (Fiocruz), which is attached to the Brazilian Ministry of Health as its research arm in order to promote health and social development to forge and disseminate scientific and technological knowledge. He earned his Ph.D. in 2010 at Federal University of the state of Santa Catarina for a thesis concerning the results of a mediation process supported by the *Grupo Transdisciplinar de Pesquisas em Governança de Bens Comuns* (GTHIDRO) group that took place in that state as part of a project called Social Technologies for Water Management. Fernandes Neto acts now as a researcher of the Public Policy, Health and Environment group at Fiocruz.

**Véronique Fraser** is a law professor in the master's program in dispute prevention and resolution at the law faculty of the Université de Sherbrooke (Canada). She is a lawyer and a member of the Quebec (civil law) and Ontario (common law) bars. She holds a doctorate degree in Law (Ph.D., University of Ottawa, common law section), a master's of laws in dispute resolution (LL.M., Pepperdine University, California) and a master's in transnational law and common law (LL.M., Université de Sherbrooke). Professor Fraser has mediated cases in Quebec and California, and participated in the conception of training material for judges and Quebec's crown corporations' lawyers in the context of the implementation of judicial mediation in the Quebec Administrative Tribunal. Professor Fraser acts as a resident researcher in the Group for the Prevention and Resolution of Disputes and in the International Task Force on Mixed Modes Dispute Resolution, a joint effort of the College of Commercial Arbitrators, the International Mediation Institute and the Straus Institute for Dispute Resolution. She is also a visiting scholar at the Straus Institute for Dispute Resolution, Pepperdine University School of Law (Malibu, California).

**Pierre-Yves Guihéneuf** is a mediator and a facilitator for concertation and public participation processes related to environment and management. As an

Agro-economist engineer, he also works in the Geyser association and the DialTer cooperative. He performs dialogue processes between stakeholders or in public participation within fields such as environment, management and urban policy. He is a lecturer at the University of Montpellier and at the Université of Paris 1 Panthéon Sorbonne. He supervises the 'Comédie' program (concertation, mediation, environment) that proposes online training in territorial dialogue and organizes national or regional meetings between local actors, researchers and public policy makers. He is also the coordinator of the Institut de la Concertation – a national network for concertation and participation practitioners.

**Nadiya R. Kobetska** is Professor of Law and the Head of the Department of Labor, Environmental and Agrarian Law. She holds a doctorate in law and the title of her Ph.D. dissertation in environmental law is "Ecological Rights of Citizens of Ukraine". Author of more than 120 scientific and methodological publications including: the textbook, approved and recommended by the Ministry of Education and Science of Ukraine, "Environmental Law of Ukraine" (2007, 2009 (2nd edition)); the textbook, approved by the Ministry of Education and Science of Ukraine, "Corporate Law of Ukraine" (2010, co-author); the scientific-practical commentary to the Water Code of Ukraine (co-author and editor); and six collective monographs as co-author. She is the Executive Secretary of the International Scientific Journal *Law and Society* from the Vasyl Stefanyk Precarpathian National University. Member of the editorial board of the scientific collection "Actual Problems of Improvement of Legislation of Ukraine". Representative of the Vasyl Stefanyk Precarpathian National University at the IUCN Academy of Environmental Law and a member of the Scientific Advisory Board of the Supreme Economic Court of Ukraine.

**Patricia Overmeyer** works in the U.S. Environmental Protection Agency's (EPA) Office of Brownfields and Land Revitalization and serves as the Agency's Land Revitalization Coordinator. Ms. Overmeyer also serves as team leader for the Brownfields Policy Team, which coordinates brownfields and land revitalization research, partnerships and outreach activities. Ms. Overmeyer is responsible for overseeing the implementation of EPA's regulations governing required standards and practices for conducting environmental site assessments or 'all appropriate inquiries' under the Comprehensive Environmental Response, Compensation, and Liability Act. She coordinated the development of the final rule that establishes standards and practices for conducting all appropriate inquiries and served as EPA's Designated Federal Official for the Agency's Federal Advisory Committee that was tasked with developing the proposed regulation on all appropriate inquiries. Ms. Overmeyer earned her M.S. from Carnegie-Mellon's School of Urban and Public Affairs and has a B.A. in economics from Indiana University of Pennsylvania.

**Susan Podziba**, a public policy mediator at Podziba Policy Mediation for more than 25 years, is author of *Civic Fusion: Mediating Polarized Public Disputes* (ABA Books 2012). She has designed and mediated scores of cases across the policy spectrum for clients including the U.S. Departments of Commerce, Defense, Education, Energy, Health and Human Services; Housing and Urban Development; Interior; Labor; Transportation; EPA, U.S. Senate; U.S. Institute of Peace; and the United Nations. She is Director of the Sacred Lands Project of the MIT-Harvard Public Disputes Program and faculty for the Harvard Negotiation Institute course titled the Advanced Mediation Workshop: Mediating Complex Disputes. Ms. Podziba has served as a Fulbright senior specialist in peace and conflict resolution and is listed on the United Nations mediator roster. She holds a bachelor of arts degree in philosophy from the University of Pennsylvania and a master's in city planning from the Massachusetts Institute of Technology.

**Hanna D. Tolsma** is an assistant professor in the Department of Constitutional Law, Administrative Law and Public Administration at the University of Groningen, the Netherlands. She received her Ph.D. in 2008 for a thesis concerning legal aspects of the use of mediation by administrative authorities during the decision-making process. She worked as a postdoc on a research project "Integrated Environmental Permitting: An Exploration of the Legal Possibility's" sponsored by the Netherlands Organisation for Scientific Research. Her publications mainly relate to general administrative law and environmental law. She is an honorary judge at a District Court.

**Lise Vandenhende** is a Ph.D. research fellow and academic assistant within the Centre for Environmental Law at Ghent University. Her Ph.D. research concerns the creation of an elaborate framework for the legal selection of protection worthy immovable heritage in Flanders. Lise Vandenhende is a member of the Flemish Commission for Immovable Heritage. This commission advises the Flemish Government in decisions concerning the protection of immovable heritage in Flanders. She is also a guest lecturer at the Faculty of Design Sciences of the University of Antwerp and a member of the editorial board of the Journal of Environmental Law and Environmental Policy (Tijdschrift voor Omgevingsrecht en Omgevingsbeleid). Furthermore, Lise Vandenhende is a lawyer at Odigo (Ghent). As a member of the bar in Ghent, she specialized in spatial planning and immovable heritage.

**Geert Van Hoorick** was born in 1968 in Lokeren, Belgium. He graduated at Ghent University (master's in law in 1991, master's in town and country planning in 1993). In 2000, he obtained a Ph.D. at Ghent University with a dissertation entitled "Legal Instruments for Nature and Landscape Conservation" awarded with the Belgian VDK-Award for Sustainable Development in 2001. He is professor in administrative, town and planning and environmental law at Ghent University within the Centre for Environmental and Energy

Law. He gives courses in environmental law, nature conservation law, notarial administrative law, town and country planning law, heritage law and animal law. He was promoter of several scientific projects for the Flemish Government (e.g. drafting legislation on landscape protection, forest management and nature conservation). He often publishes in environmental law, nature and landscape protection law, and town and country planning law. He is also a member of the IUCN Commission on Environmental Law and the European Environmental Law Forum. He is also a lawyer. He is president of the Flemish Society for the Protection of Birds (since 2013).

**Svitlana M. Romanko** is an associate professor at the Department of Labor, Environmental and Agrarian Law. The title of her upcoming doctoral thesis is titled "Climate Change Law: Theory and Practice". She is co-author of the scientific-practical commentary to the Water Code of Ukraine. In 2012, she was awarded the Young Scientist of the Year 2011 prize from the Ivano-Frankivsk Regional State Administration. She is a member of a governing board (Eastern Europe, Caucasus and Central Asia) and is on the Research Committee of the IUCN Academy of Environmental Law. She is also a member of the editorial boards of professional Ukrainian journals such as the *Environmental Law* and the *Small and Medium Business* (Kyiv), as well as on the international advisory board of the *Natural Resources – Management and Practice* from New Zealand.

**Brecht Warnez** is a Ph.D. research fellow and academic assistant within the administrative law research group. His Ph.D. research is a critical analysis of the diffuse legal system on administrative law enforcement by local administrations in Flanders. He is a lecturer at the Training Institute of the Federal Government and a member of the editorial board of the *Journal of Municipal Law*. Furthermore, he is a local councillor and a member of the council of a police district.

**Shijun Zhang** is Professor at the Law School of Shandong University and the director of the Research Institute of Economic Law. He is the standing director of China's Society of Environment and Resources Law. His current research focuses on environmental lawsuit, environmental dispute resolution, climate change and environmental governance.

# Acknowledgements

Our acknowledgements go to all the contributors whose text helps to acquire a better understanding of the development of the environmental mediation process worldwide and hopefully contributes to its improvement.

Many thanks also to the students Charles Gauthier, Kayla Brinda, Emily Alberton, Flavie Moyen-Sylvestre, Félix Deschamps and Camille Cloutier for the translation and formatting of many texts.

This book has been funded by the Fondation du Barreau du Québec and the Chambre des notaires du Québec.

# Introduction

The world is filled with cultural, political and legal diversities, but one aspect remains common across jurisdictions: behavioural propensities to conflicts or disputes over diverging interests. The international community also shares to some extent the same vital concerns about environmental protection. Over the last 20 years, the practice of mediation has evolved considerably in most countries and has been often perceived as a satisfying method for resolving different types of disputes. Mediation processes and procedures are increasingly developed and tailored to the specifics of particular types of dispute. This book aims to compare the development of mediation in the context of environmental disputes across different countries or jurisdictions in order to learn from successes and failures and to stimulate, hopefully, the evolution of environmental mediation worldwide.

Mediation is generally understood as an informal process in which a third-party neutral assists two or more parties to reach a consensual solution or agreement. In the specific case of environmental mediation, in addition to the necessity that the parties be satisfied with the solution, there is the question as to whether the agreed upon solution also really contributes to the protection of the environment. The quality of the environment affects the citizens and communities across the world and jeopardizes the living standards of future generations. What weight should be given to the public interest of protecting the environment versus the specific interests at stake of the parties to an environmental dispute? Where the protection of the environment is a central element to the resolution of a dispute, experts' technical knowledge and assessment of environmental impacts may become fundamental to a successful mediation. In such a case, the role of the mediator may not be limited to facilitating a mutually acceptable agreement, but may also include the oversight of a learning process based on knowledge sharing and mutual understanding of the environmental issue.

Environmental protection deals with a large gathering of major and smaller issues or events that all have a potential impact on the quality and sustainability of the environment. Some projects or policies that affect the environment are planned by public authorities or by the private sector, while other environmental issues result from a fault, negligence or unforeseeable circumstance (act of God). But, in all cases, mediation is a simple and effective tool to assist parties reaching an amicable and collaborative solution. Environmental mediation may either appear upstream of projects or policies to reach a consensus from all concerned actors, or downstream of a dispute to reach a peaceful agreement to the conflicting views. Mediation may take place at a variety of levels, including judicial, administrative or even private civil, each level displaying its own specific corpus of legislation.

In a judicial, administrative or private environmental dispute context, the use of mediation is often seen as a less costly alternative than trials, as well as a more equitable and adapted process to the specifics of the dispute, especially where no specialized environmental tribunal exists. The mediation process may involve a high number of plaintiffs, or be restricted to only a few. Sometimes, mediation takes place in the context of public or private consensus-building process regarding either a proposed development project or a proposed policy. In such instances, the objective of mediation is to provide a forum for information exchange in order to improve knowledge of the diverse interests involved and thus adapt the project or policy to population needs and field realities such as climate change. This type of mediation, often called facilitation, is perceived as a fundamental step towards environmental protection, social acceptability and sustainable development in the context of a democratic society. It may involve only a few participants, but usually requires the participation of numerous stakeholders to represent the vast array of interests concerned with the project or policy. In the latter case, the mediation process needs to be adapted to ensure a constructive dialogue among the numerous participants.

The development and implementation of mediation vary greatly among countries. Historical and cultural contexts may explain this discrepancy. In some countries such as Canada and the United States, lawsuits are common and the practice of consensus building is rather weak. In others, such as China or Brazil, courtrooms are generally avoided and the culture of dialogue is well developed. It can however be expected that environmental mediation will evolve rapidly for three main reasons. First, in recent years, the environmental governance, based on public participation and information disclosure, has become a fundamental approach in many democratic countries. It emerges with force in some legislation, less clearly in others, but the tendency towards environmental governance in democratic countries seems irreversible considering the widespread development of shared environmental values combined with greater expectations of consultation from public authorities. Second, the heavy judicial costs linked to environmental disputes make people reticent to seek remedies in the judiciary system. Third, the protection of the environment is, in many countries, considered a fundamental right embodied within their Constitution, which has the effect of enhancing further the involvement of concerned actors and boosting the pressure on governments to act. In many cases, mediation or facilitation processes may become a key factor to ensure the success of the implementation of a regulation, the resolution of a conflict or the social acceptance of a development project.

This book is a collection of selected papers received after a call of contribution through the IUCN Academy of Environmental Law in 2013. The book contains two parts. Part I explores the legal framework of environmental mediation, which includes the judicial, administrative and private procedures and the criteria for accreditation of mediators. In the first chapter, **Kobetska and Romanko**, from Ukraine, offer an overview of the causes and issues that give rise to environmental conflicts and the different ways available to resolve those disputes including the alternative means of dispute resolution. As many other European countries, Ukraine's legislation was drawn from the Aarhus Convention on access to information, public participation in decision making and access to justice in environmental matters and by the Directive 2008/52/EC of the European Parliament. Environmental mediation is still at an early stage of development in Ukraine, but the contributors argue that the momentum could quickly pick up with the adoption of a law totally devoted to mediation. **Deng** shows the amazing recent evolution of environmental protection activities in China. Alternative dispute resolution (ADR) is already an integrated part of the Chinese system of conflict resolution, which includes administrative conciliation, judicial mediation, people's mediation and civil mediation. After describing each mediation modes, Deng explains the difficulties in their implementation at the legal level as well as at the organization and training level. The contributor proposes a range of solutions to improve the efficiency of the Chinese mediation system. **De Graaf and Tolsma** provide an overview of the development of mediation and mediation techniques in administrative decision making and administrative adjudication in the Netherlands. They explore some of the legal constraints for environmental mediation and provide insight about giving the use of mediation and/or mediation techniques a legal status in administrative decision making and administrative adjudication in the Netherlands. **Van Hoorick, Vandenhende and Warnez** contend that mediation in Belgian environmental law is still in its infancy, but its necessity is clear. The federal and Flemish legislators have chosen to provide some forms of mediation during the administrative procedure and the judicial procedure with a relative success. Mediation mechanisms vary within court jurisdictions and within permit divisions such as urban or environmental permits. This is partly due to the specific federal state structure and partly due to the lack of a specific environmental law. The contributors analyze and compare the mediation procedures and propose other forms of mediation and advocate for a global legal framework concerning mediation in Belgian environmental law. Finally, **Choquette and Fraser** describe the legal framework of environmental mediation in the Province of Quebec, the only civil law province in Canada. They show that even though mediation is codified in the new *Code of Civil Procedure* and that it also appears in certain specialized environmental laws, many improvements are still needed in order to consider environmental mediation as a valuable and credible process for the prevention and resolution of environmental conflicts. Some of the improvements needed are revealed by an expert survey and include, among others, specific training in environmental mediation, transparency of the process and its compellability.

Part II explores more specifically practical experiences while analyzing the efficiency of different mediation processes. In the first chapter of Part II, two French mediators, **Barret and Guihéneuf**, share many years of practice in the context of environmental disputes at the judiciary level and at the decision-making level where development projects of public interests are evaluated. According to them, the crisis of confidence regarding state institutions and the growing interest regarding the environmental protection have forced the concerned stakeholders to turn towards what they called a 'territorial dialogue'. A few French laws encourage or even force public authorities to adopt dialogue approaches. The 'territorial dialogue' combines three practices: concertation, negotiation and mediation. Even though mediation is not mandatory, the use of mediation is rising rapidly. The contributors argue that the territorial dialogue must be adapted to the specifics of a situation and advance that the use of a mediator is a measure of success. They provide insightful advice regarding the role of the mediator, the conduct of a decision-making process and the use of experts. **Podziba and Overmeyer** present a case study, which describes in great details the negotiated rulemaking process used by the U.S. Environmental Protection Agency to establish federal standards and practices for the 'all appropriate inquiries' of potentially polluted properties. The contributors show that this complex negotiation, involving a wide range of stakeholders with very diverse interests, was held within a very structured and precise framework but still flexible and adaptable enough to tackle stakeholders' sub-issues and public concerns. The importance of the mediator or the facilitator or the mediation team, as in this case, is shown from the beginning of the process when the likelihood of success is evaluated, through the different phases of the negotiation (committee members, work groups, offline communications) and until the end where a consensus is reached. The contributors find that the negotiated regulation process seems to have provided all involved actors with beneficial results and contributed to public and stakeholders education in terms of specificities of the case and government limitations within decision-making processes. **Bousbaine and Bryant** present a specific consensus-building process called 'co-construction', which involves all concerned stakeholders from the very beginning of the projects. This process is slowly being adopted in North America as well as in Europe. Although mediation is not mandatory in this process, the contributors reveal that it is a sound investment and a frequent guarantee of success. Environmental mediation is also compared with the public hearing process that also aims at public participation. However, environmental mediation in a context of co-construction of projects seems highly preferable in terms of trust building, information sharing and participation to decision making. **Browning-Aiken, Fernandes Neto and da Silva** advance that environmental mediation in Brazil offers a model and a process for identifying different kinds of environmental conflicts, a system for constructively managing those conflicts, and an opportunity to transform conflicts into productive learning experiences. While Brazil initiated a legal mediation and conciliation process to be used in courtrooms in the 1990s, GTHIDRO or, *Grupo Transdisciplinar de Pesquisas em Governança de Bens Comuns*, a transdisciplinary group of researchers at the Federal University of Santa Catarina, created another form of mediation used outside the courtroom to address potential problems in local (community and state) governance of natural resources (referred to as 'socio-ecological learning'). The transdisciplinary group of researchers has put forth a dynamic and complex model of participatory 'cycles of learning' that brings six southern Brazilian community committees in the state of Santa Catarina to a common understanding of socio-ecological processes, laws and potential for collective action. Finally, **Zhang** offers a thorough analysis of the complaint letters and visits system in China that he considers a sound and valuable vehicle for peaceful and efficient resolution of environmental disputes. He demonstrates how China has a long history with the use of ADR processes and why the complaint letters and visits mechanism respond to the Chinese needs. Zhang nevertheless argues that the system is still perfectible and he proposes many improvements, such as a specialized institution for environmental dispute resolution like it exists in Japan, South Korea and Taiwan.

This book, based on a comparative study, is an attempt to induce research and innovation in the specialized field of environmental mediation. It is our hope that the process of environmental mediation will continue to develop and evolve in different jurisdictions across the world in a manner that will take into account the very specific nature of environmental conflicts. International dialogue and comparative work are necessary to continue learning from the successes and failures of different processes and programs implemented in different parts of the world.

# Part I

# The legal framework of environmental mediation

# 1 Recent developments in Ukraine

*Nadiya R. Kobetska*[1] *and Svitlana M. Romanko***[2]

## 1 The content, causes and the main impacts of environmental conflicts in Ukraine

Environmental law emerged as a means for individuals and societies to preserve the natural basis of their existence. As Ukraine makes important changes in its state policy, new ecological regulations are outlined or implemented that take into consideration the various interests of the parties involved.

The human society, particularly through its economic activities, has a powerful impact on nature's cycles. These activities have forced the growth of environmental requirements and have complicated their immediate implementation. Fundamental socio-political changes in the Ukrainian society paved the way, after 1991, for the recognition of the right to a healthy environment and other citizens' environmental rights in the legislation. Securing the basic environmental rights through the Constitution of Ukraine, in 1996, has defined the role of the state within environmental matters and shifted the 'centre of gravity' and the priorities in environmental policy. A number of specific lawmaking and law enforcement measures have since been carried out to ensure the implementation of the rights.

The most important feature of an environmental conflict rests within its object, which are the actions taken (or that should have been taken) to protect the environment. Environmental conflicts in Ukraine are usually the result of inefficient policies. They manifest themselves in various ways such as: urban development, land ownership, restrictions on the use and access to natural resources, oil and gas production. These conflicts are related to the citizens' right to a safe, healthy and wealthy environment.

In Ukraine, one of the most urgent social problems is the issue of providing public access to forests and water. In recent years, the practice of preventing

1 Head of the Department of Labour, Environmental and Agrarian Law of Law Institute of Vasyl Stefanyk Precarpathian National University, Ph.D., professor of law.

** Professor of law, Law Institute of Prykarpatsky National University, Ukraine

2 We are very thankful to our university and IUCN Academy of Environmental Law for the opportunity to get knowledge about this opportunity. Most of all we thank the Université de Sherbrooke for involving us in this important process.

citizens from going into forests and waterfronts belonging to the state and municipalities has become very common. For instance in 2009, under the resolution of Cherkasy regional state administration and in accordance with the norms of the Forest Code of Ukraine, a forest plot of 9.9 hectares, which was in constant use of the state enterprise 'Kanev forestry', was allocated to a private company for cultural and recreational purposes for a period of 49 years. Similarly, 6 hectares of forest were allocated to private companies for a period of 49 years. A peculiarity of the allocated forest was its unique location in one of the most picturesque corners of Cherkasy region – on the coast of Kanev reservoir and the Dnieper river. When word got out that the local residents of the village of Liplyave were being banned from reaching the river by the security guards of the private companies, they were asked for what kind of purpose the plots had been taken. The representatives of the company defiantly replied, "And what's the difference to you? If we wish, we'll study flying of mosquitoes". Perhaps, that is why, this conflict has got its name from the media.[3]

Serious conflicts arise in hunting areas. The peculiar feature of hunting areas (as it is stated in the Law of Ukraine "On Hunting Grounds and Hunting") is that they cover land plots of dozens of different land users. The interests and activities of the landowners or land users may come into conflict with hunting. Here is an example of a judicial practice. A landholder appeals to the court to remove obstacles to the use of his land – namely, the permission of hunting on the plots of land leased to him. According to the landholder, the presence of armed individuals on the plots of land that are used by the fish industry and the agricultural industry could represent a threat to the workers. The courts (the first and the appellate court), did not find any evidence of violations in holding the hunting activities on the lawfully granted hunting areas, and refused to meet the plaintiff's claim.

There are numerous widespread and permanent so-called junk conflicts in Ukraine. The accumulation and subsequent treatment (disposal, recycling) of waste is problematic in Ukraine. Since the solution of that problem requires a comprehensive approach and significant financial resources, regional communities are often unable to solve it effectively. Moreover, when a community has a bad experience with a landfill, neighbouring localities become very reluctant to construct new landfills on their territory. They are not convinced by the promises of the officials that modern environmental-friendly technologies will be used to reduce environmental threats or that the investment will be adequate to meet the needs. The settlement of these environmental conflicts is usually based on the least efficient (in terms of achieving long-term goals of conflict resolution) and the most intensive (as the problem of waste disposal is solved in a short-term perspective) solutions.

3 Zelenko, L., S. Yu and V. Ivanchenko, "16 Hectares at the Dnieper Were Leased to Study Mosquitoes" in *Gazeta.ua*, 2010. Access: http://gazeta.ua/articles/ukraine-newspaper/_16-gektariv-bilya-dnipra-zdali-v-orendu-dlya-doslidzhennya-komariv/332533; Limarenko, V., "Who Does Not Sleep Because of Lozinsky's 'Glory', or Who Is Going to Study the Flights of Mosquitoes in the Woods near Kanev" in *Friends of Forests*. Access: http://pryroda.in.ua/lis/komu-ne-daye- spaty-slava-lozynskogo / # more-59

There are also many environmental conflicts related to illegal construction. Construction may be carried out without any right to do so or in disregard of the requirements specified in the contract or permit. Between 2014 and 2015, the city of Ivano-Frankivsk (Western Ukraine) sparked outrage when it turned a blind eye to the destruction of green spaces and the illegal pumping of water from the lake. Another common situation is the legalization of illegally constructed buildings, including those in recreational areas, which violate the right of the community to a healthy environment.

## 2 Solutions to environmental conflicts

### 2.1 *Traditional and alternative ways of resolving environmental conflicts*

To ensure the most effective solutions, one should distinguish three different phenomena: offences, disputes and conflicts. An offence is the violation of a legal norm. It results in being held accountable by the state for legal liability. A conflict is the clash of different social interests while a dispute is the result of such a clash.[4]

In environmental matters, various and sometimes opposite interests are present simultaneously. The search for an optimal solution must take into account the interests of the parties and the society in general. The solution should be legitimate and socially acceptable to all participants. Modern conflict studies dealing with the problem of resolving problems rest on two opposing approaches: the confrontational struggle (traditional approach) and the compromise and cooperation (alternative dispute resolution (ADR) approach). The first one, based on achieving unilateral advantages, is usually associated with the ability to influence the opponent in a courtroom. The efforts of the participants are mainly directed against each other and the result of the confrontation can only be the defeat of one or both sides. The main point of the second approach is the reconciliation of positions through direct interaction between the parties or with the help of a third independent party, in order to reach a mutually acceptable agreement. ADR methods, such as negotiation, conciliation, and mediation, must adapt to the given situation, take into account the interests and requirements of the parties in order to help to overcome the conflict and save the possibility for further communication and cooperation. Disputes settle peacefully without harming public relations.[5]

### 2.2 *The evolution towards citizen's interests in the Ukrainian legislation*

In the Soviet totalitarian society, a vertical, hierarchical system of authorities, and the imperative positive law, aimed to prevent all conflicts. Accordingly, in

4 Leyba, L., *Legal Resolution of Land Disputes*, Ph.D. thesis, Kharkiv University, 2005, 8.

5 Hoyko, O., "From Court Protection to Alternative Dispute Resolutions" (2010) 6(56) *Theory and Practice of Intellectual Property* 54.

case of conflicts, a public authority had at its disposal almost unlimited possibilities for its suppression, without aiming to reach a peaceful settlement of the conflict. Since Ukraine's sovereignty in 1990, many changes in the socio-economic structure have occurred. Our society faced new challenges, which needed the domestic law to adapt. Building a 'developed civil society', as a necessary condition for the existence of a democratic state, required to strengthen the position of the public to enhance its capacity to truly influence the state decision-making process.

For the first time in 1991, Article 9 of the Law of Ukraine "On Environmental Protection" secured the system of environmental rights, including those that involve public participation in restoring, improving and protecting the environment. The legal recognition of the rights of the citizens to influence environmental policies initiated the formation of a new system of conflict resolution taking into account the interests of the community. The ratification by Ukraine in 1999 of the Convention on Access to Information, Public Participation in Decision-Making and Access to Justice in Environmental Matters played a crucial role in this process. For its implementation, Ukraine adopted a number of significant legal acts, in particular, the procedure "On public participation in decision-making in environmental protection". Public hearings became an important tool to find the best solutions to the existing problems and to mobilize resources. While assuming that community resources are limited and that there are various individual opinions on how to use these limited resources, public hearings are useful platforms for the community members to discuss environmental problems and alleviate diverging opinions.

There are examples of successful public environmental hearings in Ukraine such as in Artemivsk, a city in the Donetsk region, in 2000. Some central authorities decided to create a radioactive waste storage site inside the salt mines of the 'Artemsalt' enterprise. The officials were supported by several publications in national newspapers of well- known scientists affirming that the sealed waste containers represented no danger for the environment. What should the community do in such a situation? On the initiative of a non-governmental organization 'Bakhmat', in cooperation with local authorities, it was decided to organize a public hearing to voice the residents' opinion on the impacts of the storage. It was important not just to listen to Kiev ministerial specialists and to open the debate to other expertise. As a result, the hearing was attended by representatives of environmental organizations from Russia, Kazakhstan, Germany and Japan, as well as by representatives of the Committee of Environmental Protection and Nuclear Safety, the Ministry of Emergencies and the Department for Nuclear Industry. The city could defend its position and the potential harm of the disposal site was ultimately demonstrated.[6]

6 Gorodok, M.D., AV Kartashov, O.O. Radchenko and V.Y. Stasyuk, *Public hearings as a tool of solving the problems of local communities: a practical guide*. Kyiv: 2015. 108. Yelcheva, L. and I. Ibrahimova, *A Tutorial on the Community Development: a Practical Reference Book for Those Who Care*, Kiev, 2007, 230.

However, public discussions of projects are too often a formality where residents cannot really influence the fate of the project. They are either invited to discuss only when the project has actually started or there is a lack of information on the place and time of the hearing, or hearings are held in small buildings, or they involve uninterested people or people obviously dependent on the developer of the project. In such cases, the results of hearings do not reflect the true interests of the citizens. For example, in 2015, public hearings were held in Ivano-Frankivsk on the city development plan. The authorities did not inform the population about the hearings and only 4 persons attended the first public hearing out of a population of 20,452 residents. The hearing was cancelled, and it was decided that the consultation would take the form of written comments which, of course, exclude the dynamic of a debate and minimize the public participation on urban plan decision making.

According to the Ukraine law "On the Fundamental Strategy of Ukraine's state Environmental Policy for the Period until 2020 adopted by the Verkhovna Rada of Ukraine on the 21st of December, 2010", a very important tool for implementing the national environmental policy is the development of partnerships. This multisectorial cooperation is based on taking into account the interests of various entities such as the manufacturers, scientists, public organizations and local authorities, including those of economic, social and environmental characters. The legal basis for this cooperation became the Law of Ukraine "On Public – Private Partnership", adopted in 2010. Public-private contractual partnership is an equal and mutually beneficial cooperation between the state, local communities (relevant state or local government) and private investors within projects, which are aimed to solve important social and economic problems in the area. The law defines the scope of public-private partnerships: prospection, exploration and extraction of minerals; collection, purification and distribution of water; waste recycling, etc. In 2013, the state enterprise 'National Project Clean City' signed two agreements with the private company Ukrvtorresursy for the construction of solid waste recycling infrastructures in Kyiv and Chernivtsi. The conclusion of the agreements was preceded by a public discussion on the investment proposal which involved the investors, the Ukrainian Environmental League, the representatives of executive authorities of the cities and the region, deputies, public organizations, scientific institutions and the citizens. It is of common practice in Ukraine to sign the so-called social contracts and social partnership agreements.

The mediation, in Ukraine, is only making its first steps but it is producing its own standards and seeking ways to be implemented in public life.

## 3 Environmental mediation in Ukraine

### *3.1 Mediation definition in Ukraine*

Mediation is another form of protection of environmental rights which is inherent to higher form of environmental consciousness or socio-environmental law in the twenty-first century. Mediation is not a government coercion but a voluntary agreement on the principle '*sponte sua, sine lege*'.[7] It has extended in many countries as an alternative procedure to judicial settlement of disputes. Usually a mutually acceptable agreement is reached not based on legal formalities but on the balance of the parties' interests after the expression of opinions, negotiations and proposals by a mediator who acts on the premise of independence and impartiality and contributes to the mutual understanding of the conflict by the parties.

> Mediation means a structured process, regardless of name or reference to it, whereby two or more disputing parties attempt, on a voluntary basis, to reach an agreement to resolve the dispute with the support of a mediator. This process may be initiated by the parties or as a result of an offer or court order or prescription for the implementation of legislation of a Member state.[8]

A survey conducted by "Lawyer & Law" showed that approximately 60% of lawyers have a very vague idea about mediation, approximately 30% have training in mediation but do not use it in their practice, and only 10% of respondents successfully practiced it.[9]

Mediation in Ukraine is still mostly associated with restorative justice. From September 2006 to February 2007, the Ukrainian Centre of Common Ground carried out an intermediate evaluation of the implementation of restorative justice in the ten regions of Ukraine. Over this period were conducted 41 restorative justice programs including 39 mediations in criminal cases and two family conferences.[10]

The practice of restorative procedures demonstrated that mediation in criminal proceedings has many advantages in comparison with the general judicial order of solving the 'criminal conflict'. Mediation ensures a more effective solution to the compensation of moral and/or material damages, enables the parties to influence the decisions taken in the case and helps to reduce the emotional tension. In addition, mediation exempts judges from a heavy load of work in eliminating pending minor cases and gives them the opportunity to focus on major cases.

U.S. Agency for International Development (USAID), under the project 'Fair Justice', has provided a grant to the Law Institute of Vasyl Stefanyk Precarpathian

7 Latin expression, "voluntarily, without coercion of laws".

8 Directive 2008/52/EC of the European Parliament and of the Council of May 21, 2008 on certain aspects of mediation in civil and commercial matters OJ L 136, May 24, 2008, 3–8 Special Edition in Croatian: Chapter 19, Volume 9, 281–286.

9 Yakushenko, D.V., *Mediation in Ukraine: "For" or "Against"*, Sumy State University, 2013. Access: http://essuir.sumdu.edu.ua/bitstream/123456789/34131/1/Yakushenko_Ukrainian%20legislation.pdf

10 Quarterly Bulletin of the "Restorative Justice in Ukraine" Swiss Agency of Development and Cooperation SDC and Ukraine Ukrainian Centre of Common Ground № 1–2, 2009. Access: www.commonground.org.ua/dld/RJU_bulletin/RJU.Vol.1-2%2813%29.pdf

National University for the program 'Mediation as an Alternative Means of Dispute Resolution'. The project took place from October 2014 to May 2015. There were four certified mediators: three in civil, family conflicts and one in criminal, civil, family and corporate conflicts. The grant provided for 52 cases. Sources of cases were the parties appeal – 7, courts – 4, legal clinic – 41 (court staff provided the parties with information regarding the legal clinic). Pre-mediation was conducted in 26 cases and 16 mediations finally took place. In 12 of them, an agreement was successfully reached. The duration of the mediations was from a minimum of one to three days, including 'shuttle' mediations[11] to a maximum of almost two months. It has to be noted that the legal framework for mediation was developed only for criminal cases, regarding the other types of cases, mediation is carried out only on a voluntary basis.

As the judge of Volyn region Court of Appeal Oksana Marchuk – Zavydovska said, there are over 15 million Ukrainians passing through the judicial procedure every year and "I believe that the parties of a conflict must be offered alternative methods of dispute resolution so that they would not go immediately to court". The establishment of mediation could create peace and harmony in society. The mechanism of cooperation with mediators at the legislative and procedural level is not yet fixed. However, Article 175 of the Code of Civil Procedure about reconciliation of the parties as well as Articles 29 and 30 about the procedural rights of the parties can be actually used. The court also explains to the parties their right to conciliation.[12]

Mediation, despite its relative newness and limited use, could be very useful in cases related to the environmental protection not only in judicial proceedings but also in pre-trial stages and extrajudicial dispute resolution.

### 3.2 Mediation legislation

Ukraine is taking its first steps towards the regulation of mediation through the Law of Ukraine "On mediation" № 2480 from 27 of March, 2015 which has been adopted in first reading on November 3, 2016. This is the fourth regulation effort over the recent years but it looks promising.

In 2011 and 2013, three different draft laws "On mediation" were developed, which had one common drawback – they had ignored disputes arising from land and ecological relationships that can also be resolved through mediation.

11 Kind of mediation in which a mediator goes back and forth between the parties to work out the details of agreements. This method can be helpful in dealing with the particular issues in a case, but may not enhance communication and positive relationships among stakeholders because the participants are not present in the same room. See *The National Center on Dispute Resolution in Special Education, USA*. Access: www.directionservice.org/cadre/ctu/practicesA.cfm?id=31.

12 Mediation in the courts: experience and prospects. *Materials of the Conference for Program Initiative Support on "Human Rights and Justice" International Fund "Renaissance"*. – Lutsk, June 22, 2015r. Access: www.irf.ua/knowledgebase/news/mediatsii_v_sudakh_dosvid_ta_perspektivi/

The Law "On mediation" will cover the environmental disputes arising from the implementation of management and ownership over natural resources, environmental protection and safety. The main impacts, that are expected, concern the environmental mediation of disputes related to major companies and foreign investors.

Adopting this law will ensure the conformity of the Ukrainian legislation to EU standards and regulations implemented by Directive 2008/52 / EC of the European Parliament and Council, which aim to create general rules for all European mediators.

But how should it be enshrined in legislation? The Law "On mediation" doesn't contain provisions for a foreign mediator's activities in Ukraine, in contrast to the previous editions. A foreign mediator must receive a permission (license) for such activities in Ukraine to prove his knowledge of the Ukrainian law. Despite the existence of the UNCITRAL Model Law on International Commercial Conciliation with Guide to Enactment and Use,[13] these activities should be controlled because there are countries where mediation is not regulated by law. It would be rational to establish clear requirements to organizations and programs emitting certificates recognized by the state. It is the duty of the Ministry of Justice to keep a national register database of certified mediators. Some of these functions could later be delegated to non-governmental organizations of mediators. This is a controversial issue because if the state pays for mediation it will be eager to control the sphere. This would negate the role of mediation as a voluntary based process. Ukraine will probably choose another direction that is the deregulation of the mediation process to minimize the impact of the state on this sphere, which represents the formula closer to the actual reality.

### 3.3 *Pecularities of mediation procedures under the Law of Ukraine "On mediation"*

This law takes into account remarks to previous drafts. In particular, it was noted that previous drafts did not cover the establishment of a material and technical base for the implementation of mediation in Ukraine, the procedure for licensing entities for the training of mediators, and the controlling authority (council of mediators, mediator's chamber, etc.). The Law of Ukraine "On mediation" defines the legal professional basis of mediation and its access in society, informs on extrajudicial methods of dispute resolution and ensures a well-balanced relations between mediation and the judicial system.

The law defines the basic concepts in the field of mediation:

- Mediation: alternative (non-judicial) method of dispute resolution whereby two or more parties in dispute attempt on a voluntary basis to reach an agreement through a mediator.

13 UNCITRAL Model Law on International Commercial Conciliation with Guide to Enactment and Use, *United Nations, New York, 2004*. Access: www.uncitral.org/pdf/english/texts/arbitration/ml-conc/03-90953_Ebook.pdf.

- Mediator: a person who meets the requirements established by the law and a mediation clause (mediation agreement), and has been chosen by the parties.
- Mediation parties: physical, legal persons and/or groups of persons who wish to settle their dispute by means of the mediation procedure.
- Participants in mediation: the mediator, parties, representatives, legal representatives, translators, experts and other persons permitted by the parties.
- Organizations: providers of mediation – physical and legal entities of any ownership, organizational and legal form that are engaged in the technical preparation of the mediation procedure; and entities that provide training for mediators – physical and legal entities of any ownership, organizational and legal form, including educational institutions, that conduct professional training of mediators and issue certificates under this Act.

Mediation is conducted with the mutual consent of both parties and under the principles of equality, self-determination, independence, neutrality and privacy. Parties have the right to organize it as they see fit, to terminate it at any time and file to court or arbitration. Any pressure put on the parties for the purpose of carrying out or ending the mediation is prohibited. The principle of voluntary participation in mediation extends to the mediator and other participants. Participation in mediation cannot be regarded as an admission of guilt or as a waiver of the plaintiff's claim. Discrimination of mediation parties on any basis is prohibited. The law stipulates that the details about the mediation are confidential unless otherwise agreed by the parties. The mediator, parties and participants in the mediation are not entitled to disclose any information without the written consent of the parties.

The mediators cannot be forced to testify in court or in arbitration for what they know from the mediation except when it is required to protect the interests of children, to prevent harm to the physical or psychological health of individuals, or to enforce the mediation agreement. The parties may add a clause in the agreement stipulating that all or certain future disputes between them should be submitted to mediation. Mediation clauses, however, are not an obstacle to judicial procedures.

Article 10 of the Law of Ukraine "On mediation" defines the following features of mediation:

- Mediation can be done by a mediator independently or with the assistance of an organization that provides mediation.
- The parties choose their own mediator or mediators. The mediators themselves choose the means and methods of the mediation procedure in compliance with applicable laws, rules of mediation, and professional ethics.
- Mediation starts either when the parties agree upon the mediation procedure or within 30 days from the date one party has proposed the mediation or again at the moment specified in the proposal. The proposal can also be rejected.
- Mediation ends with: the signature of the mediation agreement, the statement of the parties or one of the parties addressed to the mediator to end the

mediation, the statement of the mediator that further efforts to reach agreement are no longer justified or if the dispute concerns the legitimate rights and interests of these persons the involvement of a third party is impossible.

The agreement reached by the parties may be summarized in written form. The agreement is a civil contract which must respect the laws of Ukraine, the interests of the state and the society, and its moral principles. If the mediation was conducted in criminal proceedings or arbitration, the results are made in an amicable agreement, an agreement based on accountability and reconciliation. The mediations of judicial proceedings in criminal, civil or commercial cases as well as arbitration, also have their own characteristics:

- The judge or arbitrator has the right to recommend the mediation procedure to the parties whenever he/she deems it appropriate.
- The judge or arbitrator has no right to recommend to the parties a mediator in particular. Parties that agree to a mediation procedure during a trial in a criminal, civil or commercial matter or during an arbitration, should be given information on existing organizations or mediators who could potentially provide the mediation.
- Upon request of the parties, the judge or arbitrator court suspends the proceedings for the mediation to take place but no longer than 14 days.

### *3.4. Requirements for mediators*

In the third chapter, the Law "On mediation" establishes requirements for mediators. Mediators must be at least 25-year-old, have a higher or vocational and technical education and 90 academic hours of certified professional training, which must include at least 45 hours of practical skills. Vocational training of mediators is provided by individuals, legal entities, programs provided by accredited mediators associations or institutions. The mediators association which conducts the accreditation of training programs adopts and makes public the provisions which set out the requirements for such programs. After the training, mediators receive a certification. This document contains the name of the training organizations; the surname, name and patronymic of trainers, the name of the curriculum; and the number of theoretical and practical training hours. The mediators are required to do the following:

- adhere to the law on mediation, to the rules of business and to respect professional ethics as well as the rules of confidentiality;
- check the credentials of representatives and/or legal representatives participating to the mediation;
- inform the parties about any conflict of interests or other circumstances that make it impossible to participate in the mediation;

- inform the parties about the procedure and the legal implications of the mediation;
- manage the mediation procedure;
- provide the parties with an opportunity to verify the legal and ethical standards of the mediation agreement.

The importance of professional training is very significant. For example, a mediator has been called in a conflict over polluting pig farms opposing the inhabitants of the village of Kopanky in the Kalush district of the Ivano-Frankivsk region to a Ukrainian agricultural company associated with a Danish investor 'Danosha'. The citizens has written a complaint to the World Bank which had funded the company. The organization called the 'Institute of Peace and Understanding' served as mediator to resolve the conflict. But instead of negotiating an agreement, the parties were given proverbs and folk wisdom and were asked to choose which ones matched their own view. Furthermore, even though the conflict concerned land use and public interest, the mediator tried to persuade the parties that the meetings should be kept confidential in order to "develop mutual trust between the parties to the conflict". Basic requirements for mediation were violated. This case could have been solved successfully if the mediator had had basic knowledge in conflict resolution. Also, the mediator must possess relevant work experience in the subject of the dispute.[14]

According to the Law "On mediation", the mediator does not have the right to determine the issue of the dispute between the parties. He is not entitled, unless the parties agree otherwise in written form, to provide guidance and recommendations on options for the resolution of the dispute, to assess the behaviour or attitudes of the parties, except for the explicit violations of legal or ethical standards and procedures.

The Law "On mediation" also emphasizes the need to comply with the principles of independence and neutrality of the mediator. The principle of independence is ensured by the fact that the mediator is not linked to any parties of the mediation, government agencies or businesses. The principle of neutrality means that the mediator is impartial to the conflicting parties. He is a neutral person who establishes and conducts the negotiation between the parties and helps them to reach an agreement. During the mediation procedure, he must commit himself to an impartial approach in any circumstances of the case. The mediator should report any situations that may cause reasonable doubt about his neutrality and/or independence.

In other countries in Europe, we can find similar legislative requirements. In Austria, the mediator is legally required to be impartial and to take special care to serve the parties without giving preferential treatment to either or any one of

14 Belikov, O., "The Conflicts in Business and the Possibility of Its Settlement" (2007) 5 *Law Journal* 1. Access: http://justinian.com.ua/article.php?id=2664

them. Mediators are bound by the legal obligation of secrecy. If they infringe their obligation to secrecy, they will face prosecution under criminal law. Certified persons may only act as mediators to guarantee that they have the required expert qualifications.[15] In Canada, the purpose of mediation is not to determine who is right or wrong but to find solutions that satisfy everyone. Often the solutions can be more creative than a court could provide. Participation in mediation may or may not be voluntary. For example, in certain cases you must attend mediation before a trial can be scheduled.[16]

### 3.5 *Additional requirements for acquiring the status of mediator*

The law restricts the circle of mediators to persons that

- are not found incapable or partially capable by a court;
- have not been convicted by a court;
- have not been dismissed from a position of judge, prosecutor, investigator from public services or from the service in local government bodies for breach of oath or corruption offence;
- have not seen their status of mediator terminated under the Article 22 of the Law "On mediation".

The mediator is responsible for the violations of the Law "On mediation", for the respect of codes of ethics and for any contractual obligations towards the parties. But the parties, who consider that unlawful acts or omissions have caused them a material and/or moral damage, may complain to the organization that has provided the mediation, the mediator's association, or may turn to courts to protect their legitimate rights and interests. After reviewing the complaint, the organization or the association of mediators may decide to remove the mediator from the registry, expel him from the membership of the organization, or to terminate the certification. Such a decision is published on the official website of the organization or the official site of the association of mediators. Reintroducing the mediator cannot take place earlier than in three years.

### 3.6 *Legal controls on mediators and internal codes of conduct*

The Law "On mediation" provides controls over the organizations that provide mediation and associations of mediators which develop and supervise the respect of voluntary codes of conduct or codes of ethics. The law requests to implement an effective quality control mechanisms over mediation services, to check the

15 *Alternative Dispute Resolution – Austria // European Judicial Network in Civil and Criminal Cases.* Access: http://ec.europa.eu/civiljustice/adr/adr_aus_en.htm

16 *What Is Alternative Dispute Resolution?* Access: http://settlement.org/ontario/legal-services/lawyers-and-other-legal-help/other-kinds-of-legal-help/what-is-alternative-dispute-resolution/.

level of professional training of mediators, to maintain a public registry of mediators, to ensure the congruence between the professional training of mediators and their offer of services. The organizations or associations must develop codes of conduct, which include the following provisions:

- the types of disputes subject to the codes;
- the procedure for the choice of a mediator or mediators;
- the procedure for the disqualification of a mediator;
- the allocation of costs between the parties;
- the procedure for the conduct of the mediation including the rights and obligations of the parties.

All supporting information should be disclosed to the public through websites. The review of complaints must be performed by disciplinary committees that are established on a regular basis. The review of a complaint is realized within a month from the reception by the responsible person. The Committee's findings are communicated to the parties in written form.

Another important issue is the remuneration of the mediators, which is definitely a good incentive for the fulfilment of their obligations. The Law "On mediation" specifies that the costs of mediation comprise the remuneration of the mediator(s) and the expenses related to the mediation. The costs are covered by the parties in equal shares, unless the parties agree otherwise. In our opinion, the activities of the associations of mediators should be financed by the state and local budgets, charitable contributions and from other allowed sources, as it is done in other countries. In Poland, for example, the remuneration of mediators comes from the state budget. The Mediation Service in the Czech Republic is a governmental organization under the jurisdiction of the Ministry of Justice. In Austria, the Department of extrajudicial resolution of conflicts works together with the Association of Approbation and Social Work, a private organization, which is subsidized by the Ministry of Justice.[17]

It should be noted that the compliance with the aforementioned standards and requirements does not guarantee the success of a mediation or of acceptable results, especially in environmental conflicts which always combine private and public interests. For example, there has been a mediation in a dispute regarding constructions near the city of Ivano-Frankivsk. The conflict was linked to a protected area where sports and recreational activities were taking place. A construction company, established by officials of the local government under faked names, built several nine-storey residential buildings, despite the fact that land lease agreement was for a single four-floor sports centre. Multiple public hearings, which in our country sometimes replace mediation, gave no result because the citizens knew nothing about the date and time of those public hearings. The

17 Khruslova, L.A., "Forms of Implementation of the Restorative Justice in Criminal Proceedings" (2007) 4 *Restorative Justice in Ukraine: Quarterly Bulletin* 29–31.

developer plans to build 10 other buildings of 800 apartments that will not only destroy the park but also the urban lake ecosystem. Two criminal proceedings and five lawsuits for invalidation of the lease have been initiated by the community. But the developer continues to move forward. A mediation was attempted with the builder, local authorities and the public but did not bring any result. The community refused to recognize the illegal construction, and the developer refused to stop or to compensate for the environmental damages. In this case, the developer is clearly not interested by any mediation because he does not intend to compromise. This is the biggest obstacle that slows down the development of the application of mediation.

With improper enforcement of laws, mediation does not work. If the offender (in our case, the illegal developer) knows that he does not need to make any concessions to the community because he can bribe a judge and the Architectural and Construction inspector, he has no incentive to undertake a mediation. The disruption of normal enforcement has very negative impacts not only on the respect of the law but also on the development of the mediation process. Ukraine's main tasks are to destroy the corruption that causes 80% of environmental violations and conflicts in the country and to ensure the true implementation of the general principles of law; otherwise, mediation will never be successful and widespread.

## Conclusion

The Law "On mediation" will play a major role in the development of mediation in Ukraine. This step of legitimization of mediation is very important in order to establish the credibility of the process within the Ukrainian society. The law also guarantees the full compliance with all directives and recommendations from the European authorities.

Regarding more specifically the development of environmental mediation in Ukraine, the next steps could include the following:

- research on the level of awareness of the community on the possibilities to participate in shaping and implementing environmental policies, and solving environmental conflicts;
- analysis of the use and effectiveness of ADR methods in environment;
- development of informational campaigns to raise awareness of the community about alternative ways to protect their environmental rights and resolve environmental conflicts;
- development of informational and educational materials concerning environmental mediation;
- development of a two-level training for mediators:

  i) First level – basic skills, solving environmental conflicts through alternative methods.
  ii) Second level – training coaches (mediators who would subsequently train specialists in environmental mediation).

# 2 Environmental mediation deficiencies in China and potential remedies

*Haifeng Deng*[1]

## Introduction

Starting from the promulgation of *Environmental Protection Law (Trial)* in 1979, Chinese environmental law has experienced more than 30 years of development and improvement. However, in contrast, due to the compressive economic growth, the overall environment in China tends to deteriorate, which results in a large number of environmental disputes. Since 1980s and 1990s, the number of environmental letters and visits has been increasing progressively. According to relevant officials in the State Environmental Protection Administration (SEPA), group incidents arising from environmental problems throughout the country increased by 11.6 times over the past decade, with average annual progressive increase of 28.8%.[2] The continuous increase of the environmental letters and visits and group incidents shows that the existing legal settlement mechanism of environmental disputes is not perfect and it cannot deal with the environmental interest demands within the system and institution. Therefore, it is necessary to carry out in-depth discussion and analysis on the existing environmental disputes settlement mechanism, in order to develop and improve the legally legitimate and rational environmental disputes settlement mechanism that conforms to China's social practice situation. In China's environmental disputes settlement mechanism, the environmental disputes mediation system wanders between facts and norms, between compromise and enforcement, and between administrative power and judicial power. It is necessary to deeply investigate how to balance the legal legitimacy and indigenous characteristics of China's environmental disputes mediation system and guarantee its validity.

1 Associate professor of law school, Tsinghua University, Beijing, China. Email address: denghf@tsinghua.edu.cn

2 Yulin, Z., "Dynamic Mechanism of the Environmental Degradation and Conflict Intensification in Chinese Rural Areas – Judging 'the Political and Economic Integration' from three 'Group Incidents' " in Wu Jinglian and Jiang Ping, eds., *Hongfan Review (Vol. 9)*, China Legal Publishing House, Beijing, 2007, 196.

## 1 Development and evolution of China's environmental disputes and current situation of the environmental disputes mediation system

Mediation refers to a way of settling the dispute between two parties, who invite a third party or agree to the active intervention of the third party to assist in the negotiation in a non-confrontational manner. The third party involved does not have the right to judge, which is different from reconciliation, negotiation, arbitration and litigation, etc.[3] China's mediation system mainly includes judicial, administrative and people's mediation.

### *1.1 Development and evolution of the environmental disputes*

According to the *National Environment Statistical Bulletin* issued by the Ministry of Environmental Protection, administrative authority of Chinese environmental protection over the years, the environmental cases accepted in 1997 included 203 administrative reconsideration cases, 90 administration lawsuit cases, and 44 administrative compensation cases. At the interval of five years, in 2002, there were 100,103 administrative punishment cases, 285 administrative reconsideration cases, 993 administration lawsuit cases and 62 administrative compensation cases, as well as 4 settled environmental crime cases. In 2007, decision was made on 101,325 environmental administrative punishment cases, 520 administrative reconsideration cases and three environmental crime cases. In 2012, there were 117,308 administrative punishment cases and 427 administrative reconsideration cases, as well as 892 348 calls/online complaints, 107,120 letters and 53 505 visits (visit/person).[4] Furthermore, according to the statistic estimation made by some Chinese scholars, there were 92,404 administrative punishment cases and 208 administrative reconsideration cases in 2006 and 2,418 cases entered the judicial process.

> The ratio among the number of environmental disputes, the number of cases entering the administrative procedure and the number of cases entering the judicial process is 255 : 38 : 1 based on the above data and it is thus clear that only a few of environmental cases enter the judicial process.[5]

3 Xingmei, Q., et al., *Study on Legislation, Theory and Practice of Chinese Mediation*, China University of Political Science & Law Press, Beijing, 2014, 11.

4 Ministry of Environmental Protection of the People's Republic of China, "National Environment Statistical Bulletin" Access: www.zhb.gov.cn/zwgk/hjtj/qghjtjgb/(Last access time: November 20, 2014).

5 Main estimation base for the about 2,418 cases entering the judicial process: "Work Report of the Supreme People's Court in 2006". In 2006, there were 4,382,407 first-instance civil cases nationwide, 95,052 administrative cases and 701,379 criminal cases with the ratio of total civil cases/administrative and criminal cases = 5.5: 1. According to the "National Environment Statistical Bulletin (2006)", in that very year, there were 372 cases, including 353 environmental administrative proceedings, 15 administrative compensation cases and 4 environmental

This shows that, although China's environmental disputes were 'multiplied' over the past 15 years, the judicial process is never a main channel to settle the environmental disputes. A large number of cases from the environmental disputes were treated with the environmental disputes mediation system, which means that the role of the environmental disputes mediation system playing in the settlement of China's environmental disputes cannot be ignored.

## 1.2 Current situation of the Chinese environmental disputes mediation system

At the moment, there are mainly three environmental dispute mediation modes, including judicial, administrative and people's mediation.

### 1.2.1 Judicial mediation

Judicial mediation is the most general mediation method. After 2002, the Supreme People's Court and the Ministry of Justice issued successively *Certain Regulations on Hearing the Civil Cases Involving the People's Mediation Agreement*, *Certain Regulations on People's Mediation Rules*, and *Certain Regulations on Applying the Summary Procedure into the Deliberation of Civil Cases.* In 2007, the Supreme People's Court established a 'New Sixteen-Character Guideline' that "consider the situation and combine mediation and judgment to close the case and resolve all conflicts".[6]

Generally speaking, courts at all levels, under the guidance of the superior court and the influence of the Supreme People's Court, always "start with the mediation" in dealing with most civil and commercial cases besides the cases which should be mediated as specified. In judicial practice, some environmental dispute cases were closed with the lawsuit mediation. Some Chinese scholars made the statistics on this matter, the proportion of environmental civil judgment paper, civil ruling paper, and civil mediation paper among judgment documents is '598: 145: 39', and the mediation accounts for 4.99% only. According to the current *administrative procedural law*, administrative proceedings are not suitable for mediation, so the environmental administrative case cannot be mediated. In the collection of judgment documents, no mediation document on the environmental crime was found. Furthermore, the contradiction between the plaintiff and the defendant in environmental civil cases is more intensified and difficult to mediate than that in ordinary civil cases. With regard to environmental civil cases, the 'communication space' is insufficient and it is difficult to apply non-legal

crime cases. Thus, it was estimated that the number of environmental civil cases entering the judicial process was (353 + 15) × 5.5 = 2046, adding up to 2,418. Please refer to Zhongmei, L., ed., *Ideal and Reality: Current Situation of Chinese Environmental Infringement Disputes and Construction of Relief Mechanism*, Law Press China, Beijing, 2011, 14.

6 Xi, X., ed., *Mediation: China and the World*, China University of Political Science & Law Press, Beijing, 2013, 53.

rules and procedures and settle disputes.[7] Environmental criminal mediation is reflected in the application to punish environmental crimes and its characteristics should embody the 'ultimate severity'. In this context, combined with the tense opposite relation between two parties in the environmental disputes, it is decided naturally that the environmental disputes judicial mediation cases are of small quantity, have little impact and remains to be developed in reality.

### *1.2.2 Administrative mediation*

Administrative mediation is currently the main form of environmental dispute mediation in China which is in the charge of environmental administrative department. It combines the practical features of China's competent environmental administrative department having both 'law enforcement administration power' and partial 'administrative legislation power'. This kind of mediation is usually easier and more operable in settling environmental disputes than judicial mediation. In recent years, there have been some professional environmental disputes administrative mediation organizations in China, such as Weihai and Penglai in Shandong Province, and environmental petition and administrative dispute mediation departments have been set up in the Environmental Protection Bureau. Some coastal developed areas have also formulated county-level regulated documents on the environmental disputes mediation. For example, the *Legal Basis Combing and Summary Table of the Provincial Department of Environmental Protection* issued by the Environmental Protection Department of Jiangsu Province classifies and systemizes the mediation process, specific matters, reference type and competent authorities and it covers relevant content in national laws, administrative laws, local policies and regulations at all levels.[8] The county-level administrative departments also actively compile summary text materials concerning the environmental protection mediation, which indicates that the environmental disputes in Chinese coastal areas and developed areas are more serious than those in other areas, and the local authority has high performance ability and transparency. It is proved through the aforementioned practices in grassroots areas that a rational and credible mediation system structure can only be constructed in the mediation process by enhancing the participation of both parties, intensifying the service orientation of competent authorities, limiting improper intervention of administrative power, and improving the transparency to release advantages of this negotiated dispute settlement mode and facilitate the purpose of the environmental disputes mediation.

7 Zhongmei, L., ed., *Ideal and Reality: Current Situation of Chinese Environmental Infringement Disputes and Construction of Relief Mechanism*, Law Press China, Beijing, 2011, 17.

8 Environmental Protection Department of Jiangsu Province, *Legal Basis Combing and Summary Table of the Provincial Department of Environmental Protection*, Chinese Government Public Information Online. Access: http://govinfo.nlc.gov.cn/jssfz/xxgk/jsshjbht/201210/t20121009_2843461.shtml?classid=451 (Last access time: October 22, 2014).

### *1.2.3 People's mediation*

People's mediation refers to the dispute mediation performed by the People's Mediation Committee. In August, 2010, the Standing Committee of the National People's Congress issued the People's Mediation Law of the People's Republic of China to systematically regulate the people's mediation and related supporting systems. The People's Mediation Committee is a mass organization at the basic level in China to solve people's internal disputes with the neighbourhood committee as the unit in cities and the village committee as the unit in rural areas. At the moment, such organizations officially solve a large number of basic level disputes in a proper way and such mediation mode is also applied in the environmental dispute field. For example, in July 2012, Lin'an Environmental Protection Bureau and Judicial Bureau of Hangzhou City, Zhejiang Province, jointly issued the *Opinions on Strengthening the People's Mediation of Environmental Protection Disputes* and set up the People's Mediation Committee for Environmental Protection Disputes. Besides, Shijiazhuang City in Hebei Province founded the People's Mediation Committee for Environmental Protection Disputes in all counties (cities and districts) with intervention of judicial departments for the judicial confirmation. Furthermore, Suzhou, Yunxiao County in Fujian Province, Lu'an City in Anhui Province and other places all set up such professional 'People's Mediation Committee for Environmental Pollution Disputes' or called 'People's Mediation Committee for Environmental Protection Disputes'.[9] Such institutions mainly concentrate in Chinese coastal areas and developed areas, where the mediation is selected more frequently than the vast Central and Western China, indicating that the people's mediation system on environmental disputes still have a broad influence space. In addition to the three aforementioned methods, some specialized agencies and organizations emerge as the civil mediation has developed rapidly in recent years, but their role in the environmental field is very limited.

In conclusion, with regard to the current environmental disputes mediation system in China, the administrative mediation of the environmental administrative department plays a main part with partial judicial mediation which, however, mainly focuses on the environmental civil disputes. The people's and civil mediation systems and methods are developing continuously, but they grow slowly environmental dispute mediation field due to their different development degrees in different areas, uneven resource allocation, insufficient influence and limited roles.

9 Daily, H., *Shijiazhuang Sets up the "People's Mediation Committee for Environmental Pollution Disputes"*, China Daily Website. Access: www.chinadaily.com.cn/hqgj/jryw/2013-12-20/content_10859743.html (Last access time: October 23, 2014); Lu'an Environmental Protection Bureau, *We Set up the People's Mediation Committee for Environmental Pollution Disputes*, Official website of the Lu'an Environmental Protection Bureau. Access: www.laepb.gov.cn/DocHtml/1/2014/6/5/4603894811435.html (Last access time: October 23, 2014).

## 2 Difficulties and defects of China's environmental disputes mediation system

### *2.1 Deficiency of legal basis*

The environmental administrative mediation system has been using Article 41 of the *Environmental Protection Law* (1989) as the main legal basis. The Article specifies

> A unit that has caused an environmental pollution hazard shall have the obligation to eliminate it and make compensation to the unit or individual that suffered direct losses. A dispute over the liability to make compensation or the amount of compensation may, at the request of the parties, be settled by the competent department of environmental protection administration or another department invested by law with power to conduct environmental supervision and management. If a party refuses to accept the decision on the settlement, it may bring a suit before a people's court. The party may also directly bring a suit before the people's court.

However, in this Article, the understanding of different subjects on the nature of 'settlement' is different, thus there are a lot of cases in practice where the party who refuses to accept the decision on the settlement brings an administrative proceedings instead of civil action to before the people's court. On November 26, 1991, the former SEPA (Ministry of Environmental Protection now) asked the Commission of Legislative Affairs of the National People's Congress (NPC) for instructions regarding whether the 'settlement' specified in Section II, Article 41 of the *Environmental Protection Law* was actually in accordance with the administrative proceedings or civil proceedings. On January 31, 1992, the Commission of Legislative Affairs of NPC replied, "The compensation responsibility arising from the environmental pollution hazard and the amount of compensation belong to civil disputes". According to Section II, Article 41 of the *Environmental Protection Law of the People's Republic of China*, the competent department of environmental protection administration shall settle the dispute over the liability to make compensation or the amount of compensation, at the request of the parties. If a party refuses to accept the decision on the settlement, it may bring a suit before a people's court. "But this is a civil suit between both parties of the civil dispute, thus an administrative suit cannot be filed with the competent department of environmental protection administration which makes the decision on the settlement as the defendant".[10] It can be seen from the reply

10 The reply said, "The compensation responsibility arising from the environmental pollution hazard and the amount of compensation belong to civil disputes. According to Section II, Article 41 of the *Environmental Protection Law of the People's Republic of China*, the competent department of environmental protection administration shall settle the dispute over the liability to make compensation or the amount of compensation, at the request of the

that although the Commission of Legislative Affairs of NPC believed that the compensation dispute arising from the environmental tort should be settled by way of civil actions, it did not give a clear explanation with regard to the nature of the 'settlement'. Apart from the *Environmental Protection Law* (1989), terms concerning the environmental disputes mediation in other relevant environmental legislations are also fuzzy and uncertain. The *Environmental Protection Law*, *Grassland Law* and *Forest Law* use 'settlement'; *Water Law* and Water Pollution Prevention and Control Law use 'mediation'; and *Air Pollution Prevention and Control Law*, *Environmental Noise Prevention and Control Law* and *Law on Prevention of Environmental Pollution Caused by Solid Waste* use 'mediation and settlement'.[11] From the point of these concepts, the understanding and determination of mediation in China is still unclear. Article 58 of the new *Environmental Protection Law* (2015) specifies that partial subject can bring a suit in terms of the environmental damage case before the people's court, but it does not provide special stipulations for the environmental disputes mediation. As a result, the environmental disputes mediation system is excluded from the dispute settlement framework determined by the *Environment Protection Law*.

In terms of the judicial mediation, the court attempts to mediate the civil compensation or incidental civil action for partial judiciary cases involving environmental disputes, but the mediation is mainly carried out before litigation. Most environmental cases entering the litigation phase do not have single legal relation and clear facts, thus it is difficult to close the case by way of mediation. In terms of the people's mediation, some places issue specialized regulations and opinions in relation to the environmental disputes mediation and set up the People's Mediation Committee for Environmental Protection Disputes. However, its biggest problem is that the settlement of environmental disputes requires a lot of scientific judgment and even anticipation of uncertain factors, while the People's Mediation Committee does not have such capacity. Therefore, this mode is rare in practice. With regard to the mediation practice, the most important legal requirement lies in clear legal basis, including the basis in the substantial law and procedural law. Without normative procedures, the mediation process will be full of arbitrariness, and without a substantially legal basis, the mediation result will be optional, leading to the chaos in the executive and judicial power. Eventually, the mediation will lack the given power and effectiveness that it shall have.

parties. If a party refuses to accept the decision on the settlement, it may bring a suit before a people's court. But this is a civil suit between both parties of the civil dispute, thus an administrative suit cannot be filed with the competent department of environmental protection administration which makes the decision on the settlement as the defendant. Please refer to Yunjiao, X. and Z. Jijun, "Realistic Implication and System Improvement of the Environmental Administrative Intermediation" (2010) 6 *Journal of Wuhan University of Technology (Social Science Edition)* 866.

11 Chao, L., "Omission and Complementation: Environmental Administrative Mediation System in a Dilemma to Settle Environmental Tort Disputes" (2011) 3 *Journal of Henan Administrative Institute of Politics and Law* 109.

On the whole, some current specialized laws in the environmental field stipulates for the mediation.[12] But basic environmental law includes fundamentally principled stipulations and explanations, making it difficult to give proper instructions and guidance in the specific mediation practice. The legislation of the environmental disputes mediation, for the most part, scatters in multiple department laws and specialized laws in the patter of 'piecing together'. Therefore, the environmental disputes mediation and related systems are short of unified and specialized legislation action and explanation in regard to environmental disputes mediation on the whole, which is adverse to integral development of the environmental disputes mediation system, restricts the practice of environmental administrative and judicial practice, and affects the settlement of environmental cases. Moreover, the legislative absence occurs to both specialized legislation and exception provisions of the environmental disputes mediation and involved environmental problems. In the traditional mediation process, the administrative organ serves as 'the third person' only to play the role of cooperation, facilitation and guidance, without intervening into the mediation process subjectively. Nevertheless, it is hard to settle environmental disputes with mediation in a large number of environmental cases. As stakeholders are usually unspecific residents and local government in the region and the case determination and settlement involve complex legal relations, such case needs to be solved by way of lawsuit and other methods. But there are no separate provisions and explanations regarding such case in the environmental disputes mediation stipulation.

## 2.2 *Unified construction thought and action*

From the practical development in recent years, China's disputes mediation system has developed gradually from 'empirical' selection to institutional construction, but it has been short of uniformly constructed thoughts and actions. As mentioned earlier, some places make specialized legislative stipulation with regard to the environmental disputes mediation and some places even set up specialized environmental disputes mediation institutions. However, seen from the present situation of legislation and dynamic state of the judicial administrative, China does not have unified construction thought and action. The current environment related lawsuits' focus on the environmental non-profit litigation, lacking attention to the other ways of settling disputes. Unified construction thought and action are the precondition for establishing and developing the environmental disputes mediation system and the fundamental premise for running the system normally on a regular basis. If the local government goes ahead of the central government to pay attention to the environmental disputes mediation, the environmental disputes mediation system will certainly lack unified institutional norm and

12 For example: *Water Pollution Prevention and Control Law of the People's Republic of China* (2008), art. 86; *Air Pollution Prevention and Control Law of the People's Republic of China* (2000), art. 62; *Law on the Prevention and Control of Environmental Pollution by Solid Wastes* (2004), art. 84; *Water Law of the People's Republic of China* (2002), art. 57.

guarantee, causing chaos to the practice. Just as some scholars say, the tendency of China's environmental disputes settlement mechanism requires the integration of environmental litigation system and non-litigation system, and in a society with judicial resource shortage and sharply increased litigation cost, the disparity expansion in applying judicial resources will lead to new social inequality, thus all countries carry out judicial reform widely to seek the reasonable construction of the disputes settlement mechanism.[13] Nevertheless, these countries lack both the response to such appeal and unified construction thought and action. Therefore, China must give priority to the unified construction thought and action in the development process of the environmental disputes mediation system.

## 2.3 Lack of professional mediation organizations and employees

The features of the environmental disputes include wide scope of influence, strong technology, and close stake. For this reason, the factors related to the environmental disputes are very complex, including diversified interests involved, universality of environmental disputes, and application of science and technology in the environmental disputes. Besides, the strength of both parties is imbalanced, including different economic strength and information asymmetry.[14] Thus, it is necessary for professional institutions and employees to involve in the environmental disputes settlement process. Whereas, for the administrative mediation, the new *Environmental Protection Law* does not specify the subject of the administrative mediation, it is still unclear which institution will act as the professional mediation organization. With unique features, environmental disputes cases require that the employees shall be professional and well trained in terms of the environment. These employees shall not only be simple practitioners with legal background but also include people of environmental specialty and technicians with certain quality and background. In the context of present actual condition and system arrangement, China lacks professional environmental disputes mediation organizations and most mediation employees are legal professionals, in badly need of the participation of people with other industry background.

## 2.4 Single mediation mode and procedural chaos

In practice, the administrative mediation is the normal state of the environmental disputes mediation and the administrative mediation subject plays an irreplaceable

13 Yong, W., "Discussion on the Communication and Coordination of the Environmental Litigation Mechanism and Non-litigation Mechanism" in Z. Zitai, ed., *Research on Forefront Issues of Environmental Disputes Settlement- Talks of Chinese, Japanese and South Korean Scholars*, Tsinghua University Press, Beijing, 2007, 283.

14 Yong, W., "Discussion on the Communication and Coordination of the Environmental Litigation Mechanism and Non-litigation Mechanism" in Z. Zitai, ed., *Research on Forefront Issues of Environmental Disputes Settlement- Talks of Chinese, Japanese and South Korean Scholars*, Tsinghua University Press, Beijing, 2007, 282.

in the environmental disputes mediation by virtue of its abundant administrative resources. From the point of efficiency, the environmental administrative mediation has some comparative advantages, but the administrative power is 'expansive' and 'arbitrary' in nature, which goes against the balance between fairness and efficiency in the environmental disputes settlement process. The judicial mediation and people's mediation have the comparative advantages that the administrative mediation lacks, especially the people's mediation, which starts trying to set up professional people's mediation institutions with personnel allocation in some places of China to resolve environmental disputes. It is also a solution that the environmental disputes mediation mode shall not be limited to the administrative, judicial and people's mediation.

Furthermore, due to different standards and system designs for the environmental disputes mediation in different places, provisions on the procedure have nothing in common with each other, resulting in the procedural chaos, which has a large influence on the actual effect and credibility of the mediation. It is also hard for the party to express its intention and claim completely in the case of such procedural chaos, reducing the credibility of the environmental disputes mediation system. Some scholars think, the administrative mediation does not have to waste too much energy on the procedure and it can quickly settle disputes by virtue of the administrative body's human resource, materials and familiarity with the situation.[15] As far as I am concerned, this is open to discussion. It is because of the advantages of administrative bodies and administrative power in the administrative mediation that more attention shall be paid to the procedure construction in the mediation process. Right mediation procedure guarantees the legally appropriate intervention of the administrative power, facilitating the credibility of the environmental disputes mediation system.

### 2.5 *Insufficient legal effect and low executive force of the current environmental disputes mediation system*

In respect to the legal effect, the environmental administrative mediation agreement has weak legal effect and relies mostly on the consensus and conscientiousness of both parties to keep promise and supervision by public opinions. Some scholars put forward that the reason why the legal effect of the environmental administrative mediation is insufficient mainly lies in its inherent difficulty, special environmental tort disputes and poor popularity of legal knowledge on the environmental protection.[16] However, I think the biggest difficulty rests with the authority and given power of the mediation. In particular, the confidence of the

15 Chao, Z. and Z. Guanglei, "Discussion and Analysis on the Improvement of Chinese Administrative Mediation System for Environmental Disputes" (2011) 21 *Knowledge Economy* 39.

16 Chao, L., *Problems and Logic: Empirical Research on Environmental Tort Relief Mechanism*, Law Press China, Beijing, 2012, 234.

party to settle disputes will be greatly reduced in contrast with the environmental litigation activity. In addition, Profession Cai Shouqiu believes that, failure to apply for the legal compulsion that the people's court directly executes or implements the administrative enforcement according to law is not equal to the absence of any legal effect, binding effect and execution, and the administrative mediation agreement has the legal effect similar to that of a contract, so that when one party fails to perform the mediation agreement or go back after the agreement takes effect for no reason, the other party shall have rights to bring the civil actions before the people's court to enforce the performance on the other party.[17] It proves that the environmental administrative mediation has certain legal effect, which is insufficient. The *Several Opinions on Establishing and Improving the Connected Litigation and Non-Litigation Contradiction and Disputes Settlement Mechanism* issued by the Supreme People's Court encourages the administrative organ to exercise official powers, supports the administrative mediation action and guarantees the given power of the mediation agreement, but it refers to civil rights and obligations mostly and does not match the environmental damage cases completely. It shows that the effect of the environmental administrative mediation cannot rely fully on the substantial law and thus it is greatly reduced. In the people's mediation mode, the Supreme Court defines the nature of the people's mediation agreement in the *Certain Regulations on Hearing Civil Cases Involving the People's Mediation Agreement*, which strengthens the legal effect of the people's mediation agreement. But it must be clear that the starting point for formulating polities is, to a great extent, civil and commercial disputes, rather than environmental disputes. The legal effect of the mediation system directly determines the effectiveness of the environmental disputes mediation system and if it is weak, it will go against the system construction and operation and against the coordination of the relationship between the environmental disputes mediation agreement and court trial.

The main reason for the executive power to be low rests with the administrative mediation. In the administrative mediation of environmental disputes, as the mediation agreement does not have direct enforcement power, the administrative resources will be wasted and the expected purpose of saving judicial resources will not be realized either, if both parties regret their non-performance or turn to purse the litigation. With low execution, the authority of the decision made by administrative organs is challenged and the enthusiasm of the party is also greatly affected. The mediation agreement formed by the people's mediation has been given the nature of contract and basis of the substantial law. In terms of the judicial mediation, the mediation agreement in payment nature is enforceable, and the execution issue of the judicial mediation for environmental disputes is not as serious as those in the two aforementioned modes since the judicial mediation refers to currently general rules.

17 Juan, Y., "Construction of the Administrative Alternative Dispute Resolution (ADR) Mechanism for Environmental Disputes" (2003) 12 *North Environment* 25.

## 3 Countermeasure design for improving China's environmental disputes mediation system

### *3.1 Make professional laws and regulations to fill in the legislative blank*

At present, China lacks specialized legislation in the environmental disputes mediation system and needs to make specific environmental disputes mediation laws. In the legislation process, the following points attention. First, integrate, systemize and sum up scattered partial laws, and relevant laws and regulations among legal fields and make specific stipulation. Second, highlight and repeatedly demonstrate the 'uncertainty of science and technology', 'public interest' and other features of the environmental dispute and make the legislation flexible to leave enough space for the 'uncertainty of science and technology'. Combine the 'principled generalization' and 'detailed description', especially the latter. Third, focus on procedural rules. Procedure is an effective way and path to limit public rights, to guarantee the mediation legal and effective, and to enable the mediation to have 'both fairness and efficiency', and it must be confronted and taken into account. Fourth, the integration and association of four mediation modes shall be taken into consideration, and in the environmental disputes mediation system, the administrative, judicial, people's mediation and even civil mediation need to be considered and arranged legislatively with a positive interactive mechanism of the environmental disputes mediation. Just as some scholars say,

> We cannot just emphasize official litigation and trial system blindly, or simplify the governing by law and rejuvenating the country as litigation supreme, or the private disputes settlement by the people as ignorance of the law, or ignore the legitimacy of Chinese civil mediation similar to alternative dispute resolution (ADR), while we are thinking how to carry forward the justice concept of the procedure.[18]

The ADR also needs to be embodied and highlighted in the legislation, thus the legislation shall consider and arrange the aforementioned modes on the whole to prepare specialized legislation to balance different mediation modes instead of applying general rules uniformly. Like appropriate division of labour in hearing the environmental disputes cases, the scope of accepting cases can be determined legislatively in different ways, including summarizing, positive and negative enumeration, etc., and the corresponding mediation mode can be chosen according to the case facts of disputes. Last, connect the ADR with the litigation mechanism in the legislation process. According to some scholars, excessive lawsuits will make the social relations more adversarial and tense and increase public cost. ADR has both the significance to expand the legal application and value to

18 Bo, C., "Analysis on the Institutional Principle and Reference Significance of ADR" (2004) 9 *Seeker* 84.

improve the judicature.[19] It is important to note that because of the characteristics of the environmental disputes, ADR is not applicable to all disputes cases. Therefore, the litigation mechanism shall be integrated and connected with the ADR, without separating them. Only when they are considered and affirmed in the legislation can their coordination and interaction and action be provided with construction precondition and institutional guarantee.

### 3.2 *Define and improve the existing laws and regulations on the environmental disputes mediation system*

The following points need attention to define the existing laws and regulations on the environmental disputes mediation system. First, define the legal language, normalize and unify the words like 'mediation' in the *Environmental Protection Law of the People's Republic of China* and other environmental legislations, and sort out partial laws on this basis; secondly, define the nature of the environmental disputes mediation, provide the legal interpretation for vague laws and regulations to explain the nature difference in different environmental disputes mediation modes and thoroughly clarify the relations among the administrative, judicial, people's and civil mediation; thirdly, define the procedure, arrange the mediation procedure institutionally in unity and strengthen the existing procedure, and clarify the vague parts in the procedure. For specific procedure arrangement and construction, some scholars put forward their own construction and explanation,[20] but in my view, the attention shall be paid on the control of the mediation procedure for the intervention of the administrative power. Furthermore, it is important to note that the ADR and litigation mechanism shall be associated and connected in the procedure design to facilitate and enhance the executive force of the mediation agreement and effectiveness of the environmental disputes mediation system. Last, it needs to be clear that the effect of the mediation agreement is directly related to the achievement transformation of the environmental disputes mediation. There is no consensus for the discussion in the theoretical cycle either. Most people think that the mediation agreement shall only have the effect in contract law, but not res judicata in the procedural law. The general impression of partial scholars also indicates that it will be, beyond doubt, a big blow to the confidence of the party without unclear provisions on the effect of the mediation agreement or lack of enforceability.[21] I think, if the

19 Yong, W., "Discussion on the Communication and Coordination of the Environmental Litigation Mechanism and Non-litigation Mechanism" in Z. Zitai, ed., *Research on Forefront Issues of Environmental Disputes Settlement- Talks of Chinese, Japanese and South Korean Scholars*, Tsinghua University Press, Beijing, 2007, 283.

20 Weiwei, X. and L. Yan, "Discussion and Analysis on the Improvement of Chinese Administrative Mediation System for Environmental Disputes" (2014) 6 *Journal of Liaoning Administration College* 37.

21 Gang, W., "Current Situation and Problems of the Environmental Dispute Mediation in China" (2013) 1 *Ecological Economy* 154.

environmental administrative mediation is given the compulsion, it will bring adverse effect to the proper and prudent settlement of environmental disputes, which must be treated carefully and maintained as it involves the environmental problems. It is suggested that the environmental administrative mediation agreement shall be given the basis in the substantial law and based on this, the appeal of the party can be realized by taking a different approach according to the facts of the disputes, which is conductive to obtain a better result with the environmental disputes considered and weighed by multiple parties.

### 3.3 *Establish professional mediation organizations and train professional employees*

At the moment, partial provinces and cities try to set up the professional mediation organizations, most of which are people's mediation institutions. Some scholars suggest, the Environmental Disputes Mediation Committee shall be established inside the competent department of environmental protection administration of the people's government above county levels to be responsible for specific disputes mediation by combining with the reality of the environmental law enforcement management system in China.[22] It is necessary to set the special mediation institution, but I do not agree with the idea of setting up the mediation organization inside the competent department of environmental protection administration. In the environmental disputes mediation process, the intervention of the administrative power is enough to domain the whole process of the environmental administrative mediation. However, as the administrative power is endowed with 'expansion' and 'arbitrariness', the environmental administrative mediation cannot be taken up by the competent administrative department entirely. For this reason, it is suggested that the attention shall be paid to the 'quasi-neutral status' and 'public interest' of the mediation organizations in their foundation, so that the mediation organizations are not completely neutral and independent or installed in the competent administrative department. In terms of the authorized strength, staff composition, formation and capital source are critical. The staff composition and formation, in my view, can be treated in different ways. The personnel can be selected and transferred from the competent department of environmental protection administration to the administrative posts, while the mediation post must be taken up by professionals of environmental protection and it shall be formed independently from the competent department of environmental protection administration. The capital source shall rely on the planning and coordination in many ways, instead of depending on the support of the administrative fund only. For the mediation institution, it can maintain a certain number of administrative personnel to keep the normal operation of the

22 Yunjiao, X. and Z. Jijun, "Realistic Implication and System Improvement of the Environmental Administrative Intermediation" (2010) 6 *Journal of Wuhan University of Technology (Social Science Edition)* 868.

institution. It is not necessary to set up a special permanent mediation post, but to select mediator from the expert database and other talent groups in case of the environmental disputes to form a temporary mediator collective. In this way, it guarantees the daily operation of the institution, reduces unnecessary wasting of administrative resources and makes for a fair and open mediation process.

Professional mediators need to be screened and selected from employees in different industries with different background. Just as some scholars conclude, the environmental disputes usually settled by temporarily transferring personnel or turning the case to other government sectors in that the function positioning of the administrative mediation institution is incorrect and the technology strength falls behind,[23] thus the importance shall be attached to the selection of professional mediators to carry out the environmental disputes mediation. In addition, the mediators shall bear some legal liability with different consequences of responsibility according to different behaviours. The consulting system can also be applied to invite some specialists, scholars and practitioners to the mediation process to give opinions in their subject and field in combination with the current situation of the mediation and actual details of the dispute case, so as to enhance the success rate of the environmental disputes mediation.

### 3.4 Enhance communication and connection of non-litigation system and litigation system; promote public engagement

Mediation system of environmental disputes in China mainly includes administrative conciliation, judicial mediation, people's mediation and civil mediation. But the solution is mainly relied on the first three. Here is about the issue of executive power and judicial power. The executive power has a direct influence on society. It is mandatory and full of scalability.[24] Thus, on the basis of realizing the self-control and procedure control of executive power, there is also the need to strengthen the censorship and control for executive power from the judicial power. During the process of the administrative mediation of environmental disputes, 'abnormal intervention' in the name of mediation often appears. Faced various social contradictions, the attitude of executive power has a distinct tendency, and the judicial power is neutrality.[25] During the process of the mediation of environmental disputes which led by executive power, the phenomenon about 'valuing the fact and neglecting the program' often occurs. It is propitious to enhance attaching 'rightful' importance to the program during the mediation process by envisaging the judicial power anew. To know the executive power

23 Hongfei, X. and G. Chengyun, "Discussion on the Institutional Deficiency and Improvement for the Administrative Mediation of Environmental Disputes" (2013) 3 *Environmental Technology* 72.

24 Niansong, Y. and X. Gangling, "Study of Executive Power" (2001) 4 *Tribune of Political Science and Law* 55.

25 Xiaoxia, S., "The Nature of Judicial Power Is Judgment-Ten Distinctions Between Judicial Power and Executive Power" (1998) 8 *Legal Science Monthly (Faxue)* 34.

and judicial power again in the mediation process is also conductive to searching the balance between the prior determinative force and ultimacy in the mediation result and keep the steady and indemnificatory of judicial power.

When we review the executive power and judicial power in the mediation system of environmental disputes, a new view is also provided for us to regard the connection of the non-litigation system and litigation system in mediation of environmental disputes. Environmental administrative conciliation and environmental people's mediation are non-litigation activities and environmental judicial mediation is litigation activity. There is no doubt that non-litigation system plays a more and more important role in the mediation system of environment disputes. As the scholar says,

> The non-litigation system of mediation system of environment disputes can promote the reforming and perfecting of legal institution and make people access the controversy better. We shall perfect the ADR system, establish a more diverse dispute resolution, give the parties the right to choose the procedure, make the resolution of alternative dispute and lawsuit draw on each other's strength, resolve disputes appropriately, save social resource and make the resolution of environmental disputes more reasonable.[26]

But how to structure the communication and connection between the two sides, affects the executive force and credibility of mediation of environmental disputes. As far as the mediation agreement of environmental disputes, only enhance the communication and connection of non-litigation system and litigation system, can provide the mediation agreement a better safeguard and the promotion of the executive force will improve the recognition degree of mediation system of environmental disputes. As far as the relationship orientation and acknowledge of environmental lawsuit and non-litigation, the point of the non-litigation system and litigation system during environmental disputes mediation shall lie in the environmental administrative conciliation area. Further extension, the point is in the transformation of executive force of mediation agreement and protection of system of mediation result.

To transform the executive force of the agreement will help develop and popularize the environmental administrative conciliation system and benefit the credibility promotion of the environmental administrative conciliation system. The protection system for mediation results will help promote the efficiency of administration and authority of environmental administrative conciliation, and play a role of external warning. In the communication of different methods and organizations in the internal of mediation system of environmental disputes, some scholars at this point put forward some advice, which are partition the

26 Yong, W., "Discussion on the Communication and Coordination of the Environmental Litigation Mechanism and Non-litigation Mechanism" in Z. Zitai, ed., *Research on Forefront Issues of Environmental Disputes Settlement- Talks of Chinese, Japanese and South Korean Scholars*, Tsinghua University Press, Beijing, 2007, 281.

environmental disputes by the standards of 'audit the fact' and 'audit the law' to realize the communication of four mediation methods.[27] The author thinks this is appropriate and suitable. But the author also deems that the premise factor of realizing the communication of four mediation methods is public engagement. Only if the public engaged, then the choice of environmental disputes mediation methods and the development of systems can possess practical significance and foundation. And only if more of the public engaged, then the mediation system of environmental disputes could progress continuously.

## Conclusion

As mentioned earlier, the mediation system of environmental disputes which is put into force for now doesn't suit the cases of China's environmental disputes, and this phenomenon grows every day. The mediation system of environmental disputes needs to be replenished, updated and completed in time. As a dispute-solving method which possesses both justice and efficiency, the mediation system of environmental disputes has good practical significance and system foundation, and it is believed to play a more important role in the solving system of environmental disputes in future. Besides, the development and progress of China's mediation system of environmental disputes needs to combine with China's long-term experience of the mediation system and be based on the environmental litigation system and establish and complete the environmental non-litigation dispute-solving system represented by the ADR system actively in order to cooperate with the environmental litigation system. By the supplement and structure of the program system, we can make an effort to push China's environmental legal construction and better serve the long-term development of China's environmental protection cause.

27 "As far as the civil mediation, pay attention to the small cases of dispute, low requirements for technical evaluation of environmental disputes, cases of environmental dispute with clear legal relation; the administrative conciliation shall be based on solving the environmental disputes with high technical evaluation requirements, large range of influence and clear legal relation; the court mainly solves the cases with complex legal relation. The civil mediation and administrative conciliation mainly are based on the mediation of disputing the fact, which is audit of the fact; the court is mainly based on the mediation of disputing the legal relation, which is audit of the law". Reference to Junfeng, D., "On the Structure of Mediation System of Environmental Disputes" in Z. Xintai, ed., *Research on Forefront Issues of Environmental Disputes Settlement- Talks of Chinese, Japanese and South Korean Scholars*, Tsinghua University Press, Beijing, 2007, 306.

# 3 A legal status for mediation in general administrative law in the Netherlands?

*Kars J. de Graaf*[1] *and Hanna D. Tolsma*[2]

## Introduction

Administrative decision making in the Netherlands frequently leads to disputes between governmental bodies and citizens. As many decision-making processes involve conflicting interests to be weighed against each other, disputes are inevitable. In the field of environmental law, conflicts come in many different shapes and sizes. Quite time consuming and complex is, for instance, the process of single-case decision making regarding the placement of a wind park for the purpose of renewable energy. Developers need all kinds of administrative decisions in order to get permission from authorities; spatial planning, nature conservation and industrial effects are all relevant aspects. Various public authorities are involved from state level to local level. Legal proceedings are almost inevitable since local residents often fear noise and light pollution and deterioration of the surroundings of their home and the view. Relatively simple is for example a conflict that may rise from amending an environmental permit for a metalworking company.

In the Netherlands, it was only towards the end of the last century that mediation became known as an instrument for settling administrative disputes.[3] In administrative disputes relating to environmental law, mediation has also proved to be an effective instrument to resolve the dispute between the parties.[4] However, the General Administrative Law Act (*Algemene wet bestuursrecht*, henceforth referred to as GALA) that provides rules predominantly for single-case administrative decision making and for legal protection does not contain any specific provisions regarding the use of mediation. Soon after the first experiences with

1 Associate professor with a chair in Public Law and Sustainability, Department of Constitutional Law, Administrative Law and Public Administration, University of Groningen, the Netherlands. Email address: k.j.de.graaf@rug.nl

2 Assistant professor, Department of Constitutional Law, Administrative Law and Public Administration, University of Groningen, the Netherlands. Email address: h.d.tolsma@rug.nl

3 Chin-A-Fat, B.E.S., "Mediation in het milieurecht" in F.C.A.M. Michiels, ed., *Recht op het doel af: Opstellen over doelmatigheid en doeltreffendheid van het overheidshandelen in de democratische rechtsstaat*, W.E.J. Tjeenk Willink, Deventer, 1998, 207.

4 Wiggers-Rust, L.F., et al., *Toepassing van mediation bij conflicten in het leefomgevingsbeleid*, BJu, Den Haag, 2000.

mediation, legal scholars began to advocate the implementation of general provisions in the GALA that would not just recognize the potential positive effects of using mediation and mediation techniques in administrative decision making and administrative adjudication but would also raise potential barriers in stimulating these methods of alternative dispute resolution (ADR).[5] However, the commonly accepted view at that time was that before being enshrined in the GALA, the concept of mediation in administrative conflicts should first take on clearer shape.

Since that time, a lot of experience has been gained with mediation in administrative law. Government policy has therefore been aimed at promoting mediation.[6] In April 2005, the Ministry of Justice implemented a number of policy measures to promote the use of mediation, including allowing courts to refer the parties to a mediator. Mediation is considered as an important alternative to the legal procedures set out in the GALA. The formal character of the implementation of those legal procedures in practice is at odds with the need of citizens and administrative authorities. 'Juridification of conflicts', 'taking too long to make decisions' and 'not listening to citizens' are typical elements of the picture that exists of the procedural approach to administrative conflicts that the GALA seems to advocate in practice. An evaluation report concerned with the GALA shows that citizens want an informal procedure with direct personal contact.[7]

In view of the aforementioned, the question arises whether the concept of mediation in administrative law has now taken shape clearly enough for it to be given a legal basis in the Dutch GALA. Is regulation in administrative law desirable in order to remove obstacles experienced in practice with regard to the use of mediation?

In our contribution, we focus on environmental mediation during the administrative decision-making process and during administrative court procedures in the Netherlands from a legal perspective. The use of mediation to increase the acceptance of the outcome of complex policy decision making is not taken into account. Relevant also is that we will focus this contribution on single-case decision making by administrative authorities; the general rules in the GALA are to a large extent also applicable for regulation in the form of general binding rules by administrative authorities, but Dutch administrative law will in general only allow an interested party to appeal to an administrative court when there is a single case administrative law decision. Furthermore, it should be noted that the term 'environment' is used in a broad sense, referring to industrial effects on the environment (such as waist, air pollution and noise) as well as to spatial planning, water, nature conservation, etc.

We start by giving an overview on the implementation of mediation in the administrative decision-making process and court procedures in administrative law. Governmental projects aimed at stimulating forms of ADR started at the

5 Kaajan, M., "Mediation in het bestuursrecht: Mogelijkheden voor een wettelijke regeling" (2001) *Ars Aequi* 64.
6 *Parliamentary Papers II* 2003/04, 29 528, no. 1 (Mediation and the legal system).
7 Committee Evaluation General Administrative Law Act 2007, *Toepassing en effecten van de Algemene wet bestuursrecht 2002–2006*, BJu, The Hague, 2007, 15–16.

beginning of this century with a clear focus on ***mediation***. At this point in time, the focus is not specifically on the use of mediation, but more on the use of ***mediation techniques*** by civil servants who have to deal with objections to administrative decisions, and by judges in administrative courts (section 1). Common view is that environmental disputes are well suited to mediation as a method of dispute resolution. However, there are some potential legal constraints on environmental mediation that must be considered. We give an overview on possible legal limitations (section 2). As mentioned before, giving the use of mediation a legal status is under discussion in the Netherlands. We will critically analyze a new proposal for an act to stimulate mediation in administrative disputes that was sent to Parliament in June 2014 (section 3). This chapter concludes with some final remarks.

## 1 Embedding environmental mediation in Dutch administrative law

This section examines the way mediation is embedded in Dutch administrative law. First, we highlight the main aspects of the Dutch system of dispute resolution (section 1.1).[8] Then we discuss the concepts of both mediation and mediation techniques and explain how these methods of ADR fit within the Dutch legal framework of administrative law (section 1.2). Finally, we present some empirical data that shows that in practice mediation plays a minor role and the focus in the Netherlands is on the use of mediation techniques by administrative authorities and courts in the process of dealing with administrative conflicts (1.3).

### *1.1 General Administrative Law Act*

Environmental law as it currently stands in the Netherlands is spread over numerous laws relating to spatial planning, environmental protection, nature conservation, water management and so on.[9] General rules for administrative decision making and legal protection are organized in the GALA. In general, a person who or organization that disagrees with a decision of an administrative authority first has to file an objection with the administrative authority that made the decision.[10] A key aspect of this pre-trial proceeding is that the administrative authority shall provide the interested parties the opportunity to be heard. It has three options to fulfil this obligation. The hearing can be conducted by the administrative authority

8 See more extensively Langbroek, P., et al., "The Dutch System of Dispute Resolution in Administrative Law" in D.C. Dragos and B. Neamtu, eds., *Alternative Dispute Resolution in European Administrative Law*, Springer-Verlag, Berlin-Heidelberg, 2014, chapter 4.

9 The government is now working on restructuring environmental and planning law into one Environment and Planning Act. See De Graaf, K.J. and H.D. Tolsma, "Country Report: the Netherlands: The Future Environment and Planning Act and the Impact of the Crisis and Recovery Act" (2015) 5 *IUCNAEL EJournal* 293.

10 *General Administrative Law Act*, art. 7:1.

itself, by a civil servant or by an advisory committee that will – after the hearing – formulate an advisory opinion for the administrative authority.[11] The GALA prescribes a full review of the contested decision bases on law, applicable policies and all relevant circumstances. The procedure gives the administrative authority an opportunity to reconsider its decision, to repair the reasoning and other shortcomings of the initial decisions. Participating in the objection procedure is a precondition to lodge an appeal with an administrative court. In Dutch administrative law, a decision from a first instance administrative district court can be appealed against at the Administrative Jurisdiction Division of the Council of State.[12]

In most cases, the procedures mentioned earlier are applicable. However, especially in the field of environmental law, there are some exceptions. In the first place, the objection proceeding is not mandatory if the initial decision is prepared using the so-called uniform public preparatory procedure.[13] This preparatory procedure applies if it is so provided by law or by a decision of the administrative authority. Usually it is applied for complex decisions in the field of environmental law, for instance a land-use plan and most types of environmental permits. One important element of this preparatory procedure is that interested parties may express their views to the administrative authority on a draft decision, either in writing or orally. Secondly, in land-use planning and some of the environmental cases, the Administrative Jurisdiction Division of the Council of the state is designated as a special first instance (and final) administrative court.[14]

### *1.2 Mediation and mediation techniques*

Complementing the formal procedures of administrative law set out in the GALA, the incorporation of both mediation and mediation techniques into the process of administrative decision making and court procedures is stimulated by policy measures. We will explain the implementation of both forms of ADR.

Mediation is generally defined as a form of dispute resolution whereby an independent neutral third party, the mediator, helps parties to find a solution for their mutual conflict. In the Netherlands, the Mediation Federation Netherland (MFN) guarantees the quality of mediators. Mediators who meet certain quality requirements and work under specified conditions are registered in the MFN-register. This is a register of qualified mediators that is recognized by the market and the judiciary. MFN-mediators have to abide by the rules and the code of conduct of the MFN. The rules contain for example provisions on appointing a mediator, on privacy, on confidentially and about the end of mediation.[15] It should be noted that parties to a conflict always start mediation on a voluntary basis.

11 *General Administrative Law Act*, art. 7:5 and 7:13.
12 *General Administrative Law Act*, art. 8:105.
13 *General Administrative Law Act*, division 3.4.
14 *General Administrative Law Act*, Appendix 2, Chapter 2.
15 Mediators Federatie Nederland, *Mediation Rules.* Access: http://mfnregister.nl (Last access time: February 15, 2017).

Parties can opt for mediation during the court procedure. As a result of policy measures of the Ministry of Justice, all courts dealing with environmental cases are given the option to refer conflicting parties to a mediator during the procedure. Referral is possible at an early stage of the proceeding (after selection on basis of a file) or at a later moment, for instance after a proposal of the judge at some point during the hearing in court. If the conflicting parties decide to try to resolve their issues using mediation with the help of a mediator, the court procedure is suspended. When mediation results in a full agreement, then the applicant of the appeal should withdraw it.

Conflicting parties can also opt to use mediation during the administrative decision-making procedure (preparatory proceeding or objection proceeding). Interesting to note is that the government sometimes employs the mediators who are used. Specifically, for these so-called internal mediators, the MFN provides a statute to ensure that this internal mediator is working in conformity with the rules and with the conditions of the MFN and to ensure that the relationship of authority with the employer is explained to the parties.

Mediation techniques can be defined as a set of communicative skills used for a solution-orientated approach. In the Netherlands, the last decade has shown an increased awareness of the value of using mediation techniques to deal with administrative disputes. The basic idea is that the way of handling administrative conflict is tailored to the specific merits of the case. Mediation techniques play an important role in this process. Since 2008, the Ministry of the Interior and Kingdom Relations promotes and supports the implementation of mediation techniques in governmental organizations through a program that provides administrative authorities practical guides, information on best practices, the possibility of knowledge exchange at national conferences, etc.[16]

Within governmental organizations, this process is known as the *Informal Pro-Active Approach Model*.[17] It should be mentioned that it depends on the policy of the administrative authority whether this approach is implemented within the organization; implementing this approach in practice is not mandatory. Also, the application of this approach in practice may differ. However, what this approach in general boils down to is that the administrative authority in question will no longer automatically initiate the formal procedures set out in the GALA. Instead, the administrative authority first informally tries to find out what the applicant who filed an objection (after a decision is made) or stated his views (on a draft decision) wants to achieve and second to determine the most appropriate way to deal with the situation. Usually a phone call is made to the person in question to

16 This project is called "Prettig contact met de overheid". Access: http://prettigcontactmetdeoverheid.nl/

17 Marseille, A.T. and K.J. de Graaf, "Criteria to Assess the Quality of the Dutch Informal Pro-active Approach Model" in D.C. Dragos and F. Lafarge, eds., *Proceedings of the EGPA Permanent Study Group: Law and Public Administration (33rd Annual Conference of the European Group for Public Administration, Boekarest, Roemenië 2011)*, Economica, Boekarest, 126.

obtain more information. If the authority decides to take an informal approach, there are several options, such as a meeting with the applicant and a civil servant or one of the administrators involved, or supportive guidance for the parties provided by an independent moderator or mediator. Sometimes parties opt for initializing a formal procedure after all.

Within courts, a similar approach is known as the *New Case Management Procedure*.[18] In 2010, administrative courts agreed to manage their cases in accordance with this new way of dealing with court cases. An important feature is that in cases of judicial review, a hearing is scheduled as quickly as possible. Task of the judge at this hearing is to find out what is exactly dividing the conflicting parties and discuss with parties how the case can best be handled, including the possibilities of ADR. The new case management is meant to deal with a case in the way that is suited for that specific dispute and that only cases in which that is necessary end with a judgment by the court. The court and the parties will explicitly think of the possibility to reach a settlement agreement, with or without the guidance of the judge or a mediator.

## *1.3 Empirical data*

How often is mediation used to resolve administrative disputes relating to environmental law? In the Netherlands, there is no empirical data available that specifically relates to environmental mediation. However, based on the existing empirical data on mediation in administrative law it is possible to give an indication. A general conclusion is that mediation as an instrument to deal with administrative disputes still plays a minor role in comparison to remedies provided by the law.

Research shows that from 2005 until 2008 the total amount of referrals to mediation by district courts increased from 414 in 2005 to 3203 in 2008. Only a quarter of these cases concern administrative law disputes (29% tax law, 23% social security, 7% civil servant, 10% 'ex-arob', 31% other cases).[19] Although the category of environmental law disputes is not specified in this study, we can conclude that the share of environmental cases is relatively limited. Also, more recent data indicates that courts do not often refer parties in administrative law disputes to a mediator. The annual report of the judiciary over the year 2013 mentions in the category 'general administrative law disputes' (including environmental cases) 110 referrals.[20] In 2014, this number even decreased to 54.[21]

18 See for a review of this process: Brink, B. and A.T. Marseille, "Participation of Citizens in Pre-Trial Hearings: Review of an Experiment in the Netherlands" (2014) 7(1) *International Public Administration Review* 47.

19 Guiaux, M., F. Turn and M. Tumewu, *Mediatior Monitor 2005–2008*, WODC, The Hague, 2009, 77. A summary in English can be found at: www.wodc.nl/onderzoeksdatabase/1330c-monitor-mediation-2009.aspx?cp=44&cs=6799 (Last access time: December 15, 2015).

20 *Jaarverslag Rechtspraak*, 2013, 62, which can be accessed via www.jaarverslagrechtspraak.nl (Last access time: February 15, 2017).

21 *Jaarverslag Rechtspraak*, 2014, 61, which can be accessed via www.jaarverslagrechtspraak.nl (Last access time: February 15, 2017).

Other studies also confirm the limited role of mediation as an instrument to deal with administrative disputes. From research on the role of mediation in municipalities follows that in the majority of municipalities from 2010 until 2012 mediation was applied one to five times.[22] Earlier research provides similar results. During a pilot period at the Province of Overijssel in the Netherlands, mediation was applied 7 times on a total amount of 208 filed objections. At the Province of Groningen, there were 4 cases resolved with mediation on a total amount of 115 filed objections. During a pilot at the municipality of Zwolle, mediation was applied 4 times out of the total amount of 571 filed objections.[23]

Why does mediation only play a minor role as an instrument to deal with administrative disputes in the Netherlands? The main explanation given in research on this topic is that with the use of mediation techniques by civil servants the disputes can be solved in consultation and there simply is no need for an 'official' mediation. Experience has shown that when mediation techniques are used, the average time used to manage objections is significantly reduced, citizens' satisfaction increases and a solution can still be found in an average of 60% of the objections filed.[24]

How widespread is the use of mediation techniques by civil servants of administrative authorities? There are no exact numbers available, however it is possible to give an indication. Numbers for 2007 indicate that 18% of all municipalities implemented a form of the Informal Pro-Active Approach Model to deal with objections filed against its decisions.[25] For the year 2011, the number of 200 administrative authorities is mentioned in literature.[26] From a study about municipalities in 2013 follows that 77% of the civil servants are able to apply some form of mediation techniques because of internal (45%) or external (32%) training (205 of the existing 408 municipalities participated).[27] A study conducted in 2016 on the design of the objection procedure concludes that most administrative authorities implemented an Informal Pro-Active Approach Model, at least on paper.[28] Of 50 randomly selected administrative authorities, 10 follow the practical guidelines provided by the Ministry of the Interior and Kingdom Relations.

22 Slooijer, J., *Onderzoek bij gemeenten naar de stand van mediation: De stand van mediation anno 2012/2013*, Rapport NMI, Amersfoort, 2013.

23 Tolsma, H.D., *Bemiddelend bestuur: Juridische aspecten bij de bestuurlijke besluitvorming* (diss. Groningen), BJu, Den Haag, 2008, Chapter 6.

24 Van der Velden, L., C. Koetsenruijter and M. Euwema, *Prettig contact met de overheid 2, Eindrapportage pioniertraject mediationvaardigheden: resultaten, analyses & aanbevelingen*, Ministerie van BZK, Den Haag, 2010, 9.

25 Schwartz, A., *De adviescommissie in bezwaar: Inrichting van de bezwaarprocedure bij gemeenten* (diss. Groningen), BJu, Den Haag, 2010, 97.

26 Brenninkmeijer, A.F.M. and A.T. Marseille, "Meer succes met de informele aanpak van bezwaarschriften" (2011) 86 *Nederlands Juristenblad* 1586.

27 Slooijer, J., *Onderzoek bij gemeenten naar de stand van mediation: De stand van mediation anno 2012/2013*, Rapport NMI, Amersfoort, 2013, 12.

28 Wever, M., "Bezwaarbehandeling door de overheid anno 2016" (2016) 44 *Nederlands Juristenblad* 2289.

Others make a phone call to the person who filed the objection (6 structurally and 16 occasionally). The rest of the administrative authorities do not use an Informal Pro-Active Approach Model (14) or have no known policy concerning the objection procedure (4).

## 2 Legal constraints for environmental mediation

In this section, we highlight some possible substantive and procedural constraints for mediation and mediation techniques in environmental disputes. Several studies in the Netherlands have shown that the GALA does not create any significant obstacles for mediation. However, there are some elements in the structure and the characteristics of administrative law that scholars have deemed to be at odds with the idea of mediation and (re)conciliation. We start with the constraints relating to the rule of law (section 2.1) and proceed to discuss potential constraints like the interests of third parties (section 2.2) and the principle of equal treatment (section 2.3). After that, we will discuss to what extent the period for lodging an appeal (section 2.4) and whether the legal embedding of a successful consultation should be considered a potential constraint in stimulating mediation (section 2.5).[29]

### *2.1 Rule of Law*

Mediation and mediation techniques provide an opportunity to negotiate a solution to a conflict. One of the points of departure in mediation is that all aspects of a conflict can be involved in negotiating a solution, including interests that are not legally relevant. In Dutch administrative law, the rule of law is firmly established in the legal system. As a consequence, it is based on the principle that public authorities do not have general powers to promote the public interest, but only specific – objective-related – powers. The rule of law and the principle of legality bring out the so-called speciality principle or the 'speciality rule' which the legislator expressed in Article 3:4(1) GALA: "An administrative authority shall consider the interests directly affected by a decision, subject to any limitations following from a provision of law or the nature of the power to be exercised". Its negative equivalent is the prohibition of abuse of power, which is stipulated in Article 3:3 GALA. As a consequence, decisions and actions of administrative authorities must be to the benefit of a specific public interest. When exercising public law powers, administrative authorities may not further promote public interests other than those with a view to which the power was

29 Some of these legal issues are also quite common in other European countries that incorporate mediation and mediation techniques into their administrative proceedings. See De Graaf, K.J., et al., "Mediation in Administrative Proceedings: A Comparative Perspective" in D.C. Dragos and B. Neamtu, eds., *Alternative Dispute Resolution in European Administrative Law*, Springer-Verlag, Berlin-Heidelberg, 2014, Chapter 19. Parts of this section are published before in this comparative analysis.

conferred. Administrative authorities are not free to involve any interest they deem relevant in decision making.

From this rule of law follows that when making decisions an administrative authority is not authorized to take into account interests that are protected by other public law provisions (considered external public interests), nor is it permitted to consider the private interests of third parties if it is clear that the legislator intended to exclude those interests. However, there has been some empirical research that allows us to examine how mediation relates to these constraints to the use of mediation in administrative disputes.[30] The research shows that the fundamental concepts of administrative law mentioned earlier are not necessarily at odds with the integrated approach that mediation requires to resolve a conflict.

For instance, an example concerned with a Water Board sub-plan for the replacement of a drawbridge shows that external public interests can be taken into consideration during negotiations about a solution. In this example, the interested party had stated his views concerned with a component of the Water Board's sub-plan. The Water Board could not take this objection into account in reaching its decision because the views were primarily concerned with an access road and were not related to water management interests. The Water Board has no powers with respect to access roads. Therefore, a representative of the ministry was invited to the negotiations about a possible solution.

Another example is the conflict about a building permit for a new residence. It shows that in negotiations about a solution, interests may be considered that are not legally relevant in the decision-making process. In this case, a neighbour filed an objection to a building permit. His objection had to do with his fear that the planned development would adversely affect the social and residential atmosphere and the ownership situation. In view of the non-discretionary assessment framework when deciding on an application for a building permit, the administrative authority may not take these interests into account. In this case, a solution for the dispute was found in the legal relationship between private individuals under civil law.

In light of these experiences, it has become clear that mediation provides possibilities for dealing with some of the practical problems citizens experience in relation to the rule that powers are conferred and applied in an objective-specific manner. In practice – specifically in the field of environmental law – citizens are confronted with compartmentalized administrative powers, in which each piece of legislation has its specific assessment framework, its specific competent authority and its specific decision-making procedure. If a dispute is spread across a number of different legal frameworks, it can be difficult to apply the integrated approach that would serve the citizen's interest. Mediation also approaches a dispute in an integrated way: not only legally relevant interests but also any complaints, including complaints about the way a citizen has been treated, may play

30 Tolsma, H.D., *Bemiddelend bestuur: Juridische aspecten bij de bestuurlijke besluitvorming* (diss. Groningen), BJu, Den Haag, 2008, chapter 6.

a role in the negotiations for a solution. However, the administrative authority shall always investigate whether a negotiated solution can be implemented within the relevant frameworks of administrative law (see section 2.5).

## 2.2 *The interests of third parties*

Especially when it comes to environmental disputes, there are often third parties involved. Many conflicts either involve or will in some way influence the legal position of third parties that are not necessarily involved in the procedure. For instance, a dispute between the applicant of a building permit and the administrative authority that refused the application cannot be solved entirely by an agreement that implies that the competent authority will accept the application it first refused; any neighbour that was happy to hear the application was initially denied will probably want to appeal the new decision as soon as information on the change of position of the administration reaches him. To be certain that the use of mediation could indeed lead to a binding resolution of the conflict, any interested third party should be included in the (facilitated) negotiations. It is often these sort of issues that bring up important questions about effectiveness, efficiency and legitimacy of the involvement of the administrative authority or the administrative court in facilitating the settlement of a dispute in another manner than by judgment; it is primarily the task of the administrative authority to take a decision that is not just in conformity with the law but also reasonable. The answer lies of course in the general interest of amicable dispute settlement in a civilized society, in the fact that a judgment is seen as *ultimum remedium* and in the costs of adjudication in general.

## 2.3 *Equal treatment*

Another issue relevant for mediation in administrative decision making and in administrative adjudication is the principle of equality. This basic principle of good governance for the behaviour and decision making of any administrative authority implies that all equal cases shall be treated equally and unequal cases shall be treated differently in a way that reflects the differences between the cases on the basis of legally allowed and objective reasons. We will not discuss this principle in-depth here, but it is obviously of influence when mediating or negotiating in administrative proceedings. When an administrative authority is negotiating the manner, it shall exercise a discretionary power; there is more at stake than the use of competence in that particular instance. Any administrative authority is obliged to act and decide systematically and consistently, and treat equal cases equally. This will limit the possibilities of an administrative authority negotiating the use of a discretionary power, as the use of the power in this one instance will serve as a precedent and will have to be repeated when the same conditions are met in other cases. When the conflict revolves around exercising a discretionary power, successful application of mediation and mediation techniques to solve it is only in order when an administrative authority is willing to change the way it exercises this particular competence in any similar case that the future might bring and therefore only when it is willing to change its policy for legitimate and objective reasons. In any other situation, the result of negotiations will be considered a (unwanted) precedent for future use of the competence. The principle of equality could therefore be considered a complicating factor when considering mediation in administrative proceedings.

### 2.4 Prescribed time periods in administrative law

Mediation and the use of mediation techniques must take place within the legal framework provided by the GALA and therefore the rules regarding time limits must be complied with. In some cases, informal consultation may require more time than the statutory decision-making period or the appeal period that applies for initiating administrative appeal procedures. Although the prescribed period for decision making has been considered a serious constraint for the application of mediation in administrative law in the past, the GALA now provides sufficient possibilities to extend the decision-making period in cases where more time is needed.[31] For instance, Article 7:10(4) GALA allows the administrative authority to postpone the decision on any objection if 'all parties agree'.[32]

Another issue that parties should keep in mind is that the possibility for judicial review and legal procedures must be protected when the informal consultation fails. This means, for example, that if informal consultations begin in connection with a decision made by a public authority, the citizen in question must still file a formal objection within the applicable time limit.[33] This seems contradictory, because initiating the formal objection procedure might frustrate the attempt to reach an amicable settlement. Nevertheless, a formal objection must be filed, because there will be no legal remedy available to anyone who is considered an interested party when the informal consultations fail.

The following example illustrates that this is not always clear. A claimant whose objection was ruled inadmissible because it was lodged after the end of the time limit stated in court that his objection should not have been declared inadmissible because it cannot reasonably be held that he was in default.[34] During the prescribed time to file a notice of objection, he was in a mediation with the administrative authority over the expansion of a pig farm. The claimant agreed with the administrative authority not to institute any proceedings against each other during the mediation. He stated that based on this mediation agreement, he could have the justifiable trust that filing an objection after the mediation was

31 Tolsma, H.D., "Formele aspecten van een informele aanpak" in H.D. Tolsma, I.M.C. van Leeuwen, F. Dijk and C. Heinen, eds., *Een informele aanpak bij bestuursrechtelijke besluitvorming (Preadviezen Jonge VAR 2011)*, BJu, Den Haag, 2011, Chapter 2.

32 *General Administrative Law Act*, art. 4:15.

33 From article 6:7 *General Administrative Law Act* follows that the time limit for filing a notice of objection or appeal is six weeks.

34 *General Administrative Law Act*, art. 6:11.

still possible. The argument failed. The court referred to Article 9 of the MFN-mediation 2008, which clearly states that the parties agree for the duration of the mediation not to institute any proceedings against each other, with the exception of steps to safeguard rights.[35]

The EU Mediation Directive, although not directly applicable to administrative proceedings, stipulates in Article 8 that member states shall ensure that parties who choose mediation in an attempt to settle a dispute are not subsequently prevented from initiating judicial proceedings or arbitration in relation to that dispute by the expiry of limitations or prescription periods during the mediation process.

Interesting to note is that the duration of mediation is not taken into account when the court has to determine if in a specific case the reasonable period referred to in Article 6, first paragraph, of the Convention for the Protection of Human Rights and Fundamental Freedoms, better known as the European Convention on Human Rights (ECHR), has been exceeded and a claimant asks for damages.[36]

## *2.5 Legal embedding of successful mediation*

Successful mediation ends in agreement. In administrative law, the point of departure is that there is a decision-making process to follow, which ends with a decision. The combination of civil law and administrative law elements may lead to various legal problems if a dispute arises regarding the result of mediation – for example, if the administrative body or the citizen involved fails to comply with the agreement reached, or if the terms of the agreement are disputed. In the Netherlands, the combination of rules deriving from civil law and from administrative law may lead to a lack of clarity as regards legal remedies. The GALA does not cover agreements and is therefore not suited to settling disputes about agreements. For instance, the administrative court does not have the option of ordering the administrative body to comply with the agreement. Claiming damages for breach of contract is not possible under the administrative procedural law either.

In connection with problems relating to the binding effect of agreements, the process of negotiation for an agreement, access to documents and to legal protection, a minimum degree of regulation in the GALA had been suggested in literature.[37] This regulation would have to define an agreement under administrative law. The definition would have to make clear that the administrative body is entering into a contract which entails exercising a public power; after the contract has been entered into, the public power must therefore be exercised. It has also been suggested that there should be provisions to oblige administrative

35 Administrative Jurisdiction Division of the Council of State March 19, 2012, ECLI:NL:RVS:2012:BW4394 (Access: www.rechtspraak.nl).

36 Administrative Jurisdiction Division of the Council of State January 16, 2016, ECLI:NL:RVS:2013:BY8546 (Access: htttp://www.rechtspraak.nl).

37 Huisman, P.J., *De bevoegdhedenovereenkomst: De overeenkomst over het gebruik van een publiekrechtelijke bevoegdheid* (Diss. VU Amsterdam), BJu, Den Haag, 2012.

authorities to consult with third parties and to restrict the obligations an administrative body can impose on a member of the public. A provision should also be included stipulating that the administrative body must comply with the contract, unless there are compelling reasons not to do so, with an accompanying provision about the administrative body's liability in such cases.

There has been a great deal of discussion in literature whether statutory regulation of such agreements is necessary and whether such a regulation should be incorporated in the GALA. It should be noted that most of this discussion is not directly related to mediation or mediation techniques. It is not only in connection with dispute resolution that government authorities enter into contracts with members of the public. There is no doubt that the lack of regulation leads to unnecessary legal complications. This is why in our opinion a general regulation in the GALA is desirable.

Another question is whether the GALA should make mediation or the use of mediation techniques mandatory in the decision-making process. In that respect also, the relation between legal procedures and the promise mediation holds for an amicable solution is relevant.

Illustrative is, for instance, the following example. The first instance court ruled that the claimant had no possible legal remedies because mediation had already resulted in a settlement agreement with the administrative authority. Therefore, the claimant had no interest in bringing an action to the administrative court. However, in the appeal procedure, the claimant stated that the administrative authority had unilaterally ended the agreement. The administrative authority refused to act in accordance with the agreement and did not exert the promised effort to grant an environmental permit. According to the administrative authority, the claimant acted contrary to the agreement by not filing the documents required for the application of an environmental permit before the agreed time. At the hearing in court, the claimant indicated that he will start a civil law procedure to make sure the administrative authority honours the agreement. The Administrative Jurisdiction Division of the Council of State ruled to quash the ruling of the first instance court; in these circumstances, the claimant still has a sufficient interest in bringing an action to the administrative court.[38]

We will address the question whether the GALA should be amended in order to better accommodate mediation within the decision-making process and/or the administrative court procedures in section 3.

## 3 A legal status for the use of mediation?

### *3.1 Introduction*

The GALA in the Netherlands provides general provision on predominantly single-case decision making by administrative authorities and the legal protection in the form of judicial review by the Dutch administrative courts. Although we have shown that some aspects or provisions of general administrative law may

38 Administrative Jurisdiction Division of the Council of State March 5, 2014, ECLI:NL:RVS:2014:730 (Access: www.rechtspraak.nl).

be considered a constraint for the successful use of mediation and mediation techniques, most scholars agree that the Dutch GALA does not preclude the use of mediation in practice. The main discussion in the Netherlands has recently been whether the use of mediation and mediation techniques in administrative law should be stimulated by either codifying in the GALA the best practices of administrative authorities that implemented these instruments for dispute resolution successfully or by making implementation mandatory.

In any country with a well-developed rule of law, government ensures that disputes between citizens and administrative authorities can be submitted to an independent, impartial and competent court. However, the court is often perceived to be a last resort. Conflicting parties should attempt to resolve their dispute by mutual agreement. Dutch legislation provides a number of methods outside the judiciary to resolve disputes, including binding advice, arbitrage and mutual consultation. The starting point for choosing between methods to resolve disputes should be which method is most effective and efficient while maximizing the ability for parties to influence the outcome and therefore remain responsible for ending their dispute. Legal proceedings may not always be the most appropriate solution. For many disputes, mediation might be a suitable alternative.

Some protagonists considered that government did not sufficiently stimulate mediation as an efficient method of conflict resolution and that one of the results of this perceived negligence was a situation of insufficient legal certainty about the possibilities and the consequences of the use of mediation in administrative law. This situation triggered member of Parliament Van der Steur, in 2013, to introduce three legislative proposals to stimulate mediation as a real and valuable alternative to legal proceedings.[39] The initiative of Van der Steur as a member of Parliament was welcomed by anyone who believed that it is important to promote the use of mediation in administrative law and that it is equally important to improve legal certainty in situation where mediation or mediation techniques are used (successfully). However, before Parliament could vote on the proposal, Van der Steur retired as a member of Parliament in order to be appointed minister of security and justice on 20 March 2015. As a consequence, Parliament has opted to revoke the legislative proposal initiated by Van der Steur[40] since the government – as it did later by letter of the new minister of security and justice[41] – indicated it would propose new legislation to replace the revoked proposal and to promote mediation. The legislative proposals were transformed into draft proposals for legislation by the government. An Internet consultation about the proposal was completed in September 2016.

One of the proposals introduces a register of mediators, which shall register mediators that meet specific requirements – stipulated in an Order in Council – with regard to quality and integrity. This proposal allows anyone to select a qualified mediator. Second, Van der Steur proposes amending the Dutch Civil Code by adding provisions on a 'mediation agreement' as a new form of commissioning

39 See *Parliamentary Papers II* 2013/14, 33 727 (for mediation in administrative law see no. 5 and 10).
40 *Parliamentary Papers II* 2013/14, 33 727, no. 12.
41 *Parliamentary Papers II* 2013/14, 33 722, no. 24.

a mediator by parties to try to resolve their dispute. Also, the proposal provides that any court competent to deal with civil law suits could at any given time during the proceedings refer parties to a registered mediator. The third legislative proposal by Van der Steur – and later as a draft proposal by the government – is most relevant for our contribution for it is concerned with administrative law and proposes several changes to the GALA. We will discuss this specific proposal in section 3.2 and discuss alternative proposals to formalize the use of mediation and/or mediation techniques in the GALA (section 3.3).

### *3.2 Legislative proposal promoting mediation in administrative law*

The bill proposed by Van der Steur amends the GALA to stimulate and promote the use of mediation and mediation techniques. The proposal suggests that it is in line with the principle of good administration that administrative authorities investigate the possibilities of an informal approach or mediation for dealing with the views and objections filed by interested parties in the decision-making process. The idea behind the legislative proposal is that the use of mediation can lead to early resolution of the dispute, allowing cost savings in the objection and appeal phase. Van der Steur expects that highly significant administrative costs can be prevented. The starting point is that good governance entails that a request of any party to an administrative authority to use mediation in order to resolve their dispute, should be granted. Experience shows that there are many disputes concerned with the interpretation of facts and the perceived deficiencies in communication between the parties concerned. In such disputes, mediation provides opportunities for successful conflict resolution. Therefore, Van der Steur proposes several provisions for different situations. First, it is proposed to include a new provision in chapter 2 of the GALA that is concerned with interaction between administrative authorities and citizens. The proposed Article 2:4a GALA reads,

> The administrative authority is committed to avoiding disputes with citizens by communicating with citizen actively and at an early stage.

This Article aims to establish that administrative authorities – within reasonable limits – should make an effort to effectively communicate about proposed decisions in order to avoid disputes with citizens. Early contact with stakeholders before a decision is made, taking the time to explain the decision and to assess alternatives, can avoid disputes about the decision at a later time. The extra strain on administration should be worthwhile because experiences show that a large number of appeal procedures are prevented. Early communication is best done by telephone and possibly in the future by way of Skype or FaceTime. According to the proposal, the added value of Article 2:4a GALA is that administrative authorities should be easy to approach.

The proposal further explains that amendments are necessary in chapter 7 of the GALA, which is concerned with the objection procedure. The first provision proposed is Article 7:1b GALA ("The administrative authority promotes good communication with the person submitting the objection".) that is very similar to the proposed Article 2:4a GALA but is applicable only to the objection procedure. The aim of this provision is to avoid the formal objection procedure by initiating contact with the person that filed the objection with the objective to remove the reasons for his objections or better explain the reasons for the decision (again). This can then be achieved by using mediation but other methods of dispute resolution may also be discussed. However, the legislative proposal also introduces a new Article 7:3a GALA that reads,

1 The administrative authority may give interested parties the opportunity to participate in mediation.
2 If mediation is used, the administrative authority will inform the parties which have put forward their views on the draft decision.
3 If the administrative authority refuses a request from an interested party to participate in mediation, it shall inform the interested party as soon as possible stating the reasons for the rejection.

Pursuant to this provision, administrative authorities may give interested parties the opportunity to participate in mediation. It is intended to ensure that authorities feel the need to try mediation and to provide information. Of course, the interested party may also ask for the use of mediation. If the administrative authority refuses, such a request the provision requires it to inform the interested party as soon as possible and state the reasons for the refusal.[42] Reason could be that the administrative authority has clear indications that successful mediation is illusory or that the dispute is concerned with a question of law that should be answered by a court. When the administrative authority and the interested parties have opted for mediation to resolve their dispute, the proposal suggests that the time period for reaching a decision in the objections procedure should be extended as long as mediation lasts. The proposal therefore amends the provision stipulating the time period (Article 7:10 GALA) to accommodate for the situation in which extension is necessary in connection with mediation.

In a further effort to promote the use of mediation in administrative adjudication, a new provision applicable to administrative court procedure is proposed. A new Article 8:41a GALA is introduced to allow, for a specific moment during the proceedings, for the court to assess whether mediation could be used to

42 An earlier version of the proposal actually proposed to have administrative authorities always state the reasons for not using mediation in the objection procedure, regardless whether it was requested or not.

resolve the dispute. The idea is that it is never too late to try to resolve a dispute by way of mediation. The proposed provision reads as follows:

> 1 The administrative court assesses with the parties whether a legitimate amicable solution is possible.
> 2 The administrative court shall allow the parties the opportunity to participate in mediation if given the nature of the dispute, he deems it appropriate.

When the court refers the parties to a mediator, it will give the parties a choice between several registered mediators. The explanatory memorandum that accompanies the legislative proposal states that this provision in a sense codifies the so-called New Case Management Procedure. The use of mediation could avoid a long series of appeals against decisions and could guide the parties to a durable solution for their conflict.

### *3.3 Critical assessment and suggested alternatives*

Some Dutch administrative law scholars have given a somewhat critical assessment of the proposal by Van der Steur introduced in the previous section. Three main objects of critique can be distinguished.

The first issue is whether legislation promoting mediation in administrative law is necessary and has added value when the Informal Pro-active Approach Method in the objection procedure and the New Case Management Procedure in administrative appeal procedures strive towards the same goal.[43] The goal being that disputes between administrative authorities and citizens lead to objection and administrative appeal procedures in more cases then necessary and that those legal proceedings also cannot always lead to a durable solution for the conflict. If implemented, the informal approach by administrative authorities in the objection procedure will improve communication with citizens in order to find the best way to resolve the conflict, not just in the objection procedure itself but also in the decision-making procedure that precedes it. The use of mediation techniques would be promoted. The legislative proposal has a similar effect for the decision-making procedure since it simply obliges administrative authorities to communicate early and pro-active. However, as regards the objection procedure and the administrative appeal procedure the proposal is focused strongly on the use of mediation as a specific manner to resolve the dispute. In light of both the Informal Pro-active Approach Model and the New Case Management Procedure, the perspective of the proposal seems very narrow and limited. Also, in practice, the use of mediation techniques and the change in perspective of and the way of communicating by civil servants seems to have far better results and is applied much more than the more formal instrument of mediation for which

43 See Marseille, A.T., "Het voorstel voor de Wet bevordering van mediation in het bestuursrecht kan nog wel wat denkwerk gebruiken" (2014) *Jurisprudentie Bestuursrecht plus* 194.

an independent mediator is necessary. A critical comment is therefore that the focus of the proposed bill is too narrow since it is focused only on mediation as an alternative for the judicial review.

A second comment relating to the provisions proposed is that some issues relating to the use of mediation and mediation techniques in administrative law disputes in the Netherlands are not discussed at all. When improving legal certainty is one of the goals, it is remarkable that the issue of agreements between administrative authorities and citizens about the use of the powers of the administration remains unaddressed in the proposal. As we explained earlier, the GALA does not cover such agreements and is, therefore, not suited to settling disputes about them; administrative courts do not have the power to order the administrative authority to comply with a settlement agreement and claiming damages for breach of contract is not possible under administrative procedural law either.

A third and important issue is whether the proposed legislation would have added value over the pre-existing regulation in the GALA and the implemented Informal Pro-active Approach Model and the New Case Management Procedure. Experiences have shown that there is nothing precluding administrative authorities and courts to use mediation and mediation techniques for finding a resolution for administrative law disputes as long as the legal framework is respected. Furthermore, the proposed legislation does not provide administrative authorities or administrative courts with specific new powers to refer to mediation or to use mediation techniques. A critical question should therefore be that the proposed provisions have no added value in light of existing possibilities to use mediation and mediation techniques. In this perspective, they are, to a large extent, symbolic. Although there are other examples of such provisions in GALA (e.g. art. 8:41a GALA: "Administrative courts shall deal with cases in such a way that the dispute between parties is resolved as much as possible"), the need to adopt these sort of provisions can be easily questioned. Furthermore, one could argue that before legislation, in order more experience with the newly developed way of managing objections and court cases is needed to allow a proper assessment of appropriate provisions to promote amicable settlement of administrative law disputes.

Earlier, we discussed the provisions promoting mediation that were proposed by Van der Steur. There have, however, been others that have suggested alternative provisions in order to stimulate either the use of mediation and mediation techniques or improve the communication between administration and interested parties to avoid disputes.

One idea is to give the problem-solving intention of the objection process (Informal Pro-active Approach Model) some sort of legal status. One suggestion reads,

> Before making a decision in the objection procedure, the administrative body will try to find out if – within the framework of the statutory rules and regulations – an amicable solution between the parties is possible.[44]

44 Allewijn, D., "Naar een probleemoplossend systeem van rechtsbescherming" (2007) *Nederlands Tijdschrift voor Bestuursrecht* 154.

Another suggestion is as follows:

> Before the administrative body begins to consider its decision in the objection procedure, it will contact the party who lodged the objection to explore the possibility of finding an amicable solution to the objection.[45]

Both provisions clarify that administrative authorities have an obligation to explore the possibility of finding an amicable solution. We prefer the second suggestion because, unlike the first suggestion, it requires actual contact between the administrative body and the party that filed the objection. It also stipulates that this contact should take place at an early stage of the procedure. With regard to the first suggestion, it seems to us that it is unnecessary to set out in statutory law that an amicable solution must comply with all rules and regulations.

In our opinion, provisions like those proposed and suggested are not strictly necessary from a legal point of view. The mediatory role of administrative authorities can be based on administrative law provisions as they now stand (e.g. the 'obligation to investigate' referred to in Article 3:2 GALA and other general standards of good governance). Moreover, since we also think that it would not be easy to legally enforce such a provision, it would be somewhat symbolic in nature. After all, there is a risk that, in practice, administrative authorities would only pay lip service to the 'obligation to investigate'. Nevertheless, in our opinion, there are also strong arguments in favour of codification. Inclusion of a provision in the GALA would make clear that the legislator not only acknowledges the informal approach but also requires it as a method of avoiding or solving administrative disputes. This would lead to greater awareness among both administrative authorities and the public, which might in turn promote the use of the Informal Pro-active Approach Model. Although we acknowledge that legislation cannot bring about the required culture shift, the argument of increased awareness could be given sufficient weight in favour of legislation.

Van der Steur also proposed a provision to promote mediation during judicial review as the role of the judge in administrative procedures should also include the duty to explore finding an amicable solution, according to the proposal. Although the mediatory role of the (administrative) court is less obvious and less evolved within administrative procedural law in the Netherlands, the implementation of the New Case Management Procedure by administrative courts shows that courts feel obliged to assess which way of managing the case would be in the best interest of the parties to the dispute and that courts have acknowledge the duty to explore the possibilities of ADR. With that in mind, both the arguments in favour and against introducing new legislation obliging administrative authorities to investigate or explore an amicable solution during the objection procedure can also be used for assessing the appropriateness of such legislation to oblige courts to explore the possibility of such a solution.

45 Brenninkmeijer, A.F.M. and A.T. Marseille, "Meer succes met de informele aanpak van bezwaarschriften" (2011) 86 *Nederlands Juristenblad* 2010.

## Final remarks

In this contribution, we have given an overview of developments concerned with the use of mediation and mediation techniques in administrative (procedural) law in order to provide information on environmental mediation. Our main question was whether it is desirable to introduce new legislation in administrative law in order to remove obstacles experienced in practice with regard to the use of mediation. In answering this question, we have focused on single-case decision making and the provisions of the Dutch GALA on decision-making procedures by administrative authorities. We, however, also focused on both the objection procedure as a necessary step towards judicial review and on the appeal procedure with an independent court specialized in administrative law disputes.

As such, the Dutch GALA and general environmental law does not provide any substantive provisions that preclude administrative authorities or courts to investigate amicable solutions, either by using mediation, mediation techniques or by simply reaching an agreement that puts an end to the dispute. However, there is an inherent tension between the integrated approach of dispute resolution by means of mediation, which will include all relevant interests of all parties involved, and some of the basic principles of administrative law. We have discussed these in section 2.1–2.4 (rule of law, interests of third parties, equal treatment, time periods). Also, Dutch GALA does not provide any specific provisions about agreements or contracts between citizens and administrative authorities on the use of public law powers and it therefore allows for some legal uncertainty when parties are able to settle their dispute with an agreement (whether this happens after using mediation or not). This seems like a serious shortcoming; introducing legislation to make up for the absence needs the attention of Dutch administrative law scholars that it has not received in the recent discussions on the use of mediation and mediation techniques.

In 2013, an initiative of one of the members of Parliament, Van der Steur, has again triggered discussion on the appropriateness of introducing new legislation to promote mediation in all stages of decision making in administrative law and judicial review (draft decision, decision making, objection procedure, appeal procedure). The added value of the proposed provisions is questioned from a legal perspective. On the other hand, the provisions seem relevant to improve the awareness of both administrative authorities and courts about the advantages of using mediation or mediation techniques. One could, however, easily argue that awareness has already grown since many administrative authorities have implemented a so-called Informal Pro-active Approach Model and administrative courts have all implemented the New Case Management Procedure in order to either avoid disputes or explore the possibility of an amicable solution for the dispute. In our opinion, the scope of the proposed legislation is, however, too limited since only mediation is considered a form of ADR worth promoting. We are of the opinion that codifying existing best practices in the Netherlands would certainly require a broader scope. On top of that, we would like to point out that integrating mediation techniques within decision-making procedures has proven to be more effective in reaching positive results and in avoiding unnecessary legal proceedings than referring conflicting parties to mediation. Van der Steur has become the minister of security and justice in 2015 and resigned in January 2017. In the meantime, his legislative proposal as a member of Parliament was revoked and transformed into a draft proposal by the government. The future faith of this draft proposal is now unsure because of the minister's resignation. This seems to be a perfect moment and opportunity to really re-evaluate the proposed provisions.

# 4 Is it time for a global legal framework in Belgium?

*Geert Van Hoorick,*[1] *Lise Vandenhende*[2] *and Brecht Warnez*[3]

## 1 Mediation in environmental law

### *1.1 'Mediation': one word, different meanings*

Suzanne La Follette, an American author and politician of the first half of the twentieth century, stated, "Laws are felt only when the individual comes into conflict with them".[4] Despite the intention of the legislators to regulate and avoid conflicts between citizens and between citizens and the government, these conflicts have been present in every period of history. Consequently, in addition to litigation, there is an alternative dispute resolution (ADR). One of the oldest forms of ADR is mediation (consider, for example, the Old Testament or the Laws of Solon). This concept has been used to refer to any kind of third-party intervention, with the aim of moving the parties towards an agreement. Given the lack of legal definition, in this chapter, we use the term in accordance with the prevailing Belgian legal doctrine.

There are two lawyers and three opinions. Thus, in literature, the term 'mediation' has been defined more than once and in different ways. In our opinion, Lien De Geyter formulated the most accurate and comprehensive definition. She describes mediation as

> an alternative way to resolve conflicts between two or more persons, based on consensus and with assistance, which is organized by a neutral, impartial and independent third party that does not use any method of coercion, but possesses a right to examine and to make recommendations and tries to reconcile the parties in order to facilitate, structure or coordinate the voluntary search for a solution, and that tries to achieve a lasting solution which

1 Centre for environmental law, University Ghent, Department of European, Public and International Law.
2 Centre for environmental law, University Ghent, Department of European, Public and International Law.
3 Research group for administrative law, University Ghent, Department of European, Public and International Law.
4 La Follette, S., *Concerning Women*, A. & C. Boni, New York, 1926, 63.

the parties have agreed upon voluntarily, because it takes into account the mutual interests and viewpoints.[5]

Defining the concept gives us the ability to demarcate the essential characteristics of mediation. The characteristics of mediation, which are given next, are common elements that have been derived from the different forms of mediation in the various branches of public law (such as the regulations concerning municipal administrative sanctions, the right of education, environmental protection, urban development, social protection, housing, institutional consultation structures between the federal and regional authorities, etc.).[6] Nevertheless, they do not appear to the same extent for each of these forms of mediation.

In the first place, a **voluntary approach** is an essential requirement of mediation and its importance cannot be stressed enough. The voluntary approach applies to all of the participants in the mediation procedure. Each party should be able to choose – unrestricted – whether he or she wishes to participate in the mediation procedure and to decide whether mediation can serve his or her interests. Nevertheless, voluntary does not mean absolute permissiveness for the parties. Once they have agreed to start the mediation, the parties must act in good faith. This means that they must make an active and constructive contribution in the search to find a solution (an obligation to perform to the best of one's ability). The voluntariness also implies that a solution can never be imposed by the mediator but rather, it is a result of the agreement between the parties.

Furthermore, mediation differs from most other forms of alternative dispute. This is because the presence of an **independent, impartial and neutral third party** ('the mediator') is required. The mediator will try to get the dialogue going again. He stimulates a **clear communication process** and focuses on the interpersonal communication between the parties. A mutual understanding between the parties can arise as a result of formulating their views on the conflict as clearly as possible and actively listening to the views of the other parties. Many conflicts arise from miscommunication. During these discussions, the mediator monitors and promotes **equality between the parties**.

By listening to the parties and conducting a constructive dialogue with them, the mediator will try to make the parties come to an agreement. It should be taken into account that the conflict is not always strictly legal. Often, emotional interests also play an important part in the struggle between the government and the citizen. In order to reach a sustainable solution, it is important that all of the parties find **satisfaction in the result** of the mediation.

5 De Geyter, L., "Alternatieve methoden tot beslechting van bestuursgeschillen" (2005) 4 *Publiekrechtelijke Kronieken* 763.

6 Lancksweerdt, E., "Bemiddeling met en door gemeenten" (2003) 2 *Tijdschrift voor Gemeenterecht* 103; Santens, M., *Gewapend bestuur*, die Keure, Bruges, 2005, 173; Lancksweerdt, E., "Bemiddeling in het kader van de wetgeving op de gemeentelijke administratieve sancties: een unieke kans voor de gemeenten" (2005) 1 *Tijdschrift voor Gemeenterecht* 41.

Finally, to achieve a successful mediation, the content of the discussions should be **confidential**. Everything that is said or exchanged (documents, emails, etc.) during mediation is strictly confidential. From the beginning of the mediation process, the parties must agree that everything that is said in the mediation will remain internal and will not be communicated to third parties without mutual agreement. Any potential third party (for example, an expert) is bound by the same confidentiality. The confidential nature of the mediation must be respected during the whole mediation procedure. The mediator is bound by the duty of professional confidentiality and must follow the same rule. This increases the possible effectiveness of mediation because parties can be more open about their interests, goals and potential concessions, without having to fear abuse.

### *1.2 Not a matter of administrative law*

Although the concept of mediation between citizen(s) and the government itself was not unknown, mediation, as we know it today, is not reflected in our old laws or even in Napoleon's Code of Civil Procedure (1806). The lack of a legal framework does not mean that all kinds of mediation have been absent from the Belgian area. Mediation has always been available outside of the judicial process and some authors have even sought to provide a basis for the use of mediation during procedures.[7]

In recent decades, mediation has had tremendous success in several branches of Belgian law. The first legislation on mediation in Belgium was introduced in the field of criminal justice.[8] The modification in 1994 to the Code of Criminal Procedure assigned the possibility for the public prosecutor to propose the mediation procedure in certain criminal cases. Furthermore, mediation appears in social affairs[9] and in family matters.[10]

Nevertheless, we had to wait until 2005 for the first general mediation regulation in civil procedural law.[11] Virtue of this law, the Code of Civil Procedure provides for two types of mediation in civil matters: the voluntary mediation and judicial mediation. Anyone who follows this legally prescribed procedure can obtain an executive title. Thus, it has the same force and effect as a judgment. The Act of April 19, 2005, determines the conditions for the recognition of mediators and establishes a federal mediation committee to monitor this recognition procedure. Another act in the same year extends the scope of mediation in

7 Brouwers, S., "Bemiddeling tijdens de procesgang: Is er een wettelijke basis?" (1999–2000) *Algemeen Juridisch Tijdschrift* 193.

8 Act of February 10, 1994 on regulating the procedure for mediation in criminal cases, *Belgian Official Gazette*, April 27, 1994.

9 Act of July 5, 1998, on the collective debt settlement and the possibility of sales from the hand of the seized goods, *Belgian Official Gazette*, July 3, 1998.

10 Act of February 19, 2001, on the procedure mediation in family matters, *Belgian Official Gazette*, April 3, 2001.

11 Act of February 21, 2005, on amending the Judicial Code in connection with the mediation, *Belgian Official Gazette*, March 22, 2005.

criminal affairs by disabling the monopoly of the public prosecutor.[12] Nowadays, any interested party person may request to start the mediation process during the criminal proceedings.

Meanwhile, taxation mediation has also gained a foothold. The Act of April 25, 2007, concerning various provisions (IV)[13] set up a "fiscal mediation service" within the Federal Ministry of Finance. The tax mediation intercedes in disputes between disgruntled taxpayers and tax administration.

The current government has paid particular attention to mediation in its plan of 2015 to reform the judicial organization.[14] The aim is to give mediation an equal place to the traditional judicial resolution. Unfortunately, no particular attention has been made to mediation in administrative law.

### 1.3 The necessity for mediation in environmental practice

The conclusion that mediation is successful in other branches of law and the formalistic and little pragmatic administrative case law in Belgium has raised the call for mediation in environmental law and administrative law in general. An outstanding example of such a judicial annulment of April 28, 2011, with far-reaching and unintended social consequences is the so-called case 'Tramline Deurne-Wijnegem'. The construction of the tramline was part of Antwerp's master plan to facilitate mobility within and towards the city. Four years after granting the urban permit, the Council of State annulled the permit due to a lack of motivation.[15] Consequently, the tramline, which was already two-thirds completed, had to be demolished. This meant a loss of 45 million euros for the government. This loss could have been avoided through mediation, since the complainant was not against the idea of the new tramline. He even declared that he was surprised and unhappy about the decision of the Council of State. He had merely intended to establish a dialogue between the government and the neighbourhood about some nuisance problems. Nevertheless, the judgment of the Council of State was final.

Among both politicians and the media, a storm of criticism arose following the strictly legalistic approach of the Council of State, which seemed to have no regard for the social consequences of its judgments. In case law, the Council could not be judged by its critics. After all, the limited suspension and annulment competence of the Council of State was not to be effective for factual dispute resolution. It became clear that administrative mediation can play an important role.

12 Act of June 22, 2005, on introducing provisions on mediation in the Preliminary Title of the Code of Criminal Procedure and the Code of Criminal Procedure, *Belgian Official Gazette*, April 17, 1878.

13 Art. 116–130 of the Act of April 25, 2007, concerning various provisions (IV), *Belgian Official Gazette*, May 8, 2007.

14 Minister of Judiciary Koen Geens, *The Justice Plan: A More Efficient Judiciary for Justice*, available in Dutch at www.stapvoorwaarts.be/wp-content/uploads/2015/03/20150318-Justitieplan-NL.pdf

15 Council of State April 28, 2011, no. 212.825, Lauwers.

Finally, for the sake of completeness, we should note that not all environmental disputes are suitable for mediation. This is due to the specific characteristics of (Belgian) administrative law such as the unilateral nature of the legal protection, the special protection granted to a third party and legal certainty. For example, a contract that was the result of mediation is not binding to a citizen who was not involved in that mediation. Thus, that citizen can still lodge an appeal for annulment.

In addition, there are still a number of other legal restrictions. Lien De Geyter describes these in detail in her doctoral thesis about ADR.[16] She argues *inter alia* that the government cannot freely exercise its powers. Such a restriction stems from the Constitution, on the one hand, and the civil code, on the other. Therefore, the government may not relinquish its competences/powers, and it should exercise these in view of the public interest. As a solution, it is suggested that, in the agreement on the resolution of the dispute, a reservation should be included. This allows a certain commitment of the government, which cannot be deviated without good reason and is in the general interest. Furthermore, the government must always act within the mandatory public law framework. Therefore, it will have to take into account, among other things, the hierarchy of legal norms, the general principles of good governance and the principle of open government. Another important limitation is the scope of mediation in relation to third parties/third stakeholders. Mediation can have an effect on third parties.

Given the rather extensive contribution of De Geyter and others, this Article does not intend to discuss the legal problems and limitations of ADR in administrative law in general. Instead, it aims to focus on the specific case of environmental mediation preceding and during the administrative procedure and preceding and during the judicial procedure.

### *1.4 Environmental law in Belgian federalism*

Belgium has a complex political state structure. Unlike the normal origin of a federation, Belgian federalism was caused by the erosion of an original decentralized unitary state. It was not a result of uniting regions. In recent decades, more and more powers have been granted to the regions. Consequently, the Flemish Region, the Brussels-Capital Region and the Walloon Region have the main competences in ambient environmental law *sensu latu* such as urban planning, environmental protection of the landscape, the protection of the environment, the protection against harmful effects on water and the conservation and protection of nature.[17] The federal government retains its powers in, for example, the protection against the dangers of ionizing radiation (e.g. nuclear waste) and the protection of the North Sea. Thus, the first consequence of the federal state structure is the different types of mediations in the different regulations. This chapter focuses on the applicable regulations in the Flemish Region.

16 De Geyter, L., *Bemiddeling in het bestuursrecht*, die Keure, Mechelen, 2006, 365.

17 Art. 6, §1, Special Act of August 8, 1980, on institutional reform, *Belgian Official Gazette*, August 15, 1980.

The second consequence of the federal structure are the different administrative courts, which each has its own powers and (mediation) procedures. Later, this chapter will give a brief introduction (*infra*, no. 3.1).

## 2 Environmental mediation during the administrative procedure

### *2.1 Different permit procedures, different regulations*

Asking for a permit is a hurdle that almost everyone has to take before carrying out certain urban developments. Article 4.2.1 of the Flemish Zoning Code lists the actions for which a prior **environmental permit for urban actions** is required. This is a very extensive list, which includes building, rebuilding, renovating, cutting down trees, substantial relief modifications and changing the function of a building.[18] In addition, Article 4.2.15 of the Flemish Zoning Code requires a prior **environmental permit for the parcelling out of land.**[19]

There are two different administrative procedures for granting an environmental permit: the regular and the simplified procedure.[20] Whereas the regular procedure is applicable in the majority of the cases, the simplified procedure is applicable for permit applications for actions listed in Article 17, §2 of the Environmental Permit Decree.[21] During the procedure, an environmental permit has to be submitted with the competent authority (Flemish Government, Provincial Deputation or the Municipal Executive).[22] The competent authority has to decide within a fixed deadline.[23] If it refrains from taking a decision within this time limit, the permit application is considered to be declined.[24] Against this explicit decision or implied decline from the Municipal Executive or the

18 Maintenance is explicitly released from this duty (see Art. 4.2.1, *in fine* of the Flemish Zoning Code). Furthermore, Article 4.2.3 of the Flemish Zoning Code provides the possibility for the Flemish Government to make a list of actions that are contemporary or occasionally, or that have a minor spatial impact and are, therefore, exempted of the obligation to receive a prior planning permission. See also the Decision of the Flemish Government of July 16, 2010, concerning certain the actions for which no planning permission is required, *Belgian Official Gazette*, December 10, 2010; Van Hoorick, G., *Handboek ruimtelijk bestuursrecht*, Intersentia, Antwerp, 2011, 213.

19 See Article 4.2.1, 14° of the Flemish Zoning Code for a definition of parcelling out land. See also Van Hoorick, G., *Handboek ruimtelijk bestuursrecht*, Intersentia, Antwerp, 2011, 216; Bouckaert, B. and T. De Waele, *Ruimtelijke Ordening en Stedenbouw in het Vlaamse Gewest*, Vanden Broele, Bruges, 2004, 203.

20 Vanheusden, B., S. Betz, M. Boodts, J. De Coninck, K.J. De Graaf, D. Devos, H.D. Tolsma and K. Van Alsenoy, *De omgevingsvergunning: Een eerste analyse*, die Keure, Brugge, 2015, 9–20.

21 Decree of April 25 2014 concerning the Environmental Permit, *Belgian Official Gazette*, October 23, 2014 (hereafter, Environmental Permit Decree).

22 *Environmental Permit Decree*, art. 15.

23 *Environmental Permit Decree*, art. 32, §1.

24 *Environmental Permit Decree*, art. 32, §4.

Provincial Deputation, an administrative appeal can be lodged respectively with the Provincial Deputation or the Flemish Government.[25]

Against the decisions in administrative appeal and the decision in first instance of the regional environmental development officer or the Flemish government, no further administrative appeal lies – the applicant will have to directly address the Flemish Council for Permit Disputes (see *infra*, n° 3.3).[26]

When someone wants to exploit the business premises of noisy or obnoxious trades, a prior **environmental permit** is also required, as included in classification list in the annex of Decision of the Flemish Government of November 27, 2015, to implement the Environmental Permit Decree (hereafter 'the classification list').[27] These establishments differ in nature and size. Some of them can be associated with big firms, such as a petroleum refinery, whereas others are associated with smaller firms (e.g. a pig farm).[28] The companies that are listed in the classification list are categorized into three classes. Class one represents the business premises of higher noisy or obnoxious trades. Class three represents the business premises of less noisy or obnoxious trades. Whereas for the third class a notification will suffice, for firms in the first or second class, an environmental permit is required. The competent authority (Flemish Government, Provincial Deputation or the Municipal Executive) is determined by the nature of the project.[29]

Against the decision of the Municipal Executive or the Provincial Deputation, an administrative appeal can be lodged, respectively, with the Provincial Deputation or the Flemish Government.[30] Against the decisions in administrative appeal and the decision in the first instance of the regional environmental development officer or the Flemish Government, no further administrative appeal lies – the applicant will have to directly address the Flemish Council for Permit Disputes (see *infra*, n° 3.3).[31]

In a densely populated region, such as Flanders, acquiring the required permit is not an easy task. Even the smallest of projects can provoke protest from neighbours or other local residents because they feel that their individual rights are harmed (cfr. the increasing amount of annulment judgments; see the aforementioned). This is reinforced by the fact that, in many cases, for the same project, various permits were required. Before the entry into force of the Environmental

25 *Environmental Permit Decree*, art. 52.

26 *Environmental Permit Decree*, art. 52.

27 Decision of the Flemish Government of November 27, 2015, to implement the Decree of April 25, 2014, concerning the environmental permit, *Belgian Official Gazette*, February 23, 2016.

28 Van Hoorick, G., *Handboek ruimtelijk bestuursrecht*, Intersentia, Antwerp, 2011, 296.

29 *Environmental Permit Decree*, art. 15; annex 1 and 2 of the Decision of the Flemish Government of February 13, 2015, of designating the Flemish and Provincial projects to implement the Decree of April 25, 2014, concerning the environmental permit, *Belgian Official Gazette*, March 4, 2015.

30 *Environmental Permit Decree*, art. 52.

31 *Environmental Permit Decree*, art. 52.

Permit Decree, one could be confronted with the obligation to obtain three different permits. For example, someone who wants to establish and exploit a chemical plant will need an urban permit for building the chemical plant and another environmental permit for the exploitation of the factory. This makes it even more difficult to be in agreement with all of the different parties that are concerned.

However, the Decree of the Flemish Government on April 25, 2014, concerning the ambient environmental permit, consolidates the environmental permit, the urban permit and the subdivision permit into one ambient environmental permit, it must be emphasized that the decree only concerns the permit procedure. With respect to content, the other decrees (the Flemish Zoning Code and the decree concerning the environmental permit) still apply.[32]

For this reason environmental disputes still occurs and several procedural guarantees exists. The local authority has autonomous discretion that leaves room for policy decisions. First and foremost, it has to take the general interest into account. Additionally, the individual interests of citizens have to be considered. To advance this assessment, mediation between the permit applicant, third parties concerned and any other relevant body of government can be helpful. This mediation can take place before the administrative procedure has started. Furthermore, mediation can even be possible during the administrative procedure.

## 2.2 *Mediation preceding the procedure for planning permissions*

### 2.2.1 *The informal mediation*

Obviously, the person who wants to submit a permit application, irrespective of the kind of permit application, can always decide to organize a joint consultation with the competent authority and parties concerned. Especially when it comes to large projects, the initiator of the project can benefit from such an informal meeting. This is because a large number of complaints can be avoided. However, it is difficult to speak in the case of mediation, as usually no neutral mediator is involved. In this case, it is difficult to distinguish mediation from consultation or other forms of participation. Lancksweerdt is of the opinion that mediation occurs when the contact is made according to the principles of mediation, thus with a neutral mediator. In practice, the licensing authority takes this role. The fact that such a procedure is non-binding is not relevant. Moreover, the fact that mediation is initiated before the permit application has the added advantage that one does not have to take procedural stator provisions into account.[33]

The result of informal mediation can be diverse. First of all, it is possible that no permit application is submitted. Secondly, the mediation can result in a private

32 Vanheusden, B., ed., *De omgevingsvergunning: een eerste analyse*, die Keure, Bruges, 2015, 218.

33 Lancksweerdt, E., "Bemiddeling en milieuvergunningen" (2011) 3 *Tijdschrift voor Milieurecht* 13.

agreement. This agreement can contain certain modalities, according to which the permit applicant will have to submit its permit application. It is also possible that, in this agreement, the competent authority engages himself to grant the permit under the conditions that have been determined in the agreement or that the third parties that are concerned have engaged themselves to not lodge any administrative or judicial appeal.[34] In this way, mediation can decrease the number of complaints or appeals after the permit is granted and maybe even those that have yet to be executed.

Nonetheless, the outcome of the mediation agreement must be nuanced. In the first place, third parties that are not involved in the mediation can still file a complaint or lodge an appeal during or after the authorization arrangements. Therefore, to ensure legal certainty, it is important to aim to reach and involve all of the concerned parties.

Secondly, the question arises whether the public authority can give up its public power through a private agreement. Informal mediation between private parties does not impose any problems. When the mediation agreement is concluded between a private person (e.g. the initiator of a project) and the public authority, the consequences are less unambiguous. In principle, the powers that are attributed to the administration should be exercised. The administration does not have the power to dispose of these competences and is obliged to apply them in the general interest. The Constitution and the law indicate what powers are attributed and how these should be exercised. They also make clear that no agreement can be made concerning the way an administrative organ exercises its powers.[35] Consequently, an administrative organ cannot, by means of an agreement, engage itself to take a certain administrative action in the future. It is obliged to take the action that best serves the general interest. If it has bound itself, the organ may no longer be able to make an evaluation at the time that the decision is made. Such restrictions that are imposed on an administrative organ to conclude a private agreement do not imply that a competent authority cannot conclude a private agreement. Furthermore, they do not imply that a public authority can put aside a closed agreement just like that. Only when there is a good reason, the public authority can differ from a private agreement. This way, for example, a local authority that is competent for an environmental permit application can still decide not to grant the permit, even though all of the conditions that have been set out in the private agreement are met, *if* it has a good reason following from the objections expressed during the public inquiry.[36]

To ensure this possibility, the private agreement that results from the mediation should contain the reservation that the authority can bypass the agreement

34 Lancksweerdt, E., "Bemiddeling en milieuvergunningen" (2011) 3 *Tijdschrift voor Milieurecht* 13.

35 *Civil Code*, art. 6 and 1128; *Belgian Constitution*, art. 33.

36 Lancksweerdt, E., "Bemiddeling en milieuvergunningen" (2011) 3 *Tijdschrift voor Milieurecht* 12; Lancksweerdt, E., "*Bemiddeling in het bestuursrecht*" in D. Lindemans, ed., *Gedogen en bemiddelen in het bestuursrecht*, die Keure, Bruges, 2003, 141 and 153.

for reasons of general interest. For this reason, in practice, there is rarely a successful informal mediation that precedes the procedure for planning permission.

Given the limitations of the authorization arrangements (*infra*), preceding mediation is the most efficient. However, in practice, it is not easy to take the decision to use any form of (semi-) mediation before the procedure for planning permissions is started. Usually, problems and conflicts between the planning permission applicant, the government body and/or other stakeholders become clear during the procedure. Therefore, it is appropriate for the initiator of a project to be vigilant and detect possible tensions in advance.

### 2.2.2 The project meeting

As written in Belgian legal doctrine,[37] the only form of mediation in environmental is the so-called project meeting. Someone who is responsible for the development and implementation of major constructions or building projects[38] may request a 'project meeting' from the advisory and the licensing authorities, if a realistic project study is available.[39] The applicant has the right to ask for this project meeting and this request cannot be refused. In this meeting, possible conflicts and tensions are eliminated in advance.

The Environmental Permit Decree provides the possibility for the competent authority to invite third parties on its own initiative or at the request of the initiator.[40]

In our opinion, the project meeting cannot be called mediation. Firstly, it is not a voluntary process, as the concerned authorities cannot refuse the request. Secondly, an independent, impartial and neutral third party (mediator) is not present. Finally, there is no question of equality between the parties, since the concerned authorities also act as the advisory and licensing authorities after the mediation.

## 2.3 The mediation during the procedure for planning permissions

In the procedure for an environmental permit, citizens have the possibility for participation: the so-called public inquiry.[41] At this stage of the proceedings, anyone can submit objections to the application of the permission.[42] The licensing authority is required to take these concerns into account. Despite the possibility of a public inquiry, mediation can be useful. This is because such an inquiry is not

37 Lancksweerdt, E., "Bemiddeling en ruimtelijke ordening" (2010) 60 *Tijdschrift voor Ruimtelijke Ordening en Stedenbouw* 229.

38 What "major constructions or building projects" is understood to mean is explained in Art. 5 of the decision of the Flemish Government of March 19, 2010 concerning planning certificates, project meetings and urban information, *Belgian Official Gazette*, April 13, 2010.

39 *Environmental Permit Decree*, art. 8.

40 *Environmental Permit Decree*, art. 8, al. 3.

41 *Environmental Permit Decree*, art. 23.

42 Van Hoorick, G., *Handboek ruimtelijk bestuursrecht*, Intersentia, Antwerp, 2011, 236 and 298.

intended to adjust the planning permission but rather, aims to assess whether or not to refuse the permission.[43]

Furthermore, in some cases, the Municipal Authority can organize an information meeting within the scope of the public inquiry. For certain class, one business premises, which can have a high impact on the environment or require an environmental impact assessment, an information meeting *has* to be organized.[44] However, these instruments can stimulate participation during the procedure. Thus, it is possible that certain conflicts arise during the information meeting. This can be an incentive for the competent authority to organize mediation.[45]

However, the authorization arrangements are not equipped with a procedure for mediation during the administrative procedure. At the same time, informal mediation is not evident. It is very difficult to conduct a profound mediation. This is because the time in which the government must, by law, come to a decision on the permission is too short.[46] Moreover, there is an important legal principle that states that a permission application may not be fundamentally modified after a public inquiry.[47] In the event that mediation has succeeded, the permit application can only be modified to a certain extent. Otherwise, the applicant has to renounce its application and file a new application.[48]

For that reason, in practice, we rarely see a successful mediation during the environmental permit procedure. Given the absolute prohibition of changing the permission application after the public inquiry, the essential characteristic of mediation – the search for a satisfactory solution – is completely nullified. However, it is theoretically possible that the permission procedure is stopped as a

43 More than that, the subject of the permit application cannot be changed during the procedure, especially not after the public inquiry. Otherwise, the public inquiry should be, once again, organized. See, e.g., Council of State, February 21, 2011, no. 211.387; Council of State, November 14, 2013, no. 225.476.

44 Decision of the Flemish Government of November 27, 2015, to implement the Decree of April 25, 2014, concerning the environmental permit, *Belgian Official Gazette*, February 23, 2016, art. 25; see, e.g., Council of State January 20, 2011, no. 210 532, Naessens, X., "De informatievergadering in de VLAREM-procedure: een gewaarschuwd man is er twee waard" (2014) *Tijdschrift voor Omgevingsrecht en Omgevingsbeleid* 147.

45 Lancksweerdt, E., "Bemiddeling en milieuvergunningen" (2011) 3 *Tijdschrift voor Milieurecht* 14.

46 Act of February 21, 2005, on amending the Judicial Code in connection with the mediation, *Belgian Official Gazette*, March 22, 2005.

47 See, e.g., Council of State November 28, 2007, no. 177.326, *Bernaert*; Council of State August 10, 2007, no. 173.955, *Carron en Callewaert*; Council of State November 19, 2007, no. 172.417, *nv Prima*; Council of State February 14, 2007, no. 167.789, *Collaert*; Council of State August 4, 2008, no. 183.773, *nv D.M.P.*; Council of State, February 21, 2011, no. 211.387, *Natuurpunt Oost-Brabant en Haegeman*; Council of State, November 14, 2013, no. 225.476, *Gemeente Sint-Katelijne-Waver*; De Waele, T., P. Flamey, P. Sourbron and P. Jan Vervoort, *De milieuvergunning in het Vlaamse Gewest : een overzicht van rechtspraak van de Raad van State*, Vanden Broele, Brugge, 2009, 32.

48 Lancksweerdt, E., "Bemiddeling en milieuvergunningen" (2011) 3 *Tijdschrift voor Milieurecht* 14.

result of the mediation talks for the applicant to put in an altered planning permission application.

Finally, we should also emphasize that, in this form of (semi-) mediation, there is no question of equivalence between the parties and a neutral mediator is rarely called in.

## 3 Environmental mediation during the judicial procedure

### *3.1 A short introduction to the Belgian administrative courts*

In order to comprehend the different kinds of mediation procedures during the various judicial procedures in administrative law, it is necessary to say a few words about the specific organization of administrative courts. This has been shaped by the typical Belgian federal state structure. According to an initial reading of the Belgian Constitution, it is clear that no administrative court can be created other than by an act that is issued by the federal Parliament.[49] Thus, the Constitution does not explicitly describe the power to establish regional administrative courts for the Flemish Parliament, which is the legislator for the Flemish Community and the Flemish Region.

Nevertheless, through the legal concept of the so-called implied powers, which is contained in Article 10 of the special act regarding the reform of the institutions, it is now accepted that the regions have this power.[50] Pursuant to the implied powers, states can regulate affairs for which, in principle, they are not authorized, insofar as such provisions are necessary for them to exercise their other attributed powers. The Constitutional Court has judged that these implied powers may be used under three conditions: 1) the exercising of these powers is necessary in order for them to be able to exercise their own powers (those of the regions), 2) it only has a small impact on the federal regulations[51] and 3) the federal regulations are compatible with the differentiated regulation.[52] One of the uses of those implied powers is the competence for the Flemish Parliament to establish regional administrative courts. The Constitutional Court confirmed this

49 Article 161, introduced in 1993 into the Belgian constitution.

50 See, *Special Act Regarding the Reform of the Institutions*, art. 10. This is an act that was voted by the federal parliament with a special majority which attributes competences to the Communities and the Regions. See *Parl.Doc.* Dutch speaking Cultural Council 1973–1974, no. 122/1, 10–21 and *Parl.Doc.* Chamber of Representatives 1977–1978, no. 461/25, 4).

51 Cf. Constitutional Court September 16, 1998, no. 95/98; Constitutional Court November 28, 1996, no. 68/96; Constitutional Court October 25, 2000, no. 105/200; Constitutional Court October 31, 2000, no. 109/2000; Constitutional Court June 30, 2005, no. 114/2005.

52 Cf. Constitutional Court January 18, 1996, no. 95/98; Constitutional Court November 28, 1996; Constitutional Court October 25, 2000, no. 105/2000.

competence.[53] However, the Council of State, which was established at a federal level, continues to act as the cassation court for the regional administrative courts.

Over the last decade, Flanders has created four administrative courts:

- *The Council for Permit Disputes* is a court where appeals can be made against permit decisions concerning the delivery or refusal of an environmental permit,[54] a validation decision and a registration decision.[55]
- *The Enforcement Council*[56] is an administrative court where an offender can appeal against administrative sanctions in environmental law and spatial planning.[57]
- *The Council on Electoral Disputes* has the competence on objections to the municipal and provincial elections.[58]
- *The Council for disputes about decisions on study progress* provides judicial protection for students of higher education colleges and universities in the Flemish Community in disputes on decisions on study progress (e.g. decisions on examinations).[59]

Some Flemish politicians are thinking about having one Flemish administrative court. Given the uncertainty about the compatibility of the power to establish such a common regional administrative court and the theory of implied powers, nowadays, no such legal proposal has been submitted. Last year, however, a general Decree of April 4, 2014, concerning some Flemish administrative courts, was adopted. This tunes the main Flemish administrative courts[60] to each other and allows a far-reaching cooperation.[61] Thus, a service for administrative courts has been established where the clerks, legal secretaries and support staff are centralized.

However, the Council of State still plays a part in environmental legislation cases. A cassation appeal to the Council of State is always provided against decisions by the Council for Permit Disputes and the Enforcement Council.

53 Constitutional Court January 27, 2011, no. 8/2011.

54 *Environmental Permit Decree*, art. 105, §1.

55 *Flemish Zoning Code*, art. 4.8.2, *Belgian Official Gazette*, August 20, 2009.

56 Before February 23, 2017, this was called the 'Environmental Enforcement Council'. Due to the entry into force of the Environmental Permit Decree, the competences of this court concerning environmental permits were transferred to the Council for Permit Disputes.

57 *Flemish Decree of April 5*, art. 16.4.19, 1995, concerning general provisions relating to environmental policy, *Belgian Official Gazette*, June 3, 1995.

58 *Flemish Decree of July 8, 2011*, art. 203, concerning the organization of the local and provincial elections and amending the municipal Decree of July 15, 2005, the provincial Decree of December 9, 2005, and the Decree of December 19, 2008, concerning the organization of the public centres for social welfare, *Belgian Official Gazette*, August 25, 2011.

59 *Flemish Codification of October 11, 2013*, art. II.285 of the decree provisions concerning higher education, *Belgian Official Gazette*, February 27, 2014.

60 The Council for disputes about decisions on study progress is not included in these regulations.

61 Decree of April 4, 2014, on the organization and procedure of some Flemish administrative courts, *Belgian Official Gazette*, October 1, 2014.

## *3.2 The Council of State*

### *3.2.1 Mediation as a task of magistrates*

The idea of mediation in administrative law was first raised three years ago at parliamentary level. The proposers of these bills attributed a significant role to the magistrates.[62] In the proposal, the prosecutor could decide to initiate a mediation procedure and he was appointed as the mediator. The choice of the auditor as a mediator is remarkable. Firstly, the independence and impartiality cannot be guaranteed during the mediation assignment or during the judicial assignment. In addition, the confidentiality is put at risk. The parties must be able to show their particular interests, without fear of abuse by the prosecutor during the judicial process. Secondly, the magistrates themselves were against a possible new assignment. This fear is not entirely unjustified. The backlog of court cases in Belgium is still not resolved, and this bill could have the perverse effect that judicial procedures would be longer. Therefore, the bills were never adopted.

### *3.2.2 The federal ombudsman as a 'mediator'*

In 2014, the State Council was greatly reformed. One of the key aspects was the introduction of a mediation procedure with the Council of State. The legislator chose to achieve this objective by upgrading the existing institution of the federal Ombudsman. Since the reform of 2014, the procedure before the Ombudsman and the procedure before the Council of State have been linked to each other.

Firstly, the procedure before the Ombudsman continues to run, even if an appeal to the Council of State is pending. Upon the establishment of the Ombudsman, his position was subordinate to any administrative and judicial remedies and the submission and consideration of a complaint to the Ombudsman did not suspend. Since the reform of 2014, this subordination has been eliminated with regard to the Council of State. Nevertheless, the general principle remains intact. This is that the procedure before the Ombudsman is suspended by lodging an appeal with a court or an organized administrative appeal such as the Council for Permit Disputes, the Enforcement Council or other ordinary tribunals and courts.

Secondly, and more importantly, the period for appeal of the cancellation action by the Council of State has been suspended when a complaint is lodged to the Ombudsman.[63] The rest of the period for appeal will begin either at the time that the complainant is informed of the decision not to treat his complaint or to reject his complaint, or at the expiry of a period of four months, which starts from the filing of the complaint, if the decision of the Ombudsman did not come

62 Bill to amend the laws of January 12, 1973, at the Council of State, *Parl.Doc.* Senate 2012–2013, no. 5–1965/1, 26 p.; Bill to amend the laws on the Council of State, coordinated on January 12, 1973, *Parl.Doc.* Kamer 2012–2013, no. 2583/001, 30.

63 *Council of State Law*, art. 19.

before. In contrast to the period for appeal to the Council for Permit Disputes or the Environmental Enforcement Court, which is not suspended by an Ombudsman procedure, the applicant will always be entitled to a period of 60 days to lodge his appeal before the Council of State, whether he has or has not decided to submit a complaint to the Ombudsman.

The Ombudsman is an important form of alternative dispute resolution (ADR) with great authority in regard to the governments. The Annual Report 2015 of the federal Ombudsman shows that 85.95% of the valid complaints led to a complete rectification by the government.[64] Therefore, the upgrading of the Ombudsman as a filter on the access to the Council of State should be praised. Nevertheless, in our opinion, the legislator is wrong when he stated that this type of Ombudsman is a form of mediation.

However, the procedure before the Ombudsman has many features of mediation, which must be nuanced. Firstly, it is generally accepted that voluntariness is an essential feature of mediation.[65] This means that parties are free to use mediation to resolve their dispute and that they are able to put an end to the mediation at any time. In contrast, the procedure before the Ombudsman is unilaterally initiated by the citizen who files a complaint.[66] Secondly, the doctrine adopts the equality of the parties as an essential feature of mediation.[67] As stated earlier, the Ombudsman has great authority. He can send a negative report with recommendations to the minister who acts as higher authority to the concerned government. These recommendations hang like a sword of Damocles over the head of the concerned government. Thirdly, the mediator assists the parties during the mediation procedure without imposing a solution.[68] The parties have to come to a solution. This is where the shoe pinches for the Ombudsman. Although his recommendations cannot be imposed, the moral pressure is quite large. He is not a guide but an assessor.

Whether the Ombudsman may or may not be interpreted as a form of mediation is purely an academic discussion. However, it is regrettable that the recent reform of the Council of State consists of a non-voluntary, forced complaints procedure with an imbalance between the parties as a method of ADR.

64 See *Annual Report 2014*. Access: www.federaleombudsman.be

65 Goovaerts, L. and S. Thielemans, *Alternatieve geschiloplossing: Bemiddelaars en onderhandelaars aan tafel*, Auxis, Brussels, 2000, 361; Hubeau, B., "De bemiddeling in het Publiekrecht" (2000–2001) 11 *Rechtskundig Weekblad* 410; Lancksweerdt, E., "Bemiddeling met en door gemeenten" (2003) 2 *Tijdschrift voor Gemeenterecht* 95; Lancksweerdt, E., "Bemiddeling met en door gemeenten" in D. Lindemans, ed., *Gedogen en bemiddelen in het bestuursrecht*, die Keure, Bruges, 2003, 141.

66 Art. 8 Act of March 22, 2005, establishing the federal Ombudsmen, *Belgian Official Gazette*, April 7, 1995; Art. 12 Flemish Decree of July 7, 1998, establishing the Flemish Ombudsman, *Belgian Official Gazette*, August 25, 1998.

67 De Geyter, L., *Bemiddeling in het bestuursrecht*, die Keure, Mechelen, 2006, 217; Lancksweerdt, E., "Bemiddeling met en door gemeenten" in D. Lindemans, ed., *Gedogen en bemiddelen in het bestuursrecht*, die Keure, Bruges, 2003, 141.

68 De Geyter, L., *Bemiddeling in het bestuursrecht*, die Keure, Mechelen, 2006, 217; Lancksweerdt, E., "Bemiddeling met en door gemeenten" in D. Lindemans, ed., *Gedogen en bemiddelen in het bestuursrecht*, di Keure, Bruges, 2003, 141.

### *3.2.3 A new type of (informal) mediation accepted in jurisdiction?*

In contrast to the Council for Permit Disputes (cf. *infra*), the legislation on the Council of State provides no rules on a judicial referral to an external mediator. Nevertheless, in one case, the Council of State has implicitly allowed the external mediation procedure.[69] In this case, all of the parties asked spontaneously for a postponement of the case because a solution was sought with the help of a mediator. The Council of State agreed and postponed the case for an undefined period. Although this pragmatic attitude of the Council of State should be praised, the informal nature of this type of mediation has its disadvantages. Firstly, there is no judicial review of the essential characteristics of mediation (e.g. the independence and impartiality of the mediator). Furthermore, the Council of State cannot ratify the mediation agreement.

## *3.3 The Flemish Council for Permit Disputes*

The Flemish Parliament has introduced administrative mediation during the procedure for the Council for Permit Disputes by the Decree of July 13, 2012.[70] The regulations are now included in the earlier mentioned general Decree of April 4, 2014, concerning some Flemish administrative courts and its administrative decree stating the executory measures.[71] These provisions state that the Council may refer a dispute to a mediator during the procedure at the joint request of the parties or on the initiative of the court with the agreement of the parties.[72] However, referring to mediation is never an obligation for the Council for Permit Disputes. The start of the mediation procedure suspends the judicial procedure before the Council for Permit Disputes.

The rules provided a lot of possibilities to appoint a mediator: judges, clerks, members of the support staff or even third parties proposed jointly by the parties could be appointed by the Council as mediator. In order to respect the principles of impartiality and independence, it had to be assumed that a board member couldn't act as a mediator and as a judge in the same case. This would impair the confidentiality of the mediation. It is clear that the parties will attach no credence to the confidentiality of a mediator who can decide as a judge in the case of a failed mediation. However, it is no longer an issue since the Decree of December 9, 2016, eliminates the possibility of appointing a judge as a mediator. In the period between the January, 1, 2014, and January, 1, 2015, the Council for Permit Disputes has referred to mediation nine times; in six other cases the start

69 Council of State November 4, 2014, no. 229.034.

70 Flemish Decree of July 6, 2012, amending various provisions of the Flemish Zoning Code, which concerns the Council for Permit Disputes, *Belgian Official Gazette*, August 24, 2012.

71 Flemish Decree of April 6, 2014, on the organization and procedure of some Flemish administrative courts, art. 42, *Belgian Official Gazette*, October 1, 2014; Flemish administrative decree on the procedure of some Flemish administrative courts, art. 95–100, *Belgian Official Gazette*, May 16, 2014.

72 Flemish Council for Permit Disputes October 1, 2013, no. S/2013/0231.

of mediation failed due to the lack of agreement between the parties[73] or because to the judge deemed mediation undesirable.[74] Every time, an internal mediator, especially a clerk, was appointed as mediator.[75]

Unfortunately, the decree provides no special guarantees to ensure the mediation skills of the third party who acts as a mediator. In contrast to Dutch law or the Belgian civil procedure law, Belgium has no specialized committee for recognizing a mediator in administrative matters. It is the Council for Permit Disputes itself that has to ensure the quality, independence and impartiality of the mediator.

The mediation procedure can take up to six months. A successful mediation leads to a settlement that gives more satisfaction to the parties than a judicial procedure. The Council for Permit Disputes can only refuse the ratification of this settlement if the agreement is contrary to public order, to regulations or to the urban development prescriptions. In the absence of a mediation agreement or when the Council for Permit Disputes determines that the preconditions for successful mediation are not or are no longer fulfilled, the Council recommends the continuation of the judicial process.

The Flemish legislator saw the administrative mediation as a filter to avoid jurisdictional procedures. From a preliminary analysis of the small number of case law, it must be concluded that this goal is partly achieved. In five of the nine cases, mediation was successfully completed.[76] In the four other cases, the parties failed to come to an agreement.[77] However, it must be noted that in 2016, more cases

73 Flemish Council for Permit Disputes October 1, 2013, no. S/2013/0231; Flemish Council for Permit Disputes June 9, 2015, no A/2015/0343; Flemish Council for Permit Disputes October 6, 2015, no. RvVb/A/2015/0077; Flemish Council for Permit Disputes October 6, 2015, no. RvVb/S/1516/0071.

74 Flemish Council for Permit Disputes May, 25, 2013, no. S/2013/0171; Flemish Council for Permit Disputes May 2013, no. S/2013/0127.

75 Flemish Council for Permit Disputes, January 14, 2014, no. A/2014/0009; Flemish Council for Permit Disputes, January 14, 2014, no. A/2014/0008; Flemish Council for Permit Disputes, June 23, 2015, no. A/2015/0384; Flemish Council for Permit Disputes, August 11, 2015, no. S/2015/0103; Flemish Council for Permit Disputes, October 6, 2015, no. RvVb/A/1516/0094; Flemish Council for Permit Disputes, October 6, 2015, no. RvVb/S/1516/0087; Flemish Council for Permit Disputes, December 1, 2015, no. RvVb/S/1516/0317; Flemish Council for Permit Disputes, October 14, 2014, no. A/2014/0705; Flemish Council for Permit Disputes, April 21, 2015, no. A/2015/0250; Flemish Council for Permit Disputes, June 25, 2013, no. S/2013/0171; Flemish Council for Permit Disputes, October 1, 2013, no. S/2013/0231; Flemish Council for Permit Disputes, May 14, 2013, no. S/2013/0127; Flemish Council for Permit Disputes, June 9, 2015, no. A/2015/0343; Flemish Council for Permit Disputes, October 6, 2015, no. RvVb/A/2015/0077; Flemish Council for Permit Disputes, October 6, 2015, no. RvVb/S/1516/0071.

76 Flemish Council for Permit Disputes, January 14, 2014, no. A/2014/0009, Flemish Council for Permit Disputes, January 14, 2014, no. A/2014/0008, Flemish Council for Permit Disputes, June 23, 2015, no. A/2015/0384, Flemish Council for Permit Disputes, August 11, 2015, no. S/2015/0103.

77 Flemish Council for Permit Disputes, October 6, 2015, no. RvVb/A/1516/0094, Flemish Council for Permit Disputes, October 6, 2015, no. RvVb/S/1516/0087, Flemish Council

were referred to mediation; future analyses of this administrative jurisdiction will determine whether or not the introduction of mediation is successful.

### *3.4 The Enforcement Council*

The general Decree of April 4, 2014, which concerns some Flemish administrative courts, contains provisions regarding mediation. Unfortunately, they were only made applicable to the Council for Permit Disputes and not to the Enforcement Council. In addition, the special rules for the suspension of the period for appeal when a complaint is lodged to the Ombudsman are not applicable for regional administrative courts. Thus, the Enforcement Council is missing out on mediation.

The only possibility that mediation could be used is similar to the case of the Council of State, which was granted in an informal manner during the mediation process (*supra*, no. 3.2.3). To this very day, however, it has never happened.

## 4 Towards a fully fledged legislation for mediation?

### *4.1 A referring judge*

It appears that mediation in administrative disputes can be an added value for ADR. From the aforementioned, it is clear that neither the Ombudsman nor the judge can be considered to be the most suitable person to act as a mediator in administrative matters (*supra*). The 'judge as mediator' principle can be problematic because of his duty of confidentiality. This duty does not relieve him of his obligation to declare as a public official, as defined in Article 29 Preliminary Title of the Code of Criminal Procedure.[78] Furthermore, the inequality of power between the government and citizens provides an additional problem. Unequal power relationships are undesirable in the process of mediation. In order to eliminate these differences, more safeguards will be necessary to add to the existing means of ADR in Belgian administrative law. Unequal power relations between the government and the citizen also cause problems within the scope of a complaint with the Ombudsman. A complaint filed with the Ombudsman can lead to a moral judgment, which the government will want to avoid.

The required impartiality is another factor than can pose a problem.[79] In this context, the judge, when acting as a mediator, is not allowed to take a decision on the merits of the case if the mediation was unsuccessful.[80] Otherwise, this can lead

---

for Permit Disputes, December 1, 2015, no. RvVb/S/1516/0317, Flemish Council for Permit Disputes, October 14, 2014, no. A/2014/0705, Flemish Council for Permit Disputes, April 21, 2015, no. A/2015/0250.

78 *Parl.Doc.* Chamber of Representatives 2003–2004, no. 51–0327/7, 68.

79 See also De Geyter, L., *Bemiddeling in het bestuursrecht*, di Keure, Mechelen, 2006, 180.

80 *Parl.Doc.* Chamber of Representatives 2003–2004, no. 327/001, 9; *Parl.Doc.* Chamber of Representatives 2003–2004, no. 327/007, 53.

to a legal challenge procedure, which cannot be reconciled with the flexibility inherent to mediation.[81] In addition, it should be noted that because of the strict separation of powers, a judge is not allowed to substitute for the administration. However, at the moment, the legislature remains silent in the Judicial Code (for now).[82] It is regrettable that the Council of Permit Disputes does provide for the possibility for a judge to act as mediator.[83]

Nevertheless, it is not desirable to rule the judge completely out of mediation. In addition to writing a good judgment, the judge needs to find a solution that every party can agree on. This reconciliation is just as important as the settlement of the dispute.[84] This is why a judge can be of great importance for the court-connected mediation in administrative disputes through a referral procedure. This model already exists in the judiciary code. Furthermore, several years ago, the Netherlands also introduced the possibility of a 'referral judge'.

In fact, since 2007 (implementation started in 2007), all of the Dutch courts have had a structural referral facility that refers all of the cases that qualify for mediation to a mediation committee. According to this system, a judge can bring the possibilities of mediation, both in civil and administrative cases, to the attention of the parties. However, the use of mediation in administrative disputes has not yet been anchored in the Dutch General Law on Administrative Law (hereafter, 'Awb').[85] Currently, only the general Mediation Regulations 2008 of the 'Mediatorsfederatie Nederland' (hereafter, 'MfN') apply. These set out certain rules regarding the procedure, the competence and conduct of the mediator.[86] To meet the need for a legal framework for mediation, an act was submitted on September 10, 2013.[87] Although the rules of the MfN would still apply, the act provides for a general obligation in respect of the governing bodies. This bill

81 *Parl.Doc.* Chamber of Representatives 2003–2004, no. 51–0327/1, 11.

82 Nothing came of the proposal for a resolution (M. De Schamphelaere, et al.) concerning an improvement of the judicial organization, *Parl.Doc.* Chamber of Representatives 2008–2009, no. 52–1974/001, which argues the necessity of an explicit legal basis for a judge as mediator.

83 Decree of April 4, 2014 on the organization and procedure of some Flemish administrative courts, *Belgian Official Gazette*, October 1, 2014, art. 42, §2.

84 *Parl.Doc.* Chamber of Representatives 2003–2004, no. 327/007, 51–52.

85 Access: www.wetten.overheid.nl; The Dutch law implementing Directive 2008/52/EC article 3 does provide for a legal basis for judicial referral jurisdiction in cross-border disputes. However, a legal anchoring of mediation and, in particular, the judicial referral system in domestic disputes, including in administrative law, is still missing.

86 These regulations were drawn up by the Dutch Mediation Institute ('NMI'), responsible for the quality of mediation in the Netherlands. Since January 1, 2014, the NMI has been called the "Mediatorsfederatie Nederland (MfN)" (i.e., the association of mediators in the Netherlands). The NMI-regulations were also renamed. Henceforth, the MfN-mediation regulations 2008 have contained the rules on mediation.

87 See www.tweedekamer.nl. The original bill was amended to the recommendation of the Advisory Division of the Council of State, see bill as amended following the recommendation of the Advisory Division of the Council of State, *Parl.Doc.* Chamber II 2012–2013, 33.727, no. 5 (hereafter, *Parl.Doc.* Chamber II 2012–2013, 33.727, no. 5).

introduces a competence for judicial referral for both governing bodies[88] and the courts.[89] They are not obliged to refer the parties to mediation but, to a large extent, are urged to do so. It must be emphasized that the parties are under no obligation to try mediation.[90] It should be noted that this bill was withdrawn, together with two other proposals concerning mediation.[91] The initiator of the proposal introduced a new, most likely similar, proposal in his capacity of minister for justice and security: the 'law promoting mediation'.[92] This has been the subject of a public consultation[93] and is still the subject of much discussion.

As mentioned earlier, such a possibility has also been recently introduced in Belgian law in the procedure before the Council for Permit Disputes (see *supra*, n° 3.3). It is desirable to continue on the same lines in the procedure before the Council of State and other administrative courts. Consequently, at the hearing, or even before the start of the lawsuit, the judge can refer the case to mediation on the common consent of the parties. The actual mediation is left to a specialized and independent mediator.

The question arises as to the duty of the government to consider a mediatory proposal that is made by the court. In light of the principle of solicitude, which is set in Article 3:2 Awb, the Dutch Government can be forced to examine the possibility of mediation.[94] However, this obligation to examine the possibility of mediation does not automatically entail that the government must agree with the proposal of mediation.[95]

In Belgium, the government also has a duty of care. This implies that the administration can only make a decision on the basis of an adequate and complete examination of the specific case.[96] Additionally, during the judicial procedures, this duty of care must be observed.[97] As a result of this, in Belgium, the possibility to introduce a duty to examine the possibility of mediation can also be suggested.

88 Art. 1, C *Parl.Doc.* Chamber II 2012–2013, 33.727, no. 5.

89 Art. 1, F *Parl.Doc.* Chamber II 2012–2013, 33.727, no. 5.

90 See, e.g., HR January 20, 2006, *NJ* 2006, 75, *LJN* AU3724. Nevertheless, it appears that the parties experience a commitment to try mediation, since they are afraid that the court will not appreciate it if he refuses to cooperate. Sponselee, A.J.M., "Mediation: een strategisch verplichte omweg?" (2007) 10 *Arbeidsrecht* 48.

91 *Parl.Doc.* Chamber II 2014–2015, 33 722, n° 23, 33 723, n° 14 and 33 727, n° 12.

92 Wet bevordering mediation.

93 For the concept of the law during public consultation. Access: www.internetconsultatie.nl/wetmediation.

94 However, this obligation is limited to the relevant facts and interests to be weighed and will play especially if the government's decision has got a discretionary power, see Tolsma, H., *Bemiddelend bestuur: Juridische aspecten van bemiddeling bij de bestuurlijke besluitvorming*, Boom Juridische Uitgevers, Den Haag, 2008, 38.

95 Tolsma, H., "Mediation in de Algemene wet bestuursrecht: de hoogste tijd?" (2009) 2 *Tijdschrift Conflicthantering* 17 and 19.

96 See Mast, A., J. Dujardin, M. Van Damme and J. Vande Lanotte, *Overzicht van het belgisch administratief recht*, Kluwer, Mechelen, 2009, 55.

97 Tijs, R., *Algemeen bestuursrecht in hoofdlijnen*, Intersentia, Antwerp, 2012, 264.

However, this duty to examine whether a referral to mediation is possible will only be effective and consequently applied if the court proceedings can be suspended for the duration of the mediation. In the Netherlands, the suspension of the judicial procedure already applies when the parties use mediation with a registered mediator.[98] Additionally, in Belgian civil law[99] and in the procedure before the Council for Permit Disputes, the period of limitation is suspended when mediation is initiated.[100] This is not yet the case when a complaint is filed with the Ombudsman (*supra* n° 3.2.2) or in cases where mediation is used ad hoc.[101] Nevertheless, it would be desirable to introduce the suspension of the judicial procedure for mediation in all administrative matters.

In spite of all the advantages, in the parliamentary debate, the argument was put forward that the European Court for Human Rights (ECHR) had already condemned Belgium by reason of a violation of Article 6 of the ECHR.[102] At the basis of this condemnation was the fact that the administrative courts do not handle court cases within a reasonable time, as Article 6 of the ECHR imposes. This argument is nevertheless irrelevant because this reasonable period of time must be assessed in the light of the specific circumstances.[103] In this context, the Dutch Council of State considers that mediation should not be included in the determination of the reasonable time.[104]

In addition, Article 13 of the ECHR gives everyone the right to an effective remedy before a national authority in order to safeguard, among others, the rights that are contained in Article 6 of the ECHR. The requirement of an effective legal remedy before a national body should not be interpreted as the requirement of a judicial authority. All of the procedures that are available in a specific state will play a role in assessing whether the requirement of Article 13

98 *MfN Mediation Regulations 2008*, art. 9.1. Additionally, the draft of the Mediator Registry Act provides for an interruption of the procedure by the administrative court, see *Kamerstukken* II 2012–2013, 33.727, no. 6, 13.

99 Judicial Code, art. 1731, §3. See also Gayse, B., B. Allemeersch and P. Schollen, "De wet van 21 februari 2005 in verband met bemiddeling" in B. Allemeersch, ed., *De nieuwe wet op bemiddeling*, die Keure, Mechelen, 2005, 9 and 40.

100 Art. 42 Decree of April 4, 2014 on the organization and procedure of some Flemish administrative courts.

101 Art. 19, third paragraph Act of the Council of State, as amended by Art. 7, 3° Act of January 19, 2014, on the reform of the power, the control process and the organization of the State Council, *Belgian Official Gazette*, February 3, 2014; It is most regrettable that a pending judicial proceeding is not suspended when the parties decide to start mediation (or file a complaint with the Ombudsman). Due to this, mediation becomes a parallel dispute resolution, rather than an alternative dispute resolution, which was the initial purpose of introducing mediation.

102 Draft law on the reform of the power, the control process and the organization of the State Council, *Parl.Doc.* Senate 2013–2014, no. 5-2277/3, 18.

103 *Frydlender t. Frankrijk*, 30979/96, §86, EHRM 2000-VII; *Pizzati t. Italië*, 62361/00, §134, 29 maart 2006.

104 Dutch Council of State December 2, 2011, *JB* 2012/257; Dutch Council of State January 16, 2013, *Jurisprudence Environmental Law* 2013/311.

has been fulfilled. Here, accessibility, as well as speed and the guarantee of an effective solution, will be taken into consideration.[105] Consequently, mediation can also fall within the scope of this requirement. Mediation is accessible, cost-effective and fast, which implies that this alternative form of dispute resolution will safeguard the rights that are contained in Article 6, rather than violate them. A limitation in time for the use of the mediation will further contribute to this. By analogy with the Netherlands and the Judicial Code,[106] a maximum period for mediation in administrative matters can be an additional guarantee for compliance with Article 6 of the ECHR.[107]

### 4.2 *A general mediation committee with recognized mediators*

For the sake of both structurally and emotionally unequal power relations, a neutral mediator in administrative disputes is needed. Additionally, in the Netherlands, the Mediator Registry Act provides a legal basis for the rules on registration.[108] According to these rules, the mediator must meet the demands of quality and integrity. In Belgium, a regulation like in the Netherlands does not yet exist. However, in order for mediation to be effective, a recognized mediator is desirable, if not needed. When a mediator can be any neutral third party designated by the parties, this does not offer enough guarantees concerning the relationship between administration and citizens. A recognized mediator, on the other hand, can be guaranteed as a professional, impartial and independent third party. Therefore, a recognized mediator can be the outstanding means to rectify the unequal power relations in administrative matters, without losing sight of the intended purpose of mediation.[109] Therefore, when introducing a general referral system for the court, it can be recommended to set up a general mediation committee. All of the disputes that are eligible for mediation can be referred to the mediation committee by the court. In turn, the Committee can refer the dispute to a recognized mediator, who is specialized in the specific matter. He subsequently handles the dispute. The recognition of the mediators proceeds through

105 *Doran t. Ierland*, 50389/99, §§55–60, ECHM 2003-X.

106 *Belgian Judicial Code*, art. 1734, §2.

107 The mediation procedure before the Council of Permit Disputes already has a maximum duration of six months (*Council for Permit Disputes Procedural Rules*, art. 42, first paragraph, 4°).

108 Bill from the member Van der Steur to lay down the rules concerning the registration and promotion of the quality of mediators (Mediator Registry Act), *Parl.Doc.* Chamber II 2012–2013, 33.722, no. 5 (hereafter, *Parl.Doc.* Chamber II 2012–2013, 33.722, no. 5). Bill from the member Van der Steur to lay down the rules concerning the registration and promotion of the quality of mediators (Mediator Registry Act), *Parl.Doc.* Chamber II 2012–2013, 33.722, no. 6, 13 (explanatory memorandum); Also this bill was withdrawn, see n° 0 *in fine*.

109 See De Geyter, L., *Bemiddeling in het bestuursrecht*, die Keure, Mechelen, 2006, 128.

a flexible procedure, which is based on some predefined conditions. This already happens in both the Netherlands and Belgian civil judicial law.[110]

The administrative procedure is merely focused on participation such as the public inquiry. Therefore, mediation will play a less important role during the administrative procedure (see *supra*, n° 2.3). Consequently, a legislative framework for mediation preceding or during the administrative procedure is not as necessary as it is for mediation during the judicial procedure. However, if the parties decide on an informal mediation in this stage, they should be able to address the mediation committee and make use of a recognized mediator.

## Conclusion

All of the aforementioned makes it entirely clear that, for the sake of mediation as a form of ADR, a central mediation committee, including recognized mediators, is needed. Judges in both civil and administrative matters can refer to this body with a view to mediation. An independent, neutral mediator, who is recognized by the central mediation committee on the basis of general conditions, can lead the deliberation. Meanwhile, the basic principles of mediation, such as confidentiality and voluntariness, can be guaranteed.

110 Additionally, in the mediation procedure before the Council for Permit Disputes, there are some conditions set out. However, no recognition is needed yet.

# 5 A new code of civil procedure in Canada and needs for further developments in environment

*Catherine Choquette*[1]
*and Véronique Fraser*[2,3]

## Introduction

Over the past 25 years, mediation regulation has evolved substantially in Quebec, one of the ten provinces in Canada. The field of environment protection has also benefited from these developments especially through the Bureau d'audiences publiques sur l'environnement (BAPE) *Office of Public Hearings on the Environment* offering mediation in the context of major environmental projects. However, BAPE's cases represent only a small proportion of environmental disputes. A larger spectrum of environmental disputes need to benefit from processes offering the potential for expeditious resolution and mutually beneficial solutions.

This chapter describes the legislation, procedures and processes surrounding environmental mediation in Quebec. First, we present the mediation processes available at the judiciary, administrative and extrajudicial levels and show that environmental mediation processes are still at early stages of development in Quebec. This is true despite the entry into force of a new *Code of Civil Procedure* in January 2016, which made a step forward towards the codification of private modes of dispute prevention and resolution. Indeed, the new *Code of Civil Procedure* imposes an obligation for the parties to consider private prevention and resolution processes before referring their dispute to the courts,[4] but we can wonder whether appropriate processes are in place to follow through this legal obligation. To respond to this query, we present an overview of the institutions offering services in environmental mediation, the

1 Catherine Choquette, biologist and lawyer, professor of Law at the Université de Sherbrooke, director of the Research Group on Strategies and Actors in Environmental Governance (SAGE) and co-Director of the Regulation and Law of Governance Research Center (CrRDG).

2 Véronique Fraser, lawyer, professor of Law at the Université de Sherbrooke and a member of SAGE.

3 Acknowledgements go to the students Frédérique Tremblay, Raphaël Morneau-Bérubé, Simon Voyer-Poitras, Charles Gauthier for their excellent research work.

4 *Quebec's Code of Civil Procedure*, 2016, c C-25.01 [CCP], art 1.

general requirements to act as a mediator and as the opportunities for mediation training.

Quebec's new *Code of Civil Procedure* puts forth procedures for the conduct of private mediation. Such procedures, however, are not specifically tailored for environmental disputes. Do the existing processes and procedures respond to the needs and expectations of users and actors in the environmental sector? Are appropriate processes and procedures in place to address the demands of stakeholders with respect to environmental dispute resolution and prevention processes? We address these questions by presenting the results of a survey of environmental experts within government, associations and industries.

## 1 Description of the environmental dispute prevention and resolution processes in Quebec

Part 1 presents the range of environmental dispute prevention and resolution processes available in Quebec. More specifically, section 1.1 examines the facilitation, mediation and arbitration procedures available in the environmental sector that the citizens can readily refer to, whereas section 1.2 provides a summary assessment of the number of mediators who offer dispute resolution services in the context of environmental disputes as well as their specific qualifications and training.

### *1.1 Facilitation and mediation procedures for environmental disputes in Quebec*

In Quebec, as is the case elsewhere, the prevention and the resolution of environmental disputes are many-sided and involve different authorities, including the judiciary level, the administrative level and the extrajudicial level. The following section portrays the environmental dispute prevention and resolution procedures that exist in Quebec.[5]

#### *1.1.1 Judiciary level*

Judicial mediation, also known as 'settlement conference', first appeared in Quebec justice system when the *Code of Civil Procedure* was reformed in 2003.[6] The new *Code of Civil Procedure* states that the courts' mission, both in first instance and in appeal, includes "facilitating conciliation whenever the law so requires, the parties request it or consent to it or circumstances permit, or if a settlement conference is held".[7] To this end, courts can order to stay the proceedings at any

5 This description is not exhaustive.

6 Roberge, J.-F., *La justice participative: Changer le milieu juridique par une culture intégrative de règlement des différends*, Éditions Yvon Blais, Cowsansville, 2011, 70.

7 *Quebec's Code of Civil Procedure*, 2016, c C-25.01 [CCP], art 9.

time in order for the parties to participate in a settlement conference or a private mediation.[8] On the request of the parties, or when it is deemed appropriate, the chief justice designates a judge to preside over the settlement conference.[9] The conference is held in camera, free of charge and without formality.[10] The whole process is confidential,[11] and if the parties reach an agreement, it can be homologated by a judge upon request.[12]

Even though several cases of settlement conference are recorded in corporate, civil and family law, no example could be found in environmental law.[13]

### *1.1.2 Administrative level*

#### I) FACILITATION

Resorting to a facilitator helps to prevent potential disputes. In Quebec, the term 'facilitation', in the context of environmental law, can only be found at the BAPE *Office of Public Hearings on the Environment*, which defines it as follows: "a procedure consisting in the creation of an environment in which citizens, resource people and the promoter can exchange in a constructive way, and which aims at discussing specific aspects of a public hearing".[14] Thus, facilitation, as the BAPE defines it, is nothing but a tool for decision making. Resort to facilitation has a few objectives, including the following:

- Promoting the emergence of consensual solutions between the citizens and the promoter in order to facilitate the acceptance of the project in the community.
- Providing citizens with additional information so that they can refine their submissions in the second part of the public hearing by validating in advance the applicability of some of their proposals with the promoter and resource people.
- Giving the promoter the opportunity to address the concerns of the citizens by adapting his/her project.[15]

The facilitation is a voluntary procedure and it first appeared in 2008. It has been used only three times: for the Gros-Morne and Montagne Sèche wind

8 Art 156 and 158, para 1 CCP.
9 Art 161 et seq CCP.
10 Art 163, para 1 CCP.
11 Art 163, para 3 CCP.
12 Art 165, para 1 CCP.
13 Due to the fact that settlement conferences are confidential, such research could not be carried out exhaustively.
14 BAPE, *La facilitation*, 2011 at 2. Access: www.bape.gouv.qc.ca/sections/documentation/Facilitation.pdf [translated by authors].
15 Ibid [translated by authors].

park projects (2008),[16] the Ministry of Transport of Quebec's project to rebuild Routes 108–143 and 147 at Waterville (2009),[17] and for the project of L'Érable, a regional county municipality, to restore the natural threshold of Joseph Lake in Inverness (2011).[18]

II) MEDIATION

*a) Administrative Tribunal of Quebec, territory and environment section* The Administrative Tribunal of Quebec contains a division, the 'Territory and Environment Section', which specifically deals with cases involving environmental disputes. However, this division serves as a forum only for contesting decisions taken by a minister, a public body or a municipality under approximately a dozen laws.[19] The Administrative Tribunal of Quebec offers to citizens to take part in a conciliation session (which word is used as a synonym for mediation) with a representative of the entity that has taken the decision.[20] With some exceptions, the administrative judges generally act as conciliators and their role is to facilitate dialogue or negotiations between the parties, help them to identify their interests, assess their positions, negotiate and explore mutually satisfactory positions.[21] They do not give opinions with respect to the dispute and refrain from providing assessments of the legal strengths and weaknesses of the parties' positions and arguments. After consulting with the parties, the conciliator defines the rules applicable to the conciliation and any measure to facilitate its conduct, and determines the schedule of the sessions.[22] Conciliation sessions are held in private, at no cost to the parties and without formality, and require no prior

16 BAPE, *Enquête et audience publique : Projets de parcs éoliens de Gros-Morne et de Montagne Sèche*, 2009. Access: www.bape.gouv.qc.ca/sections/mandats/eole-gros-morne-montagne-s%C3%A8che/index.htm.

17 BAPE, *Enquête et audience publique : Projet de réaménagement de l'intersection des routes 108/143 et 147 à Waterville*, 2010. Access: www.bape.gouv.qc.ca/sections/mandats/Routes_Waterville/index.htm.

18 BAPE, *Enquête et audience publique: Projet de restauration du seuil naturel du lac Joseph à Inverness*, 2011. Access: www.bape.gouv.qc.ca/sections/mandats/lac_joseph_inverness/index.htm

19 Tribunal administratif du Québec, *The Tribunal: Origin and Role.* Access: www.taq.gouv.qc.ca/en/about/the-tribunal/origin-and-role.

20 See, generally, Tribunal administratif du Québec, *What Is Conciliation.* Access: www.taq.gouv.qc.ca/en/conciliation/general-explanations/what-is-conciliation.

21 *Act Respecting Administrative Justice*, RSQ, c J-3, art 121. However, in some cases, a personnel member may preside the conciliation session as provided for by art.120 (1) : "If he considers it expedient and if the subject-matter and circumstances of the case permit it, the president of the Tribunal, the vice-president responsible for the division concerned, the member designated by either of them or any member called on to hear the case may, with the consent of the parties, at any time before the case is taken under advisement, preside a conciliation session or allow such a session to be conducted by a personnel member chosen by the president of the Tribunal or by the person chosen by the president of the Tribunal".

22 Ibid, art 121.1 (1).

written documents.[23] The sessions are held in presence of the parties and their representatives. With the consent of the parties, the conciliator may meet the parties in private caucuses. Other persons may also take part in the sessions if the conciliator or the parties consider that their presence would be helpful in resolving the dispute.[24]

Everything that is said or written down during the conciliation remains confidential: such information cannot be revealed at a hearing before the tribunal or any other tribunal or court of law.[25] The law also provides that the conciliator cannot be required to disclose what has been said or presented during the conciliation session. No one can force him or her to disclose a document prepared or obtained in the context of conciliation.[26] However, if the parties arrive at an agreement, the details of their agreement are, in principle, not confidential.[27] The agreement reached is recorded in writing and signed by the conciliator, the parties and their representatives. It is binding on the parties and can be homologated by the tribunal to be enforceable as a decision of the tribunal.[28] If the parties fail to settle the dispute, the citizen still holds the right to go to hearing. The judge, who acted as conciliator, cannot be the judge at the hearing.[29]

*b) Quebec's Bureau d'audiences publiques sur l'environnement (BAPE)* Various environmental laws can entail the use of environmental mediation in Quebec. When a project is presented and subject to the environmental impact assessment and review process, the *BAPE Office of Public Hearings on the Environment*, according to the *Environment Quality Act*,[30] has to conduct environmental inquiries, after which mediation can be undertaken in accordance with the *Rules of Procedure for Environmental Inquiries with Mediation*.[31] The BAPE defines mediation as "a dispute resolution process in which negotiation is used in order to bring the parties together".[32] The Quebec's Department of environment can, on request or on its own initiative, proceed to mediation. The

23 Ibid, art 121.1 (2).
24 Ibid, art 121.1 (3).
25 Ibid, art 122.
26 Ibid, art 123.
27 Tribunal administratif du Québec, *Is It Confidential*. Access: www.taq.gouv.qc.ca/en/conciliation/general-explanations/is-it-confidential
28 *Act Respecting Administrative Justice*, RSQ, c J-3, art 124.
29 *Act Respecting Administrative Justice*, RSQ, c J-3, art 121.2.
30 *Environment Quality Act, RSQ, c Q-2, art 6.3* ("The function of the Bureau is to inquire into any question relating to the quality of the environment submitted to it by the Minister and to make to him a report of its findings and of its analysis thereof. It must hold public hearings whenever required to do so by the Minister.").
31 *Rules of Procedures for Environmental Inquiries with Mediation*. Access: www.bape.gouv.qc.ca/sections/documentation/proc-mediation-anglais.pdf.
32 BAPE, *La mediation*, 2012 at 3. Access: www.bape.gouv.qc.ca/sections/documentation/Mediation.pdf [translated by authors].

*Table 5.1* Number of mediation mandates at the BAPE[1]

| *1979–1989* | *1990–1999* | *2000–2009* | *2010–2016* |
|---|---|---|---|
| *4*<br>*(4 implicit mediations)* | *36*<br>*(5 implicit mediations)* | *12* | *11* |

[1]*BAPE, Tous les rapports du BAPE*, Access: <www.bape.gouv.qc.ca/sections/rapports/tous/index.htm>; BAPE, *La médiation en environnement. Une nouvelle approche au BAPE* (1994). Access: <www.bape.gouv.qc.ca/sections/documentation/Mediation_environnement.pdf>.

'Implicit mediation' refers to a mediation process by a third-party neutral, for which the term 'mediation' was not explicitly used.

mediation mandate spans over 30 to 60 days and is presided over by a BAPE member who acts as commissioner.[33] The role of commissioner consists of

> facilitating communication between the participants, helping them point out the relevant facts and determining the questions to answer, contributing by defining and developing solutions, allowing the participants to negotiate and helping them evaluate the different options and making decisions. The commissioner ensures the proposed solutions preserve the quality of the environment and do not jeopardize the rights of third parties.[34]

The people who attend the mediation are the applicant for a public hearing, the initiator of the project, as well as any other person, ministry or organism if their presence is needed in the commissioner's view.[35] The minutes and the transcription of the stenographic notes ensure the publicity of the mediation process.[36] The commissioner's report, containing his findings and his analysis, as well as the agreement (if one has been reached) are also public.[37] According to the *Rules of Procedure for Environmental Inquiries with Mediation*, the BAPE can be given a mediation mandate "on any issue relating to environmental quality that does not constitute a project subject to the environmental impact assessment and review process".[38]

Table 5.1 illustrates the number of mediations held by the BAPE since its creation.

33 Ibid.

34 *Règles de procédure relatives au déroulement de l'enquête avec médiation en environnement*, art 20. Access: www.bape.gouv.qc.ca/sections/documentation/proc-mediation.pdf [translated by author].

35 *Règles de procédure relatives au déroulement de l'enquête avec médiation en environnement*, art 10–12 and 19. Access: www.bape.gouv.qc.ca/sections/documentation/proc-mediation.pdf.

36 *Règles de procédure relatives au déroulement de l'enquête avec médiation en environnement*, art 21 and 28. Access: www.bape.gouv.qc.ca/sections/documentation/proc-mediation.pdf

37 *Règles de procédure relatives au déroulement de l'enquête avec médiation en environnement*, art 26 and 27. Access: www.bape.gouv.qc.ca/sections/documentation/proc-mediation.pdf.

38 *Rules of procedure for environmental inquiries with mediation*, art 30. Access: BAPE www.bape.gouv.qc.ca/sections/documentation/proc-mediation-anglais.pdf.

*c) Specific law mediation provisions* Since 1989, some legal provisions deal specifically with mediation in the agricultural sector. The *Act Respecting the Preservation of Agricultural Land and Agricultural Activities*[39] (ARPALAA) limits the use of mediation to the people whose "current or projected exercise of an agricultural activity in an agricultural zone is restricted or prevented by reason of the application of a municipal planning by-law or nuisance by-law".[40] Under the ARPALAA, the people suffering injury from the application "may apply for the intervention of a mediator".[41] A municipal by-law protecting the environment could thus be mediated. The request for a mediator must be motivated in writing and sent to the regional county municipality. A copy must be forwarded to the local municipality.[42] The warden of the regional county municipality must then designate a mediator acceptable to the parties.[43] Under this Act, the role of the mediator is to "allow the parties to exchange their points of view, and to foster agreement between the parties as expeditiously as possible. The mediator may also give an opinion on the dispute, if it subsists, and make recommendations".[44] It can be evaluated that the mediation process has a public character considering that the announcement of the holding of the mediation is made publically and that whoever is interested can then transmit written comments.[45] Under the ARPALAA, the mediator has to "take into consideration, particularly, generally accepted agricultural standards, and the consequences of the municipal by-law on the current or projected agricultural activities of the applicant, and on those of the other producers in the agricultural zone".[46] The mediator has the ability to convene any person to obtain his point of view and to require expert opinions from a relevant department member.[47] At the end of the process, the mediator's report and his recommendations can be sent to any interested person if considered appropriate in the circumstances.[48] The local municipality does not have to follow the mediator's recommendations but, in such a case, has to give reasons for its decision to take no action.[49]

It should be noted that the mediation process outlined in the Act does not involve the intervention of the *Commission de protection du territoire agricole* (CPTAQ) (Quebec agricultural land protection commission). If the CPTAQ were to act as a mediator, it would necessarily be outside of its statutory functions. However, in 1999, the Commission explicitly recognized that, beyond

39 *Act Respecting the Preservation of Agricultural Land and Agricultural Activities*, RSQ c P-41.1 [ARPALAA].
40 S 79.3 ARPALAA, s 79.3.
41 Ibid.
42 79.6 ARPALAA, s 79.6.
43 ARPALAA, s 79.7.
44 ARPALAA, s 79.4 and 79.15.
45 ARPALAA, s 79.7.
46 ARPALAA, s 79.9.
47 ARPALAA, s 79.10 and 79.11.
48 ARPALAA, s 79.15.
49 ARPALAA, s 79.16.

its competences granted by law, its role was to "be a neutral and independent arbitrator given the large number of actors, the nature of the interests at stake and the sensitive issues concerning agricultural land zoning".[50] In addition, the Commission stated, "In daily practice the reconciliation of divergent interests has in some cases become a reality for the Commission".[51]

Two main conclusions can be drawn from the legislative framework of environmental mediation at the administrative level. First, it should be observed that the environmental mediation process is conferred with a substantial degree of transparency, while mediation is typically held in camera and with a confidentiality agreement in other forums.[52] Second, the role of mediators and facilitators is not uniformly defined in the context of environmental mediation at the administrative level. BAPE's mediators and facilitators are attributed a non-evaluative role. Their role is to facilitate discussions and assist the parties' negotiations. This contrasts with ARPALAA's mediators, which are granted by law with the authority to give an opinion on the dispute, make recommendations and convene various experts and individuals whose presence is deemed useful to obtain their point of view on the subject matter.

### *1.1.3 Extrajudicial level*

#### I) FACILITATION

Resort to facilitation at the extrajudicial level appears to be increasingly more frequent due to the multiplication of multi-stakeholder forums, created by the federal and provincial governments, such as the watershed committees,[53] the Areas of Prime Concern committees (ZIP committees)[54] or the committees for integrated management of natural resources and territory.[55] The decision-making process of these organisms often requires the presence of a facilitator. Furthermore, environmental associations and citizens sometimes request to these committees to act as facilitators for local decision making. Resort to facilitation is informal and, for that reason, is difficult to quantify.

50 CPTAQ, *L'approche, les rôles et les responsabilités dans l'application du régime de protection du territoire et des activités agricoles*, August 1999 at 9. Access: www.cptaq.gouv.qc.ca/fileadmin/fr/publications/publications/approche_roles.pdf [translated by authors].

51 Ibid [translated by authors].

52 E.g., art 163 CCP.

53 *Loi affirmant le caractère collectif des ressources en eau et visant à renforcer leur protection*, RSQ c C-6.2 s 14.

54 The ZIP committees were established in 1993 as part of the Canada-Quebec Agreement on the St-Lawrence, see: St-Lawrence Action Plan 2011–2026, *History of the Areas of Prime Concern (ZIP) Program*. Access: http://planstlaurent.qc.ca/en/integrated_management/zip_program.html

55 *Loi sur l'aménagement durable du territoire forestier*, RSQ c A-18.1 s 55.

II) MEDIATION

Article 1 of Quebec's new *Code of Civil Procedure* (CCP) provides an obligation for the parties to consider private prevention and resolution processes (which include mediation) before referring their dispute to the courts.[56] Moreover, the CCP creates an obligation for the parties to participate in the process of mediation in "good faith", to be "transparent with each other, including as regards the information in their possession, and to co-operate actively in searching for a solution".[57] The mediator is to be chosen jointly by the parties.[58] As for the confidentiality of the process, the parties and the mediator "undertake to preserve the confidentiality of anything said, written or done during the process, subject to any agreement between them or to any special provisions of the law".[59] While the parties are free to determine together the procedure applicable to the mediation process,[60] the CCP provides that the role of the mediator is to help the parties "to engage in dialogue, clarify their views, define the issues in dispute, identify their needs and interests, explore solutions and reach, if possible, a mutually satisfactory agreement".[61] Furthermore, it is provided that the parties "may ask the mediator to develop with them a proposal to prevent or resolve the dispute".[62] If the mediator chooses to hold caucuses, he cannot disclose any information received from a party to the other party without that party's consent.[63] Any party is free to "withdraw from or put an end to the mediation process at any time at its own discretion and without being required to give reasons".[64] If the parties reach a settlement agreement, they have the option to create a transaction if so are their wishes and the circumstances permit.[65] A transaction terminates the judicial proceedings[66] and can be homologated by a judge to have the same force and effect as a judgment of the court.[67]

Due to the fact that private mediation is held in camera, it is difficult to measure how often it is used in environmental matters. However, it should be noted that the Quebec's legislator seems to have envisioned the mediator's role to be more facilitative than evaluative, although there is no provisions prohibiting the mediator from giving his opinion regarding the dispute. Indeed, the CCP provides that the mediator should help the parties to engage in dialogue (as opposed to argumentation) and to explore their needs and interests (and not exclusively

56 Art 1 CCP.
57 Art 2 CCP.
58 Art 3 CCP.
59 Art 4 CCP.
60 Art 6 CCP.
61 Art 605 CCP.
62 Ibid.
63 Art 611 CCP.
64 Art 614 CCP.
65 Art 613 CCP.
66 *Civil Code of Québec*, RSC c C-12, art 2631; Art 220 CCP.
67 Art 527 and 528 CCP.

their rights and positions).[68] In practice, the parties are free to design their own mediation procedure and are not required to follow the supplemental procedure provided for in the CCP.

### *1.2 Training and accreditation of Quebec's facilitators and mediators in environmental issues*

How to become a mediator or a facilitator in Quebec? No professional order regulates the competencies, training and ethics of the facilitators, and mediators working in Quebec because facilitation and mediation are not professions or activities that are protected by the Quebec *Professional Code*.[69] This means that no formality is required to practice as a facilitator or a mediator. In order to address the potential problems of having a non-regulated profession, some organizations have come to offering mediation training and institutional certification. ADR Institute of Canada is a non-profit organization recognized as Canada's preeminent professional organization with respect to the practice of alternative dispute resolution.[70] It provides general training leading towards certification as a chartered mediator (C. Med.), a qualification protected under the *Patent Act*.[71]

ADR Institute of Canada is active at the national level and has affiliates in most Canadian provinces,[72] such as Quebec with the Quebec Institute for Mediation and Arbitration (IMAQ).[73] In order to become an accredited IMAQ mediator, candidates either have to

(a) have been a member in good standing of a professional association recognized by the Quebec *Professional Code* since at least five years or have actively practiced mediation (minimum of 100 hours) since the past three years and have completed at least 40 hours of training in mediation recognized by IMAQ;
(b) hold a graduate diploma (30 credits) in dispute prevention and resolution recognized by IMAQ and have completed a minimum of 25 hours of clinical practice in mediation; or
(c) have been working as an institutional mediator since at least one year and have completed a minimum of 30 hours of training in institutional mediation by the University of Sherbrooke.

In addition to fulfilling these three conditions, the candidate cannot have been subject to a civil or criminal conviction, which could potentially have an impact

68 Art 605 CCP.
69 *Professional Code*, RSQ c C-28 s 24.
70 *ADR Institute of Canada*. Access: http://adric.ca
71 *Patent Act*, RSC 1985, c. P-4. For more information, see ADR Institute of Canada, *Profesionnal Designations*. Access: http://adric.ca/resources/professional-designations/.
72 ADR Institute of Canada, *Affiliates*. Access: http://adric.ca/about-adr/affiliates/
73 *Institut de médiation et d'arbitrage du Québec*. Access: www.imaq.org.

on the practice of mediation, and the candidates must commit to conform themselves to the IMAQ mediators' *Code of Conduct* and *Code of Ethics*.[74]

The Quebec Bar Association also offers mediation training, which allows lawyers to be accredited as mediators. The training focuses on different areas of law, such as the Small Claims Divisions, family law, labour law, civil law and commercial law, but not environmental law specifically.[75] To become accredited as mediator in civil and commercial law, the candidate must meet three conditions:

(a) to be a member in good standing of the Quebec Bar Association;
(b) to hold a professional liability insurance with the Quebec Professional Liability Insurance Fund or to work within the Federal or Provincial Public Service and be exempted from professional liability insurance;
(c) to have completed a minimum of 40 hours of training in civil and commercial mediation recognized by the Quebec Bar Association's Accreditation Comity.[76]

Some private centres, such as the *Centre de médiation professionnelle du Québec Inc.* (Quebec Centre of Professional Mediation), also offer mediation training, but no specific training in environment.[77]

How many mediators or facilitators, specialized in environmental dispute prevention and resolution, are there in Quebec? What type of training have they completed? Table 5.2 shows the results of a research conducted on the Internet, which aimed to compare the number of mediators offering their services in environmental dispute prevention and resolution as well as their training backgrounds.

Table 5.2 indicates that there are a total of 77 mediators advertising themselves as specialized in environmental mediation in Quebec. In addition, there are a total of 19 additional mediators offering services in environmental mediation through the Canadian Centre for Environmental Arbitration and Mediation (CCEAM) (2 mediators) and the BAPE (17 commissioners). IMAQ's and CCEAM's mediators must meet some mediation training requirements to receive accreditation from these organizations. However, BAPE's mediators are not required to have followed mediation training. Approximately half of CCEAM's (50%) and BAPE's (59%) mediators have completed scientific training as compared to only 16% for IMAQ's mediators offering services in environmental mediation. This is not surprising, due to the fact that IMAQ is a professional mediation organization in

74 IMAQ, *Critères d'accréditation – Médiateur accrédité*. Access: http://imaq.org/wp-content/uploads/2014/05/criteres-adhesion-et-equivalencemediateur-octobre-2015.pdf.

75 Barreau du Québec, *Devenir médiateur*. Access: www.barreau.qc.ca/fr/avocats/formation-continue/mediateur/

76 Barreau du Québec, *Devenir médiateur: En matière civile, commerciale et travail*. Access: www.barreau.qc.ca/fr/avocats/justice-participative/mediateur/civil-commercial/index.html.

77 Centre de Médiation Professionnelle du Québec Inc., *Formations*. Access: http://mediationprof.qc.ca/formation/formation-en-mediation/.

*Table 5.2* Approximation of the number of mediators specialized in environment in Quebec and their training backgrounds[1]

| | *Number of mediators offering services in environmental mediation* | *Percentage of mediators indicating having completed mediation training* | *Percentage of mediators indicating having completed relevant scientific training (chemistry, biology, physics, geology, forest engineering, etc.)* |
|---|---|---|---|
| **IMAQ** | 77 | 100% (not indicated but must meet IMAQ requirements) | 16% (Ten engineers, two sustainable development advisers) |
| **Canadian Centre for Environmental Arbitration and Mediation (CCEAM)** | 2 | 100% (not indicated but must meet CCEAM requirements) | 50% (1 biologist) |
| **BAPE** | 17 commissioners | 6% (1) | 59% (10 scientists) |

[1] According to the data collected online on June 1, 2017.

which its mediators offer services in multiple areas, including corporate, family and administrative law in addition to environmental law.

Results indicate that in Quebec no specific training in mediation or in sciences is required to act as a mediator specialized in the environmental sector. In addition, Quebec's most preeminent training and accreditation organizations, IMAQ and Quebec Bar Association, do not offer specific mediation training in environment. Surprisingly, it should also be noted that only one BAPE commissioner has undertaken training in mediation.

As was seen earlier, there is no specialized court in environment, but there are in Quebec and in many Canadian provinces administrative tribunals specialized in environment and which have a mandate to offer mediation or conciliation procedure. Table 5.3 compares different Canadian administrative tribunals in terms of training of their members. It shows that in Quebec, all judges from the Environmental Section of the Quebec Administrative Tribunal have completed specific training in mediation. However, this is not true for other Canadian provinces, where less than one-fourth (for Ontario Environmental Review Tribunal and British Columbia Environmental Appeal Board) and less than half (for Alberta Environmental Appeal Board) have completed mediation training. As for relevant scientific training, it seems to be more favoured in the Western provinces of Alberta and British Columbia, where more than half of the mediators have completed relevant scientific training, than in the Eastern provinces of Quebec and Ontario, where it is the case for only one-fourth.

*Table 5.3* Comparison between a sample of environmental administrative tribunals[1]

| | *Number of judges/ members* | *Percentage of members indicating having completed mediation training* | *Percentage of members indicating having completed relevant scientific training (chemistry, biology, physics, geology, forest engineering, etc.)* |
|---|---|---|---|
| **Administrative Tribunal of Quebec's Environmental Section**[2] | 4 judges | 100% specific training in conciliation | 25% (1 engineer) scientific formation not required |
| **Ontario Environmental Review Tribunal**[3] | 16 members | 13% (2) | 25% (4) |
| **British Columbia Environmental Appeal Board**[4] | 24 members | 13% (3) | 54% (13) |
| **Alberta Environmental Appeal Board**[5] | 10 members | 40% (4) | 60% (6) |

[1]According to the data collected online on June 1, 2017.
[2] Tribunal administratif du Québec, *The Tribunal's Administratif Judges*. Access: <www.taq.gouv.qc.ca/en/about/the-tribunal/the-tribunal-s-administrative-judges.
[3]Ontario, Public Appointements Secretariat, *Agency Details*. Access: <www.pas.gov.on.ca/scripts/en/boardDetails.asp?boardID=755>.
[4] British Columbia, Environmental Appeal Board, *Board Members*. Access: <www.eab.gov.bc.ca/board_members/index.htm>.
[5] Alberta, Environmental Appeals Board. Access: < www.eab.gov.ab.ca/members.htm>.

The various sections of the Administrative Tribunal of Quebec require hearings to be conducted by a panel of two judges: one of whom to be lawyer or notary, and the other to have had training in another discipline than law related to the type of disputes covered by that section. For instance, the Social Affairs Section requires two judges: one of whom to be a lawyer or notary, and the other a doctor, social worker, psychiatrist or another profession depending on the case. The same kinds of requirements apply to the Immovable Property Section, which provides that one judge has to be a lawyer or notary, and the second, a licensed appraiser. Curiously, no such condition applies for the Territory and Environment Section, where one of the two judges is required to be lawyer or notary, and there are no specific qualification requirements for the second judge.[78] This is another example that illustrates that scientific expertise is not deemed as essential by various Quebec institutions even in the context of a tribunal ruling over an environmental dispute.

78 Tribunal administratif du Québec, *The Tribunal: Origin and Role*. Access: www.taq.gouv.qc.ca/en/about/the-tribunal/origin-and-role.

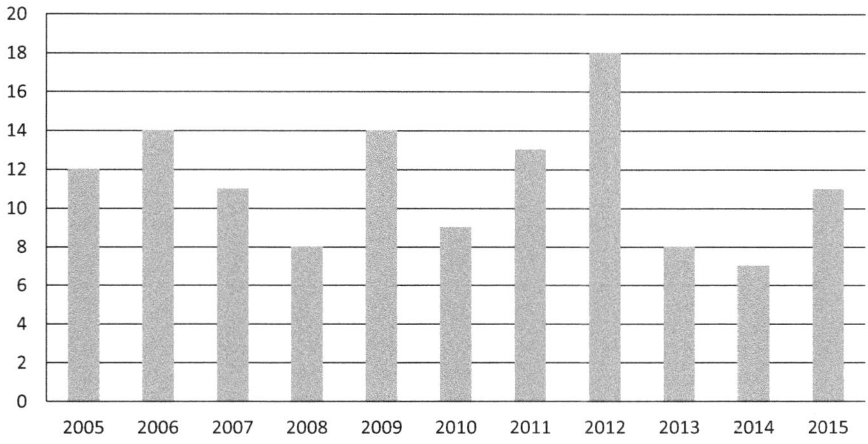


*Figure 5.1* Superior Court estimated number of judgments in environment[79]

## 2 Demand for environmental dispute prevention and resolution processes in Quebec and future development perspectives

What is the extent of environmental disputes in Quebec? How large is the demand for dispute prevention and resolution processes? What are the expectations of users for these processes in Quebec? Section 2.1 addresses the question of the potential market for environmental mediation in the light of actual conflicts and environmental issues. Section 2.2 presents the results of a survey conducted with environmental experts and analyzes the needs and future development perspectives in environmental dispute prevention and resolution.

### *2.1 Portray of environmental issues and disputes in Quebec*

Examining court cases tells us that a relatively small number of environmental disputes are brought before the Superior Court of Quebec, that is between seven and 18 judgments per year since 2005 with a slight decline in the last years (see Figure 5.1). Does this indicate that the number of conflicts related to the environmental sector is small? Not necessarily.

Several recent reports have examined the evolution of the expectations of users with respect to Quebec's judicial system. They note a phenomenon of dropout

79 SOQUIJ. Access: http://citoyens.soquij.qc.ca (June 6, 2016). The number of judgements is an approximation using the key words: (environment or ecosystem) and (conservation or pollution) and protection. Irrelevant judgements were removed.

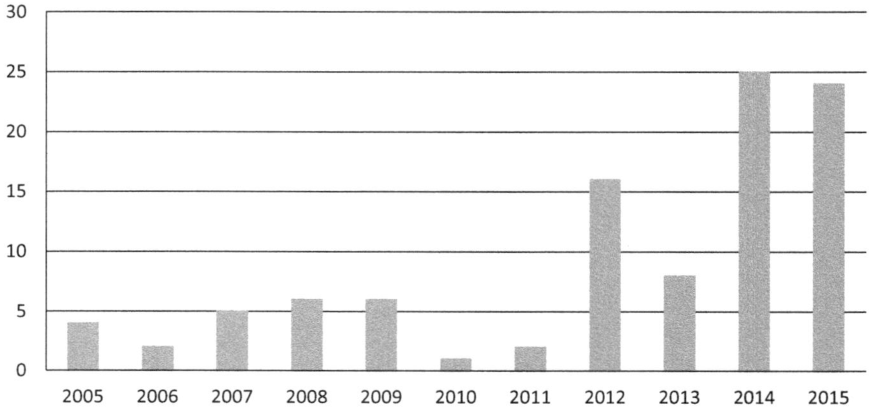


*Figure 5.2* Administrative Tribunal of Quebec (Territory and Environment Section) estimated number of decisions in environment[80]

from the judicial system[81] and a general loss of confidence from users regarding the judicial system because its delays are too long, its procedures too costly and it is generally unsatisfying.[82] In the case of environmental disputes, these factors are aggravated due to the complexity of disputes, which require the intervention of experts. Furthermore, the potential for personal gains in environmental litigation are often small compared to the costs engaged, which may discourage an individual to bring her or his dispute before the courts. It can be observed that the number of filed environmental cases does not increase, but even decline, despite the presence of various factors that should have a stimulus impact on filed environmental cases, such as an increased awareness in the population to the environmental cause, an augmentation of legislation protecting the environment and an increased difficulty of the state to enforce environmental laws. Litigating environmental disputes is more about collective benefits. This explains why lawsuits and class actions in this sector are often filled by the government or by organizations dedicated to the protection of the environment.[83] However, environmental

80 *SOQUIJ*. Access: http://citoyens.soquij.qc.ca (June 6, 2016). The number of judgements is an approximation using the SOQUIJ classification under 'environment'. All CPTAQ decisions which concern agriculture and irrelevant decisions were removed.

81 It is reported that judicial activity in Quebec has decreased from 32.5% between 2002 and 2011, see Barreau du Québec, *Barreau-mètre 2015: La profession en chiffres*, 2015, 43 and 76. Access: www.barreau.qc.ca/fr/publications/avocats/barreau-metre/

82 Ibid at 29. See also Lafond, P.-C., *L'accès à la justice civile au Québec: portrait général*, Éditions Yvon Blais, Cowansville, 2012.

83 For example, environmental lawsuits have been filed by organizations such as the Centre québécois de droit de l'environnement (*Centre québécois du droit de l'environnement* c. *Oléoduc Énergie Est ltée*, 2014 QCCS 4147, *Centre québécois du droit de l'environnement* c. *Transcanada Pipelines ltée*, 2016 QCCS 903), and the Association des résidants riverains de La Lièvre (*Association des résidents riverains de La Lièvre Inc.* c. *Québec (Procureure générale)* 2015 QCCS 5100), by the government (Québec (Procureur général) c. Gosselin* (C.S.,

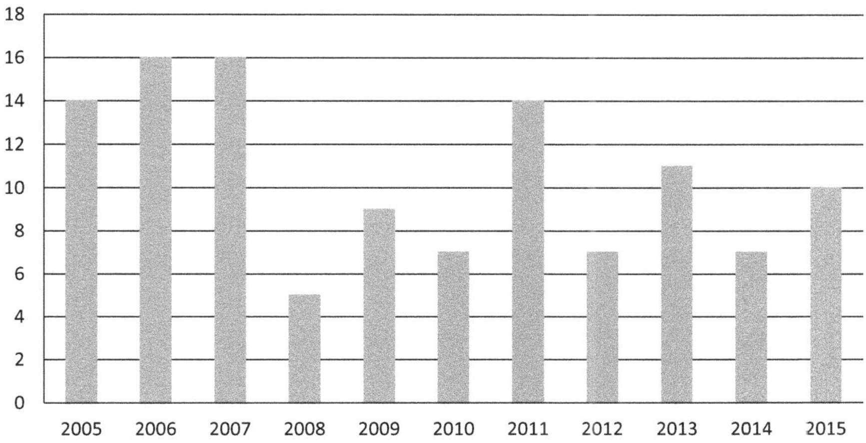


*Figure 5.3* Number of reports produced by the BAPE per year[84]

disputes are in most cases only judicially addressed when the prejudice is considerable or spectacular. Yet, this leaves unresolved several smaller disputes such as usage conflicts, neighbourhood disturbances and diffuse pollution, which proliferation can be equally harmful to the environment due to the added pressure on the balance and on the vulnerability of many ecosystems.

While the filing of environmental cases in courts appear to be in decline, the contestation of governmental decisions has, on the other hand, significantly increased in the last four years, as shown by Figure 5.2, indicating at least some increased interest for environmental protection by the government which has been substantially more active since the implementation in 2012 of the monetary administrative penalties regime.[85]

Opportunities for environmental mediation could also be found in the projects submitted to the BAPE *Office of Public Hearings on the Environment.* Figure 5.3 reveals the number of reports delivered by the BAPE's commissioners. Some reports already include a mandate for mediation or facilitation, but such processes only took place in a few cases (see section 1.1.2.) despite the fact that all projects could have benefited from at least some form of environmental mediation. The BAPE only deals with major projects that could affect the environment. Other environmental issues are much more difficult to identify, but a recent survey by Choquette and He (see section 2.2) might provide some insights regarding the occurrence of environmental disputes and the means by which they are resolved.

2003–05–16), SOQUIJ AZ-50175083; R. c. Hydro-Québec (C.S. Can., 1997–09–18), SOQUIJ AZ-97111092, J.E. 97–1792, [1997] 3 R.C.S. 213), and by municipalities (Ville de Hudson c. Spraytech Société d'arrosage (Cour municipale Hudson- 29 novembre 1995).

84 *BAPE.* Access: www.bape.gouv.qc.ca/sections/rapports/tous/index.htm

85 Environment Quality Act, art.115.13.

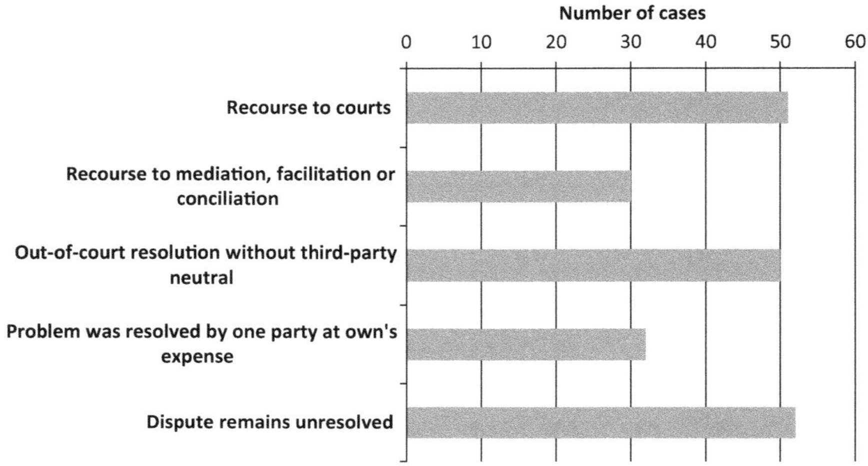


*Figure 5.4* Processes used to resolve environmental disputes

## *2.2 Survey on the needs and expectations for environmental mediation in Quebec*

Professors Choquette and He, members of the University of Sherbrooke's SAGE research group (Research Group on Strategies and Actors in Environmental Governance),[86] carried out an expert survey in 2014 to clarify the needs and expectations for environmental mediation in Quebec. The survey was circulated electronically to selected government members, environmental protection associations, industries and involved citizens, of whom 187 individuals completed the questionnaire. Most of the respondents had worked in the environmental sector for at least 15 years. The sampling is composed of the governmental (14%), community (20%), professional (21%), and educational sectors (14%) as well as of citizens (16%). The industrial sector is, however, underrepresented (2%). In addition, the respondents work in both rural and urban areas. The majority of them (82%) have been at least once confronted to an environmental conflict.

Participants, who indicated having been implicated in one or more environmental disputes in the past, were asked to identify how such disputes were resolved (Figure 5.4). It was found that the use of a mediator, a facilitator or a conciliator is not a frequent option in Quebec. But what is interesting to note is the high proportion of disputes either unresolved or resolved by one party at its own expense. These situations could demonstrate potential for environmental mediation. Furthermore, most of the environmental disputes recorded concerned usage conflicts, neighbourhood disturbances and land-use disputes, which are contexts suitable for mediation.

86 *Groupe de recherche sur les Stratégies et les Acteurs de la Gouvernance Environnementale* (SAGE). Access: www.groupe-sage.ca

Participants were also asked in the survey to determine their needs throughout the lifecycle of an environmental problem, encompassing three stages: (1) preventive measures, (2) dispute resolution process and (3) implementation. First, as for preventing the escalation of environmental disputes, the participants considered as a priority an improved access to information, an access to a facilitator, as well as an access to a pre-set dispute mechanism. Second, as for resolving an existing dispute, the respondents evaluated as a priority having access to a mediator,[87] followed by having access to a pre-established forum. The possibility of resorting to tribunals was perceived as being satisfactory. Finally, for the implementation and follow-up processes of an agreed upon solution, the respondents evaluated as a priority having access to a third-party neutral, such as an independent auditor, putting in place implementation and follow-up mechanisms for the agreed upon solutions and the enforceability of judgments. While the new *CCP* encourages the parties to opt for a private dispute prevention and resolution process to "prevent a potential dispute or resolve an existing one"[88] and creates an obligation to "consider private prevention and resolution processes before referring their dispute to the courts",[89] it does not put into place a new process to assist the parties with dispute prevention and out-of-court resolution.

### *2.2.1 Optional resort to mediation*

When an environmental dispute arises, the respondents predominantly favour resort to mediation (92%) over litigation (8%). However, the respondents were divided as to whether mediation should be mandatory (35%) or optional (48%). Seventeen percent remained undecided on this question. While the new *CCP* obligates parties to a dispute in family matters involving children to participate in a mediation information session before being allowed to proceed to trial,[90] it does not provide such an obligation for environmental disputes. The code rather states that the applicant must indicate, at the time of the originating application, if he or she is interested in mediating a resolution of the dispute.[91] Moreover, when summoned to court, the defendant can "propose mediation or a settlement conference".[92] At any stage of the proceeding, the tribunal can, ex-officio or at a party's request, invite the parties "to a case management conference or a settlement conference, or encourag[e] them to use mediation".[93] When it comes to the recovery of small claims,

> The court clerk informs the parties at the earliest opportunity that they may, at no additional cost, submit their dispute to mediation. If the parties consent to mediation, they may request the court clerk to refer them to the

87 Optional resort to arbitration was not part of the survey.
88 Art 1, para 1 CCP.
89 Art 1, para 2 CCP.
90 Art 417 et seq CCP.
91 Art 544 CCP.
92 Art 147 and 547 (for small claims) CCP.
93 Art 158 CCP.

> mediation service. In that case, the mediation session is presided over by a lawyer or a notary, certified as a mediator by their professional order.[94]

If the parties reach a settlement, the settlement agreement once confirmed by the special clerk or the court is equivalent to a judgment.[95] In the case of private mediation, it

> begins, without formality, on the day on which the parties agree to enter into a mediation process by mutual agreement or at the initiative of one of them. In the latter case, failure by the other party to respond constitutes a refusal to participate in the mediation process.[96]

The legislator could have gone further and made refusal harmful to the originator, as is the case for DNA paternity tests,[97] to serve as a strong incentive to participate in the mediation process. Under the new *CCP*, the parties, with the assistance of a mediator, determine the length and the rules applicable to the mediation.[98] Once mediation begins, the presence of the parties is mandatory but they can be accompanied by any person whose contribution may be useful.[99] The mediator can suspend the mediation process at any time in the interests of the parties or of one of them,[100] or "if the mediator is convinced that the mediation process is doomed to failure or is likely, if continued, to cause serious prejudice to one of the parties".[101] Furthermore, "a party may withdraw from or put an end to the mediation process at any time at is own discretion and without being required to give reasons".[102]

Concerning the costs of the mediation, the new *CCP* states that, due to the voluntary nature of the mediation process, the costs are borne in equal shares by the parties, unless otherwise agreed by the parties or ordered by the court if the mediation process took place in the course of a proceeding.[103] The government can also, by regulation, establish "a tariff of professional fees payable to certified mediators by the mediation service, and the maximum number of sessions for which a mediator may be paid fees in relation to the same application".[104] Although this Article is most applicable in family matters,

94 Art 556 CCP.
95 Ibid.
96 Art 608 CCP.
97 Bernard, C. and C. Choquette, « Les incidences de l'identification génétique sur le droit de la filiation québécois » in C. Hennau-Hublet and B.-M. Knoppers, eds., *L'analyse génétique à des fins de preuve et les droits de l'homme: Aspects médico-scientifiques, éthique et juridique*, Bruylant, Bruxelles, 1997, 353.
98 Art 609 CCP. Ccp.
99 Ibid.
100 Art 610 CCP.
101 Art 614 CCP.
102 Ibid.
103 Art 615 CCP.
104 Art 570 CCP.

established rates could create an incentive for parties to refer their dispute to a mediator in environment.[105]

Following the results of the survey, the proposition to share the costs equally by the parties did not receive much support. The respondents showed instead strong preference for the mediator to determine the costs each party would bear. They also favour, almost in the same preponderance, the use of a green fund, financed by money collected from environmental contraventions, to defray the costs of environmental mediation processes. The latter suggestion is specifically tailored to environmental disputes. Unlike some other types of disputes, the resolution of an environmental dispute often benefits the community as a whole, and not just the parties. Protecting the environment arguably benefits everyone, including human beings, the fauna and flora and ecosystems affected by the conflict. That is why making a party bear a large proportion of the costs seem unfair for many environmental stakeholders. In addition, due to factors such as the respondents' divisiveness concerning whether mediation should be or not mandatory, the general lack of awareness among the population about dispute prevention and resolution processes, and the particular nature of environmental conflicts, the new *CCP* should have provided for a mandatory information session on mediation.

### *2.2.2 Transparency of dispute prevention and resolution processes*

Under the new *CCP*, the parties to a dispute prevention and resolution process "are required to participate in the process in good faith, to be transparent to each other, including as regards the information in their possession, and to co-operate actively in searching for a solution".[106] They are also required "to uphold human rights and freedoms and observe other public order rules".[107]

The new *CCP* also provides for the confidentiality of the process with respect to third parties, as well as the general principle of non-disclosure of a party's information to the other party without the prior consent of the providing party.[108] In fact, parties to a dispute resolution process, such as mediation, and the mediator facilitating their dispute undertake to preserve the confidentiality of anything said, written or done during the process, subject to any agreement between them on the matter or to any special provisions of the law.[109] In addition, "no information relevant to the mediation received from a party may be disclosed by the mediator, without that party's consent, to the other party".[110] Furthermore, the mediator and mediation participants cannot be compelled, in arbitration, administrative or judicial proceedings, whether related or unrelated

105 Art 3 CCP.
106 Art 2 CCP.
107 Ibid.
108 Art 611 CCP.
109 Art 4 CCP.
110 Art 611 CCP.

to the dispute, to disclose anything they hear or learn in the course of the mediation process[111] and "no information acquired from statements made in the course of the mediation process may be admitted in evidence in such proceedings".[112] The privilege of non-compellability can only be claimed if the mediator is certified by a body recognized by the minister of justice.[113]

Confidentiality is not always appropriate in environmental matters, because, in some cases, non-disclosure of information can harm the environment for a number of reasons. First, as is the case for water, part of the common heritage of the Quebec nation,[114] every litigation involving the environment is a matter of public interest. Second, many victims can suffer from an environmental problem and these people are entitled to equitable treatment, which makes this principle virtually incompatible with confidentiality. Third, the solutions to environmental conflicts can be innovative and useful to prevent or resolve similar conflicts. Fourth, climate change influences many environmental issues and sharing the knowledge acquired in the resolution of environmental conflicts can help preventing future problems that could be more harmful to the environment. For the reasons expressed earlier, certain exceptions to confidentiality in cases of public interest matters, including for the purpose of protecting of the environment, could be desirable and even legally necessary to add to Article 606 of the new *CCP.*

### *2.2.3 Choosing and training facilitators and mediators in the environmental sector*

The results of the survey show that the respondents expect some qualifications from environmental mediators. A great majority of respondents are in the opinion that it is either 'essential' or 'very important' that the mediator be trained in law (80%) in ecology (69%), in biology (52%) and in psychology (50%). Competences in economy and in chemistry were not found as essential (Table 5.4).

The survey also measured specific skills that the mediators should possess. An overwhelming majority of respondents believe that communication (98%) is either an 'essential' or 'very important' skill to possess for a mediator, followed by the ability to popularize technical information and concepts (81%) and general empathy (65%). Respondents seem to have a preference for a mediator that would play a proactive role and adopt an evaluative and directive style (55% found it was either essential or very important), as contrasted to using a facilitative style and playing the role of a coordinator (43%).

111 Some exceptions apply, such as if the law requires disclosure, a person's life safety or personal integrity is at stake or its disclosure is necessary for the mediator to defend against a claim of professional misconduct, see Art 606 CCP.

112 Art 606 CCP.

113 Ibid.

114 *Loi affirmant le caractère collectif des ressources en eau et visant à renforcer leur protection*, RSQ c C-6.2 s 1.

*Table 5.4* Importance of knowledge of mediators specialized in environmental mediation

| *Areas of knowledge* | *Useless* | *Little important* | *Medium* **important** | *Very important* | *Essential* |
|---|---|---|---|---|---|
| **Biology** | 1 | 12 | 48 | 36 | 31 |
| **Law** | 0 | 2 | 24 | 49 | 53 |
| **Economy** | 1 | 20 | 65 | 33 | 6 |
| **Psychology** | 4 | 24 | 34 | 43 | 20 |
| **Ecology** | 0 | 5 | 35 | 44 | 43 |
| **Chemistry** | 5 | 40 | 45 | 26 | 12 |

*Table 5.5* Importance of skills of mediators specialized in environmental mediation

| *Skills* | *Useless* | *Little important* | *Medium important* | *Very important* | *Essential* |
|---|---|---|---|---|---|
| **Communication** | 0 | 0 | 3 | 46 | 79 |
| **Empathy** | 2 | 6 | 37 | 52 | 31 |
| **Bilingual (French/English)** | 2 | 21 | 49 | 33 | 21 |
| **Popularization (of technical concepts)** | 0 | 2 | 22 | 64 | 40 |
| **Leadership (proactive, evaluative, directive)** | 4 | 9 | 29 | 55 | 29 |
| **Passive (facilitative/ coordinating)** | 7 | 16 | 49 | 38 | 17 |

Respondents also indicated that mediators should possess the following specific skills: they should be good communicators and popularizers, especially when working in a scientific field as technical as the environment. Empathy was also considered as a significant asset to have (Table 5.5).

As for the need for mediator's certification, accreditation or affiliation (e.g. government, professional association, university, etc.), a large majority of respondents (92%) found it not relevant so long as the mediator is considered qualified by the parties to the dispute.

In addition to impartiality, diligence, good faith and fairness, no other qualities, skills or training are required by the new *CCP* in order to act as a mediator.[115] The mediator is chosen by mutual agreement of the parties.[116] Any interested person can be facilitator or mediator in the environmental sector in Quebec. No law requires any training or accreditation. The only exception in the new *CCP* with respect to the recovery of small claims, where the parties, upon request, can

115 Art 3, 605, and 613 CCP.
116 Art 3, and 605 CCP.

be referred to a mediation service presided over by a lawyer or a notary, certified by their professional order.[117]

## Conclusion

Environmental mediation in Quebec has evolved rapidly over the last 25 years in an informal and anarchical manner. This was caused mainly by the growing social awareness with respect to environmental issues in recent years and heightened public participation in decision-making forums related to environmental affairs. The adoption of a legislative framework would have been necessary in this context to control the quality and facilitate access to dispute prevention and resolution services due to the unique characteristics of environmental issues, being public by nature as affecting the interests of communities, and necessitating thorough understanding of scientific and technical data. Striking examples of anarchical development of environmental mediation include (1) the improvisation of various governmental agencies as mediator or facilitator to attempt to respond to citizens' needs in search for processes to resolve environmental conflicts, (2) the low level of scientific training and specific training in environmental dispute prevention and resolution of Quebec mediators and (3) the fragmented legislative framework. The rules of procedure of the Permanent Court of arbitration at the international level and training of mediators of the Alberta Environmental Appeal Board may serve as an inspiration for future developments.

Quebec's new *CCP* has been applauded for being at the forefront in terms of the codification of private modes of dispute prevention and resolution. Indeed, it provides that private modes of dispute prevention and resolution, and not trial, should be the preferred method for resolving a dispute. However, it appears that the processes in place are insufficient for stakeholders to make effective use of the existing legislation in environmental matters. The recent survey found that the principal shortcomings relate to the lack of (1) scientific training of facilitators and mediators offering their service in environmental mediation, (2) specific training in environmental mediation, (3) institutions specialized in environmental dispute prevention and resolution and (4) availability and widespread of information regarding existing potential recourses for environmental dispute prevention and resolution.

The respondents to the survey are in the opinion that training in law and in environmental sciences is necessary for a mediator to facilitate an environmental dispute.[118] In addition, the survey respondents evaluated as essential for environmental mediators to possess skills in communications, popularizing of technical information and concepts, as well as general empathy. Such abilities can be acquired through general training in environmental sciences and in dispute prevention and resolution. The new *CCP*, however, remains silent with respect

117 Art 556 CCP.

118 The respondents also indicated that training in psychology was important.

to training requirements of facilitators and mediators in the context of environmental dispute. It lets the parties to an environmental issue with little resources and guidelines to evaluate, to the best of their knowledge, the facilitators' and mediators' skills.

A majority of the respondents expressed the need for assistance in making informed decisions. It should also be noted that a small majority of the respondents would prefer that environmental facilitators or mediators make use of evaluative techniques and play a proactive role as opposed to adopting a strict facilitative approach. In the context of environmental issues, where the problems are excessively complex, a mediator without knowledge in environment will find difficult to play a leadership role or even to fulfil the role that is provided for by the new *CCP*, that is to "hel[p] the parties to engage in dialogue, clarify their views, define the issues in dispute, identify their needs and interests, explore solutions and reach, if possible a mutually satisfactory agreement".[119]

Consideration should also be given to the non-compulsory character of mediation (or other modes of dispute prevention and resolution) for resolving environmental disputes, as well as to the degree of confidentiality required for environmental mediation processes. Such reflection should be made by taking into account the specific character of environmental issues, that are public in nature, complex and generally costly. As expressed strongly by the survey respondents, thoughts should also be given to the creation of new processes that would favour the prevention of environmental disputes or minimize their escalation. There is a need to tailor specific processes for environmental dispute prevention and resolution in Quebec.

119 Art 605 CCP.

# Part II

# The environmental mediation processes

# 6 A territorial dialogue in France

*Philippe Barret*[1] *and Pierre-Yves Guihéneuf*

## 1 The French context

In France, a country marked by political centralism, public authorities have long played a role in defining the public interest and in managing the common good. While Anglo-Saxon countries often perceive public interest as an adjustment of specific interests within a state-based framework, the French tradition has long maintained that specific interests were irreconcilable and that public interests should arise from a political state vision not based on these specific interests and short-term contingencies.[2] Since the first decentralization waves in the '80s, the state and local authorities have left little room for the formation of agreements between stakeholders. Arguments underlying this position are still being brought forward, such as disregarding the majority's interest for the benefit of compromises determined by power inequalities between groups with specific interests, ignoring the interests of minorities or those of the future generations and the loss of authority of elected representatives and public institutions. Despite this, participatory practices and multi-stakeholder dialogue initiatives have been developing for a few decades in the public sphere, particularly in the areas of environment, transport, energy, urban planning, city politics, health, industrial risks and natural hazards. While not all public sectors are affected by these developments, initiatives have increased since the nineties.

### *1.1 Developing dialogue practices*

Dialogue practices are driven by two noticeable major trends. The first stems from the public's lack of confidence in the state's capacity to answer their needs. Although this confidence crisis manifests itself primarily in the mistrust of national elites and the rejection of political centralism, it also affects, to a lesser extent, the

1 GEYSER Association – Access: www.geyser.asso.fr, DialTer Cooperative society – www.dialter.fr
2 Chevallier, J., «Intérêt général" in I. Casillo, et al., eds., *Dictionnaire critique et interdisciplinaire de la participation*, GIS Démocratie et Participation, Paris, 2013. Access: www.dicopart.fr/es/dico/interet-general

relationship between elected officials and their constituents. The implementation of participatory processes is conceived as an answer to this crisis but also as an attempt to reassert the legitimacy of public decisions by involving broad sectors of the civil society. The crisis of public finances has also forced the state and local governments to seek partnerships with private actors as well as to incite the civil society to take over some institutional actions.

The second trend lies in the rise of the notion of common good as well as in the public deep attachment to its land regarded as lifestyle and territorial identity. Water, air, natural environments and landscapes are emblems from this point of view, and private interests that threaten them (such as farming and industrial development) are frequently contested. Mistrust of citizens towards political elites is frequently accompanied by mistrust in interest groups including economic actors. They are often accused of being linked to politics and of being insensitive to the concept of public interest. Even environmental protection organizations are no exception; they are sometimes accused of being unrepresentative of the majority, of being allies with the political and economic powers and of defending their own interests, such as the sustainability of their structures.

For these reasons, dialogue practices are developing. The view that prevailed until the 1980s, which considered participation a risk to the definition of public interest, has given way to a more flexible and pragmatic approach. However, public authorities play an active role in framing the dialogue and one of the main components of this development is regulation.

Indeed, the law now encourages or forces public authorities and private actors to engage dialogues in specific situations, whether in defining how they should be made, or leaving local actors the freedom to define their terms. The 'loi sur l'eau' (Water Law) of 1992, which aims to ensure water conservation and aquatic environment protection through water management plans, is a good example of a text that precisely defines how a dialogue between local actors must be organized. The 1995 law on the strengthening of environmental protection provides yet another good example, since it creates the 'Commission nationale du débat public' (*National Commission for Public Debate*) – an independent administrative authority in charge of organizing public debates on major development projects. However, the 2000 law on solidarity and urban renewal requires the establishment of dialogue processes prior to the design or the revision of planning documents in the urban planning field, without defining how such processes should be made.

Initiatives from local authorities, who want to promote citizen participation, are also prompting participatory practices and the implementation of local public political debates in several areas: urban planning and development, water and sanitation, transport and natural areas. They are encouraged by a series of regulatory measures that have been adopted since 1999, the most recent event being the creation in 2014 of citizen councils in districts considered to be a priority in terms of urban renewal.

The increase of dialogue practices legally or institutionally driven also comes with an increase of local initiatives. These are set up outside of any regulatory obligations, carried voluntarily by associations, companies or communities.

Often local in scope, these initiatives take many forms, depending on the will and resources of the stakeholders. This will be further discussed later because it is frequently in such a context that we exercise our activities as mediators.

## *1.2 Environmental dialogue's particularities*

In France, the dialogue between local actors on environmental issues contains a few particularities.

The first one relates to public actors ubiquity. In France, the general interest is intimately linked to the state, either in the regulation and administration or through elected actors and services at the local levels. State regulation fosters dialogues in areas such as water management, transports, large infrastructures and urban planning where public and private actors get together. This does not mean that any strictly private action is non-existent, but as soon as an environmental issue with a collective dimension is raised, local actors usually consider it necessary to involve at least one public actor. They do so even for their own initiatives taking place without any regulatory requirements. Such arrangement incites the public actor to become involved in the implementation of the agreement, to ensure the compatibility of the agreement with regulations or local policies and to guarantee compatible and coherent actions. However, not all pertinent actors are enthusiastic about the idea of dialogue. Local elected officials may feel deprived of their powers, and public administrations have few cultures of dialogue. They usually have difficulties with processes that challenge the procedures and schedules, question the legitimacy of the public actors and the skills of experts.

Another particularity of France is that stakeholder dialogue and public participation are part of the same process. The term '*concertation*' means either one. Historically, the environmental dialogue processes, particularly in water management, have always favoured the participation of stakeholders – that is to say organized groups such as associations and professional organizations – at the expense of individuals considered too laymen on complex matters. On the other hand, urban policies inspired by participative democracy have always favoured the citizen's contribution to the expense of stakeholders, being treated as lobbies. As for the dialogue processes incurred for major developments, such as transport infrastructures, they are trying to gather both. This mixing tendency is now expanding to all sectors, including environmental and urban policies.

Finally, a third particularity lies in the impact on public decision, which remains in France a sensitive question. While citizens and stakeholders are asking for more decision-making powers, public authorities often tend to limit their participation to a consultative role.

Traditional consultation methods such as the public inquiry collecting individual opinions are now deemed inadequate. The theories of deliberation[3] have

3 Blondiaux, L., "La délibération, norme de l'action publique contemporaine?" (2001–2004) *Revue Projet* 98; Beuret, J.E. and A. Cadoret, *Gérer ensemble les territoires: Vers une démocratie coopérative*, Editions Charles Léopold Mayer, Paris, 2010.

shown that local actors' dialogues were a source of creativity and capacity building in such a way that the notion of 'co-construction' has became a kind of ideal to reach. Co-construction leaves a large place for exchanges, collective learning, controversy management, the identification of individual interests and the search for agreements. But it really consists in the co-construction of proposals and not in the co-construction of public decisions, which remain the prerogative of the authorities. These co-constructed agreements have therefore mostly a consultative status in the decision-making process: they are intended to inform the elected officials or the administration, who may then decide to what extent they will respond, or not. Of course, if the dialogue process mobilizes influential actors, is made public or is part of the agenda of policymakers, it is more likely to have a more important impact. However, the importance of the dialogue in public decision is often considered insufficient, or at least less visible making it a major source of dissatisfaction for citizens and stakeholders. Some public actors have taken it upon themselves to show how they incorporate public proposals in their decisions,[4] but these transparency measures are sometimes considered neither sufficient nor well enough developed.

### *1.3 Environmental mediation in France*

In such a context, where does environmental mediation stand in France? With no official legal status after three decades, the environmental mediation remains a marginal practice. However, it gradually finds its place in the diversity of implemented processes.

First, mediation principles are increasingly used to reach an agreement. The search for an agreement is an old goal of dialogue approaches dealing with water management, as they have sought to actively engage stakeholders and get them to change behaviours from the beginning. But this is not the case with approaches that concern large development, urban planning and local public policies, which are rather inspired by the principles of reasoned debate that aims to bring out and confront strong opinions in order to enlighten the decision maker. This vision of dialogue, which is more in line with the French culture of controversy and debate, has often come up against the mediation spirit of listening over rhetoric, consensus over confrontation, respect of individual interests over the expression of values and principles. However, necessary pragmatism is changing the situation, and even if debate remains a well-established standard, it is becoming increasingly frequent, even on the sidelines of major public debates, to see mediation or negotiation spaces being set up. These developments however question the role of animators. While they use tools of facilitation and meeting animation in the case of debates, they are often left powerless to lead participants in their search for an agreement.

4 For example, see the 'Charte pour la conduite de la concertation' of the SNCF Réseau, a public rail society. Access: www.lnpn.fr/download/file/fid/162

Second, there has been a return of environmental conflicts in the media in the past few years. Some local conflicts have taken a national scale, such as those concerning the airport of Notre-Dame-Des-Landes, the dam of Sivens, the Roybon recreational centre or the nuclear waste landfill of Bure. These have shed light on the inadequacy of the current tools used to express discontentment and even more so to find alternatives. The increase of environmental conflicts is certainly linked to a variety of causes: greater sensitivity of the population against attacks on their environment, development of social networks that facilitate a broader mobilization, citizen disaffection towards inefficient dialogue initiatives. Nevertheless, the management and the prevention of conflicts make room for environmental mediation. Although the use to mediation in an official manner does not yet appear to be relevant at this time, the mobilization of its principles by animators seems essential.

## 2 An independent team's approach

For the past 30 years, a French non-profit association known as Geyser has brought together professionals from both rural and environmental worlds committed to promoting meaningful initiatives in regards to participatory democracy, and our relations to the natural world.

Before getting involved in ecological engineering, and agricultural and rural policies, this association extensively worked on agri-environmental issues Since 2000, Geyser has been mobilizing conflict mediation know-how to develop new participatory approaches that combine concertation, principled negotiation[5] and mediation methods with citizen participation practices. All these approaches were consolidated under the generic name 'territorial dialogue'.[6] In 2008, Geyser created the cooperative society DialTer, which specializes in the preparation and performance of the territorial dialogue's process.

The **territorial dialogue** regroups three practices that are relatively similar:

- The **concertation** process aims the co-construction of projects or solutions to solve a problem or conflict. The suggested solutions are submitted to decision makers. The concertation is driven by one of the stakeholders.
- The **negotiation** process aims to reach an agreement (to decide together) on a project, actions, changes in practices; each stakeholder commits to contribute to the project's implementation.
- The **mediation** is a concertation or a negotiation that is facilitated by a neutral third party.

5 Fisher, R. and W. Ury, *Getting to Yes: Negotiating Agreement Without Giving in*, Penguin Books, New York, 1983.

6 Barret, P. and P.-Y. Guihéneuf, *Guide pratique du dialogue territorial: concertation et médiation pour l'environnement et le développement local*, Éditions de l'Aube, La Tour d'Aigues, 2012.

The territorial dialogue's main characteristic is the establishment of a constructive dialogue in which all concerned actors take part. It aims to attain a comprehensive agreement or to develop a common project. Dialoguing primarily consists in listening and understanding the other party, in combining different types of knowledge and in highlighting individual needs rather than prioritizing positions or procedures.

In order to conduct a territorial dialogue process, DialTer's mediators base their practice on the **principled negotiation** and, particularly, on the following three principles:

- Focus the negotiation on the needs or interests rather than positions.
- Separate the various negotiation phases: expression of the needs (common diagnosis), open research for solutions, choice of solutions and drafting of the agreement.
- Be accommodating with the other stakeholders: mutual understanding requires accepting that various forms of rationality exist. Understanding, however, does not necessarily mean agreeing with.

While adopting these principles, we need to accept the expression of specific interests, not to sum them, but as a starting point to build a general interest.

Implementing the territorial dialogue requires a **preliminary diagnosis** from the mediator. The diagnosis is based on a series of interviews with the main protagonists. It allows to verify if the conditions for dialogue are met, in particular the following three: the protagonists agree to the dialogue; the object of the dialogue is real; there is a relative balance of powers. Also the preliminary diagnosis makes it possible to design an appropriate process while taking into account the stakeholders' expectations and concerns.

At the heart of the territorial dialogue rests the various **instances of dialogue** such as the steering committee, the select committee, working groups. Their composition is based on the non-exclusion principle or instead on the integration of all concerned parties. It might be difficult to attain but the dialogue should gather the actors of sectors of our society that are generally absent or more discreet in public debates (immigrants, multi-active farmers, hikers, mushroom pickers) and not only the institutions or the dominant organized stakeholders.

Of course, dialogue instances are rarely able to reunite all the concerned people. Thus, through the various stages of the process, it is important to provide for the **establishment of connections with the entire population**: public meetings, newsletters, websites, medias. The connection between the dialogue instances and the population is essential in order to avoid the rupture between the people who have worked together and the diverse interest groups they represent.

Once the process's components are in place, it is therefore possible to engage the dialogue itself through the instances.

The meeting room's layout must allow the mediator to place himself in a focal point that all parties can see, at least most of the time. Most importantly, the mediator must be able to move between the participants. Actually, to DialTer, **mediation is the art of movement**: the movement which allows participants to understand each other better and, consequently, to get closer allowing them to freely change their positions and opinions. The mediator must be in motion, as it enhances the communication with and between the participants. The mediator relies on his voice, words and looks but also on his gestures and movements to signal the parties to either express or restrain themselves.

Introducing the dialogue is a delicate exercise. The animator must briefly, yet clearly, answer the following essential questions: *Who am I? Why are we meeting? What will we discuss? How will we proceed?* The animator then suggests the **operating rules and principles** (e.g. respect of interlocutors, confidentiality, time management, decision making). This step is even more important if the parties oppose one another in a conflict.

One of the animator's most important skills is **active listening**, which implies a supportive attitude and reformulation as well as validation. Through the personal validation, the animator ensures that the reformulation satisfies the party from who originated the information. The personal validation is sometimes followed by the collective validation, through which the animator ensures that all the participants properly understand the expressed key points.

Who can animate a territorial dialogue process? Nowadays, most of these processes are animated by one of the stakeholders who is not, *a priori*, neutral. Nevertheless, it is strongly recommended that the animator learn to adopt a neutral position, at least for most of the reunion. The ideal situation is when the stakeholder facilitating the process designates two persons: the first one participates in the dialogue in order to defend his/her organization interests and enforces their needs while the second person focuses on animating the dialogue and on co-constructing the propositions. This being said, if the conflict is significant, it is always preferable to get a mediator involved. Whatever the situation may be, the animator must gain legitimacy amongst all stakeholders and confirm it throughout the entire process. To accomplish this, the animator must demonstrate his ability to equally listen and respect all involved participants.

*In summary, the success of a territorial dialogue's process is based on four key pillars:*

- **The elaboration of an appropriate method**: goals targeted by the dialogue and the predicted outcomes, creation of various instances of dialogue, connection with the population, experts and decision makers.
- **The elaboration of an operation frame** for the instances: division of tasks, operating rules, time management.
- **The development of a simple, progressive and flexible process**: identification of needs, open solution research, choices of solutions.
- **The selection of an animator, guardian of the process, able to adopt a neutral position**: to gain legitimacy amongst stakeholders.

## 3 Lessons and questions drawn from our experience

### *3.1 Defining the role of the mediator*

DialTer is a small team of environmental mediators who intervene in a variety of issues (water management, biodiversity conservation, industrial activities, etc.) in order to fulfil several types of missions such as the followings.

#### *3.1.1 Studying the dialogue's feasibility*

The mediator intervenes only beforehand to meet with the stakeholders and assess the dialogue feasibility. A harbour development project to which local residents strongly oppose was an example. In such case, the mediator listens to the parties in conflict, determines if they are ready to take part in a dialogue and, if so, under what conditions. Subsequently, the mediator issues a report, which also includes recommendations on how to execute the dialogue. Finally, the contractor (who usually is the project leader) chooses whether the recommendations will be implemented or not. He may decide to conduct the concertation, or ask a mediator to do so.

#### *3.1.2 Preparing and launching a process*

Here the mediator goes a bit further than previously. Not only does the mediator define a strategy for the concertation, but he also facilitates the first meetings. This was the case of a project willing to reduce the introduction of invading species in La Reunion Island. DialTer met the actors and then facilitated a first meeting; this unblocked the dialogue's process. Once that was done, the mediator's presence became superfluous, because the project leader was able to lead the collective work with only some advices given by the mediator.

#### *3.1.3 Carrying out the mediation from the beginning to the end*

It is possible that the project leader does not wish or does not have the capacity (availability, animation skills) to conduct the dialogue (or both situations at once). In such circumstances, the mediator is responsible to ensure the process's execution through its various stages, whether it is the diagnosis phase or the proposition phase. However, it is quite common for the mediator's mission to end before the acceptance of the final agreement because: final steps of the process are longer than expected; the technical aspects and, consequently, the role of experts are relatively important compared to the stakeholders' role, or the actors, have gotten closer during the process and are now able to complete it without the mediator.

Furthermore, it is not unusual that the project leader takes note of the main points during the meetings, sometimes even providing the reports' drafting and editing. Of course, the mediator must review the reports before they are shared to participants to make sure they are coherent with the mediation's spirit.

### 3.1.4 Sharing the facilitation of the dialogue with the project leader

In this case, the mediator is not the only one to conduct the process, he is working in collaboration with the sponsor. Although the mediator still conducts the initial interviews and elaborates a concertation strategy, its implementation is performed with the sponsor: joint reflection on the strategy, division of the facilitation and secretarial tasks according to the difficulty and the timeline.

### 3.1.5 Advising the dialogue facilitator

The mediator is not leading the process. He does not accomplish the initial interviews, nor does he directly intervene in the dialogue's facilitation. Instead, the mediator advises the project leader throughout the dialogue's various phases: the interviews, the elaboration of a dialogue strategy, the preparation and facilitation of the meetings. The mediator is sometimes present during the meetings to intervene if necessary as well as to observe the animator (and the stakeholders!). This presence and monitoring allows the mediator to give recommendations to the animator after the meetings.

### 3.1.6 Occasionally intervening to animate one or two meetings

The mediator intervenes in an ongoing concertation to animate a meeting that deals with a delicate subject. The mediator benefits from the experience that was acquired during the previous steps. Nevertheless, the mediator meets with the main stakeholders before the meeting.

These missions listed earlier demonstrate that environmental mediation may take a variety of forms, which are considerably more diverse than other types of mediation such as family and commercial mediation. Also, these missions' particularities seem to sometimes move away from the conventional mediation structure, where the mediator intervenes throughout the entire process, from A to Z, in order to reach an agreement that suits the parties involved in the conflict. So why can we still qualify them as being environmental mediation? What is the common ground for all these different situations?

For the mediator, it is a question of facilitating a dialogue while being neutral, and therefore by not defending the interests of a specific stakeholder including the sponsor's interests. The essential characteristic of mediation must be clearly stated right from the very beginning, and written in the contract binding the sponsor and the mediator. Another aspect of this neutral position is that the DialTer team does not intervene on the dialogue's content, unless it is to make sure that the information shared by the different parties throughout the process is properly understood by everybody. DialTer focuses its attention on the process itself, more precisely on the dialogue's progression, to ensure mutual comprehension and recognition as well as to reach an agreement or common proposals. In addition, in the fourth and fifth situations listed earlier, where the project leader is either the dialogue's conductor or the co-conductor, the mediator recommends to the animator he is assisting to adopt a relative neutral position. This means that the animator only intervenes occasionally on the content and, if possible, entrusts one of his colleagues with this task.

### *3.2 Defining the decision-making process*

In most of the cases we intervened, three levels of participation were combined as follows:

1 Consultation, to seek opinion

    1 Concertation, to co-construct proposals for decision makers
    2 Negotiation or co-decision, to implement or to realize

Each level corresponds to a body of dialogue, which comes with its own composition and methods:

- Consultation is done through public meetings or bilateral discussions.
- Concertation is carried out in working groups, representing all the concerned actors. It is at this level that the mediation takes place, including the transition from positions to needs and then the search of a collective solution.
- Negotiation or co-decision takes place within groups of decision makers where the mediator is optional. Often named steering committees, these groups gather around the table decision makers, whether they are funders or developers. First of all, their role is to steer the process, and at the final stage, to validate the proposals made by groups. However, validating is not truly deciding. Indeed, people in the Steering Committee are rarely able to commit themselves to finance or to realize. The decisions made in the Steering Committee are rather 'pre-decisions' to be submitted to the ultimate decision makers (assembly of elected representatives, State services, executive committee of a company). To clarify, the third level (negotiation or co-decision) should be split in a level of validation or pre-decision, followed by numerous decisions coupled (or not) with negotiations between several decision makers (e.g. a negotiation between a public funder and a developer). In some cases (for instance, case 3 in Table 6.1), the ultimate decision makers are the people or groups that are using the resource or the area. A validation by a steering committee is not enough to ensure that every person will comply with the new rules developed during the mediation process, even if the users were represented. Moreover, it is difficult to characterize the processes at work in this level. When the concertation has worked well, that is to say,

*Table 6.1* Various cases of mediation processes

| *Goal of mediation* | *Decision-making process* | *Relevant actors* | *Experts' involvement* |
|---|---|---|---|
| 1/ **Building an action plan** for the management of a natural site or watershed. This plan will be used as a reference for a choice of actions to undertake. | Adoption of the plan by a limited steering committee (decision makers) or opened committee (all actors). The implementation of each action will depend on the subsequent involvement of the concerned actors (managers, owners, financers). | State, local and regional authorities, water or site users and managers, environmental associations. | The need for expertise is important, in particular to evaluate the situation and to further study key points. |
| **2/ Preparing and executing a specific action,** whether or not it originates from the plan (for example: the construction of a water reservoir, or the introduction of a new species). | Approval of the co-constructed project by a steering committee. The project is submitted to a public consultation (and sometimes it is also submitted to an evaluation done by an official commission, such as the national commission for the protection of nature), followed by a state decision. | State, local and regional authorities, water or site users and managers, environmental associations. | The need for expertise is important, for the diagnosis as well as for the project's development, preceded or not by scenarios. |
| **3/ Solving a use conflict** (for example, in a natural area). | The suggested solutions are approved by a steering committee and/or by the managers. The compliance with the new usage rules will depend on their advertisement, as well as on the decisions made by each individual user. As for the solutions, their execution will depend on the decisions made by the managers. | Local and regional authorities, site users and managers, scientists, environmental associations. | The need for expertise varies. |

(*Continued*)

*Table 6.1* (Continued)

| *Goal of mediation* | *Decision-making process* | *Relevant actors* | *Experts' involvement* |
|---|---|---|---|
| 4/ **Solving a conflict** that concerns an industrial project (wind turbines) or an ongoing industrial activity (quarry). | The suggested solutions are either integrated or not by the project dealer. This project, more or less modified after the mediation, is submitted to a public consultation, which is followed by a state decision. Similarly, the industrial actor who is already in activity adopts or not the propositions, knowing that the state can intervene and impose certain measures. | Local and regional authorities, businesses, inhabitant associations, environmental associations. | The recourse to expertise requires the parties' consent. |
| 5/ **Implementing a permanent body for dialogue or cooperation** (between the stakeholders who are concerned by industrial pollution). | Operating rules of the permanent body written by a limited group of people, are designed and modified by a larger group in which all concerned actors are involved. These documents are subsequently submitted to the main members of the instance for approval. | State, local and regional authorities, private companies, environmental associations, scientists. | There is a low need for expertise. |
| 6/ **Facilitating cooperation** to produce common tools (such as technical data sheets that encourage the production of native plant species). | The tools prepared by ad hoc working groups are improved and validated by a steering committee, and by a monitoring group that brings together all the concerned parties. | It varies significantly depending on the project. | There is a low need for expertise. |

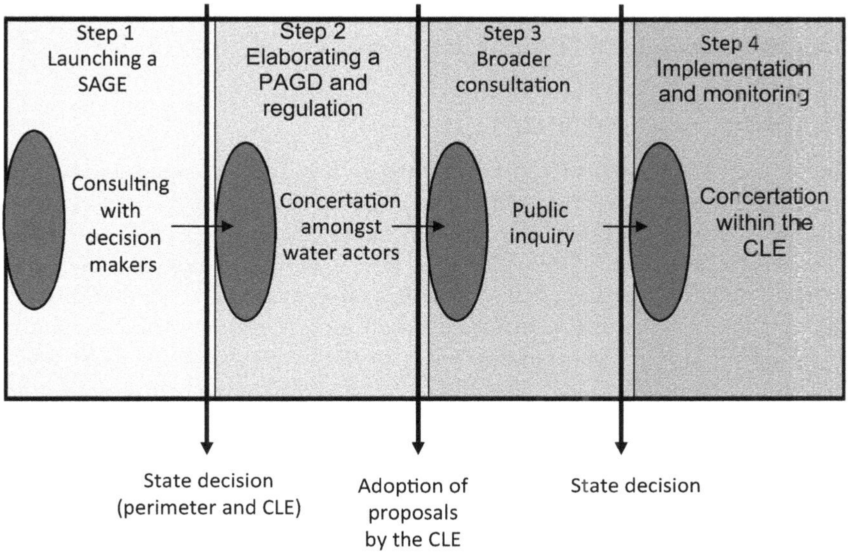


*Figure 6.1* Water management plan (SAGE)

when the working groups (where decision makers are represented) produced propositions that seem to satisfy stakeholders, it is simply a matter of informing and consulting the steering committee and to gather its remarks and approval. But if some issues remain unsolved, the steering committee will have to choose, or come up with its own and start over the consultation or negotiation phase.

Table 6.1 shows at least one case (case 4) where there is no instance of validation or pre-decision. The ultimate decision maker is the company or project/activity initiator that arouses opposition or even conflict. He must, however, comply with all the requirements of the state. A corollary of this situation is that environmental mediation, unlike other types of mediation, produces documents such as action plan, drafts, land-use plan, uses or territorial charts that have no compelling value, before optionally leading to the signing of agreements or conventions.

Another complicating factor is that in some cases, including case 1 of Table 6.1, mediation is part of a broader process that alternates between participating steps and deciding steps. Figure 6.1 shows an example of a 'Schéma d'Aménagement et de Gestion des Eaux' (SAGE).[7] For each SAGE is appointed a 'Water Local Commission' (CLE),[8] which brings together the state, local authorities and users.

7 A SAGE is a water management plan.
8 A CLE is a local commission on water.

The CLE is in charge of developing a 'Plan d'Aménagement et de Gestion Durable'[9] and a regulation. In this example, the heart of the mediation is in step 2 and proceeds to step 4; the other steps run as consultation.

## 3.3 Identifying the stakeholders

One of the fundamental principles, adopted by DialTer, is to open the dialogue to all concerned actors.[10] Most often, an environmental subject involves a wide range of actors (see Table 6.1) and given categories of actors may even gather hundreds to thousands of individuals. In fact, we invite representatives of each category (or interest group), and we schedule information and consultation activities for those who were not invited. How do we identify the concerned actors? By asking first the project initiator and then the people we meet. How do we choose a representative? The choice belongs, most often, to the organization of each category of actors (e.g. Hunting federation).

Specific situations call for adaptations of this general principle.

### 3.3.1 How are non-organized actors represented?

If it is possible to gather them in a meeting (e.g. the inhabitants of a hamlet), the mediator explains to them the purpose of the mediation; listens to their concerns, expectations and suggestions; and then suggests they appoint a representative. If they are too dispersed (e.g. motocross practitioners in a natural area), the mediator will seek a local representative (a motorcycle seller or repairer established near the concerned area) or, conversely, a regional one (a regional motocross association).

In our view, it is not necessary for an organization to be registered and to have a legal status in order for it to be represented. A membership list is sufficient to measure the importance of the group before inviting it.

### 3.3.2 Which role for the experts in a mediation?

From our perspective, the experts contracted to conduct a study related to the object of the mediation, or the experts invited to give an opinion are not stakeholders if they are not affected by the topic of the mediation. Nevertheless, in some cases (cases 3 and 5 in Table 6.1), scientists become stakeholders in the mediation because they are linked permanently to the given territory and play a significant role (e.g. a scientific council of a natural reserve) or because they are going to be associated with the permanent dialogue process that is to be set up.

9 A PAGD is a management and sustainable development plan.

10 Warning! This principle applies to instances of mediation/concertation and not to a steering committee, which answers to different principles.

### *3.3.3 How to treat highly polarized situations?*

High conflict situations introduce two threats to representation of concerned actors: first, a disproportionate imbalance between those approving and those opposing and, second, to reduce the dialogue to a confrontation between two extreme positions. The general principle is, then, supplemented by the two following points:

- The mediator ensures balance between the number of people who are supporting the project and the number of people who are against it.
- The mediator includes people who do not have a clear position, who are undecided, waiting for further information or longing for a compromise.

### *3.3.4 How to combine two territorial scales?*

When the project concerns a relatively large area, the mediation must combine a global vision and a detailed understanding of the local issues at hand. This is the case for projects in the field of watershed management (alluvium management, ecological restoration of river stretches). It is therefore wise to design a process that allow global and local actors to express themselves, to understand and co-construct consistent and relevant solutions at both levels. One possibility is to create a steering committee (or a watershed concertation group) responsible for the global vision and several local concertation groups such as one group per geographic sector (upstream and downstream) or per concerned site. The watershed group essentially invites representatives of the regional organization, while local groups bring together half local actors and half delegates of the watershed group. In this way, the dialogue between the global and local levels is held in the local concertation groups.

### *3.3.5 Should organizations without a permanent presence on the territory be excluded?*

Some conflicts carry important policy or activist issues, which extend far beyond the territory where the environmental mediation is taking place. For examples, representatives of a national association, which is opposed to wind turbines, might invite themselves to the concertation organized for a specific local wind project. Should we consider them as concerned actors? It depends.

If the same interest (or position) is already defended by local actors, it seems preferable to avoid the presence of regional or national activists. Indeed, we risk to 'politicize' the dialogue in generalizing it and to enter into strategic considerations and therefore to move away from the 'specific' needs of the actors, which is at the heart of the mediation process. This is one of the points on which mediation differs from public debate.

If, however, an interest is not defended by locals (e.g. wind turbines can affect the movement of birds), then the presence of a regional association (defense of birds) is justified if they focus on the local situation.

### *3.3.6 Should ordinary citizens be invited?*

Mediation is neither a public meeting nor an open debate (although these forms of participation can be part of a process of environmental mediation). The heart of mediation is when a process gathers concerned parties, or their representatives, within a balanced composition, as we have said earlier. It is therefore difficult to integrate all who wish to participate, though it would be interesting to save some seats for 'ordinary' citizens wishing to be involved. By 'ordinary' we mean people who are not part of any of the represented organizations. They may have relevant opinions or proposals not already expressed by the other stakeholders.

## *3.4 Articulating expertise and mediation*

In environmental mediation, the use of an external expertise is, to stakeholders, particularly important in the first two cases of Table 6.1. Two options are possible for the project initiator: either he recruits a technical expert and a mediator or he launches only one invitation to tender which integrates the two functions. The second option is a more desirable one because the process places the experts from the start at the service of the stakeholders.

Indeed, the most commonly made mistake is placing technical expertise at the heart of the dialogue and only soliciting the input of stakeholders in order to complete or comment on the experts' vision. In reality, the perceptions and needs of the concerned actors are essential to mediation, whilst the expertise should serve to shed light on and enrich the vision and proposals made by the actors.

### *How do we ensure experts are at the service of stakeholders?*

The first basic precept is to encourage a back-and-forth discussion between the input by the experts and the production of stakeholders. At least two round trips are necessary: to diagnose and to develop proposals (which will later on make up the action plan or the project). These steps are sometimes split into more. On one hand, an initial inventory precedes a precise diagnosis, which is eventually followed by additional studies, all aiming at formulating objectives. On the other hand, the proposal phase may be coupled with the development of scenarios and followed by the outline of the chosen scenario.

The second basic precept is to seek an overall balance between the contribution of experts and stakeholders. In the first phase of the process, the production of stakeholders is preferred over that of the experts (that is, the actors' expression of perceptions and needs precede the experts' diagnosis). Upon completion of the diagnosis (a shared diagnosis, if possible, amongst the visions of both groups), it is up to the stakeholders to make proposals, and only then do the experts build scenarios or outline plans of action. Subsequently, the relation will be reversed; the more we advance in the development of the final document, the more the work of experts is at the heart of the discussion. In this second phase, the success of the mediation lies within two skills: the ability of the experts to be understood by all (outreach) and their ability to pin point the 'political' choices at hand as much as the elements that compose each choice (neutrality). In this sense, the mediator plays an important role in supporting the technical experts – namely, to proofread with a layman's look the documents to be presented in meetings. This avoids two rather frequent errors: one in which the speech of the expert remains partly inaccessible to a non-specialist; and one in which the expert directs the choice towards his personal preferences.

Of course, and this is not the easiest issue to resolve, back-and-forth discussions must be paced to meet required studies deadlines, moreover they must respect time constraints as well as fulfil the expected results of the stakeholders.

Finally, it is worthy to mention three relatively original ways to facilitate expert-mediator articulation:

- using a mediation instance to define the specifications of some studies that seem necessary to respond to the problem;
- these specifications include hosting training sessions in which the stakeholders are given the necessary tools to better understand the results of the study;
- some studies include a participatory component open to all volunteers (e.g. census and wetland diagnosis).

## Conclusion

Over the recent decades, participatory approaches in environmental field have increased in France. They are often inspired by the principles of deliberation put forward by public organisms. However, approaches based on structures or tools (public debate, conference of citizens, open space forums, neighbourhood council) often dominate on approaches based on processes and adapted methods. Furthermore, because the model of debate undermines the culture of dialogue, reaching a consensus is much less important than it is in Anglo-Saxon countries.

For these reasons, environmental mediation remains marginalized. However, the methodology developed by practitioners is meeting the actors' growing demand to create pragmatic approaches on which to base effective public and private actions. It is frequent that training and methodological textbooks incorporate principles derived from mediation. In fact, one of the ways environmental mediation could gain ground in France in the coming years is probably by sharing the principles and methods so as to gradually develop better debate facilitation techniques, facilitator's posture and dialogue's bodies.

# 7 Negotiated rulemaking for the Brownfields law in the United States of America

*Susan Podziba*[1] *and Patricia Overmeyer*[2]

## Introduction

Negotiated rulemaking is a process used in the United States to create federal regulations in which representatives of a sponsoring government agency and relevant stakeholders work together to develop a consensus recommendation for the content of a proposed rule. Through mediated negotiations, government and stakeholder representatives work through every issue and detail of a proposed rule to integrate their perspectives and interests.

The U.S. Environmental Protection Agency (EPA) used a negotiated rulemaking process to establish federal standards and practices for the all appropriate inquiries (AAI) of potentially polluted properties, as required under the Comprehensive Environmental Response, Compensation and Liability Act (CERCLA) Section 101(35)(B), as amended by the Small Business Liability Relief and Brownfields Revitalization Act (Public Law No. 107–118), also known as the Brownfields Law. The final AAI rule was published in the *Federal Register* in November 1, 2005, and enacted in November 1, 2006.

Participants credited the negotiated rulemaking process with having provided an opportunity to meet public policy goals while limiting unintended consequences, and reducing regulatory uncertainty for their industries and the public.

## 1 Overview of negotiated rulemaking

Negotiated rulemaking, sometimes referred to as regulatory negotiations (reg neg), is a process for developing regulations that relies on stakeholders and government working together to develop consensus on the actual text of a proposed rule. The critical element of negotiated rulemaking is that it creates a forum in which participants engage in complex negotiations to write enforceable federal regulations that achieve the government agency's public policy goals and satisfy

1 Susan Podziba, principal of Podziba Policy Mediation, served as the convener and mediator for the All Appropriate Inquiries Negotiated Rulemaking (AAI Reg Neg).

2 Patricia Overmeyer, land revitalization coordinator of the Office of Brownfields and Land Revitalization of the U.S. Environmental Protection Agency, served as designated federal official, program analyst and primary regulation writer for the AAI Reg Neg.

stakeholders' key concerns. Reg neg offers an opportunity to integrate the differing perspectives and interests of federal, state, tribal, and local government and stakeholder constituencies that will be affected by the rule as well as relevant expert information and public concerns. Generally speaking, it brings a great deal of focus and resources to the issues embedded in the future rule. If successful, the nation benefits from publicly supported rules that achieve government and stakeholder policy goals.

Reg neg has been used in the United States since the early 1980s and was codified in the Negotiated Rulemaking Act of 1996. Many federal agencies have conducted negotiated rulemakings, but most still favour the traditional rulemaking process in which the public is invited to submit formal comments on a draft rule prepared by the government. Government officials evaluate comments and determine whether to support, reject or create alternatives to particular sections or subsections of their proposed rule. In traditional rulemakings, they do so on their own – without the benefit of deliberations with and among outside stakeholders and the public.

Reg neg uploads potential conflict to the frontend of the rulemaking process and provides opportunities to resolve conflict and clarify regulations in the context of real-world applications rather than waiting for formal comments after a rule is proposed. Whereas proposed rules developed through a reg neg process still undergo the formal comment period of proposed rules, the participating organizations agree not to submit formal negative comments on the proposed rule if the sponsoring agency publishes their consensus text as the basis of its Notice of Proposed Rulemaking (NPRM).

The reg neg process begins with an assessment to determine the potential stakeholder groups and how they may be represented, the key issues that will be discussed, the relevant history and dynamics of the situation, and the feasibility of convening representative stakeholders and government to negotiate the text of the rule. After a determination of feasibility, negotiations are initiated to develop consensus text for the proposal rule.

Negotiations typically occur over a period of six months to a year and include multi-day meetings approximately once per month, work groups to develop proposals for the negotiating committee, work groups among subsets of the stakeholders, ongoing communications among the participants and the mediation team, outreach and consultations with constituents, and expert presentations.

The initiating government agency actively participates in the negotiations and provides its substantive expertise as well as its knowledge of regulatory enforceability. The final recommendation of the reg neg committee should, therefore, effectively incorporate all the concerns raised by the sponsoring agency, thus assuring the Agency's willingness to adopt it. Although a government agency can request and receive consensus recommendations from a federal advisory committee as stipulated in the Federal Advisory Committee, it cannot transfer its authorities to such a group. Importantly, the government agency always retains and never relinquishes jurisdiction over the final rule – the Agency may reject even a formal consensus recommendation of its advisory committee.

However, organizational protocols negotiated at the outset of a reg neg process typically indicate that if final consensus recommendation is achieved, the federal agency is expected to publish the consensus regulatory text as the basis of its NPRM. In return, the organizational members of the negotiated rulemaking committee agree not to submit formal negative comments on the NPRM.

This mutual commitment among the federal agency and the reg neg committee members is an acknowledgement that the final consensus on the proposed regulation represents a collection of joint decisions that satisfies the key concerns of each negotiator within existing political and resource constraints. Negative comments from committee members on issues for which they accepted less-preferred options in exchange for more-preferred options on other parts of the 'package' of decisions would render the overall effort meaningless.

The government agency is represented on the advisory committee, actively participates in committee negotiations and must be included in all consensus decisions. The final package of decisions should therefore effectively incorporate the concerns of the sponsoring agency, thus making it possible for the Agency to accept the formal advisory committee recommendation.

Negotiated rulemakings are conducted in accordance with the Federal Advisory Committee Act and the Negotiated Rulemaking Act. For the purpose of the negotiations, the sponsoring federal agency establishes a negotiated rulemaking advisory committee in accordance with the requirements of the Federal Advisory Committee Act (FACA). Committee members are appointed by the chief official of the sponsoring federal entity – i.e., the secretary of a department or administrator of an agency. Committee composition must meet the FACA requirement of "balanced representation from affected and interested stakeholder groups".

FACA also requires the government agency to publish a Notice of Intent to Establish a Negotiated Rulemaking Committee and Notice of First Meeting (and subsequent meetings) in the *Federal Register* and file a FACA Charter with the General Services Administration and Congress. The Notice of Intent, which must be filed at least 45 days before the Committee's first meeting, includes solicitation of comments on the purpose of the reg neg, issues to be discussed, proposed stakeholder categories, and proposed committee members.

The Negotiated Rulemaking Act describes the negotiated rulemaking process including the need for a convening assessment, the use of consensus as a decision rule, and the activities of the mediator for managing the group deliberations to achieve the goal of reaching consensus on draft regulatory text for the proposed rule.

## 2 The all appropriate inquiries negotiated rulemaking

The U.S. Environmental Protection Agency (EPA) initiated a negotiated rulemaking to develop a proposed rule establishing federal standards and practices for AAI, as required under CERCLA Section 101(35)(B), as amended by the Small Business Liability Relief and Brownfields Revitalization Act (Brownfields Amendments).

The negotiated rulemaking process began with a convening assessment to determine the feasibility of proceeding with a consensus process to develop the AAI standards. After a determination of feasibility, negotiations were initiated among representatives of government and the key stakeholder groups that would be significantly affected by the AAI Standards.

The All Appropriate Inquiries Negotiated Rulemaking Advisory Committee (AAI Negotiated Rulemaking Committee) was composed of 25 members and four resource participants. It held six multi-day meetings to discuss the issues outlined in the Brownfields Amendments, such as qualifications for environmental professionals conducting AAI, required interviews to determine historical uses of properties and requirements for visual inspection, including when access to a property is denied.

After eight months of negotiations, assisted by a public policy mediator, the AAI Negotiated Rulemaking Committee reached consensus on all issues related to the AAI standards. The negotiations included 6 meetings for a total of 13.5 meeting days, a series of work group conference calls, ongoing communication between meetings, a federal government work group and consideration of intensive public input throughout the process.

The All Appropriate Inquiries Notice of Proposed Rulemaking was based upon and included the AAI Negotiated Rulemaking Advisory Committee's recommended consensus regulatory language, and was published in the *Federal Register* on August 24, 2004. Following a public comment period, EPA developed a final rulemaking. EPA published the final rule in the *Federal Register* on November 1, 2005, and it became effective on November 1, 2006.

The final standard represents the priorities and expert knowledge of the diverse stakeholder committee; provides clear, defensible rules on assessing properties for hazardous substances; and provides for both increased brownfields redevelopment and protection of public health and the environment.

## 3 Background on all appropriate inquiries

### *3.1 The Brownfields amendments*

On January 11, 2002, the Small Business Liability Relief and Revitalization Act (Pub. L. No. 107–118), also known as the 'Brownfields Amendments' to the CERCLA, was enacted. The Brownfields Amendments amended CERCLA to include liability protections for certain landowners. One of several requirements applicable to landowners seeking liability protection is the requirement to conduct AAI into past uses and ownership of a property prior to acquisition (§101(35)(B). The AAI standards and practices are relevant to

- the innocent landowner defense to CERCLA liability (§101 (35));
- the contiguous property owner protection from CERCLA liability (§107(q));
- the bona fide prospective purchaser protection from CERCLA;
- the brownfields site characterization and assessment grant program (§104(k)(2)).

The Brownfields Amendments required EPA to establish regulations setting forth standards and practices for how to conduct AAI by January 11, 2004, two years after enactment of the law. The Brownfields Amendments include ten criteria specified by Congress, which the federal standards for AAI were required to address. In addition, the Brownfields Amendments established an interim standard for the conduct of AAI that remained in effect until EPA promulgated federal standards. For properties purchased after May 31, 1997, Congress established the interim standard as the American Society for Testing and Materials (now ASTM International) Phase I Environmental Site Assessment Standard. EPA developed a direct final rule to allow for the use of the ASTM E1527–2000 Phase 1 environmental site assessment standard as an interim standard for AAI. This is the voluntary industry standard widely used prior to passage of the Brownfields Amendments.

### *3.2 Definition of all appropriate inquiries*

'All appropriate inquiries' is a term coined by Congress under CERCLA to describe a distinct process for real property 'due diligence'. An essential step in real property transactions is evaluating a property for potential environmental contamination and assessing potential liability for contamination that may be present at a property. When such due diligence is conducted as part of a process to establish a defense to environmental liability under CERCLA (e.g. the Superfund Law), that process is referred to as 'all appropriate inquiries'.

Congress first used the term 'all appropriate inquiries' with regard to environmental due diligence for property transactions when it passed the 1986 'Superfund Amendments and Reauthorization Act' (Public Law No. 99–499, 100 stat. 1613, 'SARA'). With those amendments, Congress created the 'innocent landowner' defense to CERCLA liability. To be afforded this defense to liability, a party was required to undertake prior to, or on the date of acquisition of the property, 'AAI' into the previous ownership and uses of the property consistent with "good commercial or customary standards and practices". In 2002, when Congress again amended CERCLA with the Brownfields Amendments, it added liability protections for "contiguous property owners" and "bona fide prospective purchasers". These provisions also required that prospective owners of real property conduct AAI, among other requirements, to benefit from the liability protections.

## 4 AAI negotiated rulemaking timeline

| | |
|---|---|
| August 2002 | EPA initiated the convening assessment to determine feasibility of a negotiated rulemaking |
| December 2002 | Completion of Convening Assessment |
| March 6, 2003 | Federal Register Notice of Intent to Negotiate the Proposed Rule on AAI |

| | |
|---|---|
| April 5, 2003 | Deadline for Comments on the purpose and membership of the AAI Reg Neg Advisory Committee |
| April 7, 2003 | Federal Register Notice of Establishment of the AAI Negotiated Rulemaking Committee under the Negotiated Rulemaking Act (NRA) and the FACA and Announcement of its First Meeting and Request for Comments |
| April 28, 2003 | Final FACA Charter filed with Congress |
| April 29–30, 2003 | First Meeting of AAI Reg Neg Advisory Committee |
| April–November 2003 | AAI Reg Neg Advisory Committee negotiations (total of six meetings) |
| November 14, 2003 | AAI Reg Neg Advisory Committee reached final consensus on all issues at its final meeting |
| December 18, 2003 | AAI Reg Neg Advisory Committee approved its November 12–14 meeting summary, which documented the Committee's final consensus on all issues |
| August 26, 2004 | AAI Proposed Rule published in the *Federal Register* |
| October 25, 2004 | Deadline for public comments on proposed rule |
| November 1, 2005 | Final Rule published in the *Federal Register* |
| November 1, 2006 | Effective date of final rule |

## 5 The convening assessment

### *5.1 Overview*

Prior to initiating negotiations to develop a proposed rule, a public policy mediator conducts a convening assessment to determine the feasibility, or likelihood of success, of bringing together government and stakeholder representatives to build a consensus rule.

It entails in-depth interviews with individuals and groups to identify potential stakeholders and negotiators, critical issues, expected dynamics, and the varied perspectives and interests of the stakeholders with regard to the rule. Convening assessment reports typically include a determination of feasibility, categories of stakeholders, substantive issues by stakeholder group and key issues across stakeholder groups. When there is a reasonable likelihood of achieving consensus through negotiations, the convening report also outlines procedural issues, proposed participants, provides a process design and offers protocols and procedures for consideration by the future committee.

Prior to the interviews, the convener develops an interview protocol for the interactions with parties. The protocol is a set of questions designed to obtain relevant stakeholder information needed to support the reg neg process. The questions function as a guide through interviewee narratives of the situation, including stories that illustrate the issues as well as hopes and fears related to the rule. As the narrative is told, the convener frames questions to draw out additional dynamics as well as to ensure that all information of the protocol is provided. In addition to learning of substantive issues, priorities, interests, history and dynamics, the convening also provides opportunities for clarifying and questioning assumptions held by interviewees to seed future discussions in favour of new understandings. The interviews also enable the mediator to begin building relationships with committee members, which enhance his or her ability to mediate effectively during negotiations.

The convening assessment also serves to identify potential members of the negotiating committee by differentiating those parties with a real stake in the issues from those parties with limited interests. Parties concerned with only one or few issues have little incentive to consider a range of alternative ideas and proposals because they have little need to integrate their interests with those of the other committee members.

The information obtained during these interviews is used to design the process and effectively facilitate the negotiations to ensure productive deliberations. Information derived from these interviews is treated as confidential by request of the interviewee.

## 5.2 *The all appropriate inquiries negotiated rulemaking convening assessment*

At the start of the AAI Reg Neg assessment process, Susan Podziba, serving as convener, met with Patricia Overmeyer and the EPA team to identify an initial list of interviewees based on EPA knowledge of relevant stakeholders and issues.

The convener interviewed approximately 60 representatives of federal, state, county, local and tribal government; for profit and not-for-profit developers, real estate and environmental attorneys, real estate brokers, bankers and lenders, environmental professionals, environmentalists, environmental justice advocates and insurance companies. Virtually every interviewee expressed support for addressing the issues and differences among interested parties through the negotiated rulemaking process.

Among the key findings of the convening assessment were the determination of feasibility, categories of stakeholders, key issues by stakeholder group and key issues identified across stakeholders. The findings of the convener are documented in the report titled *Convening Assessment Report on the Feasibility of a Negotiated Rulemaking Process to Develop the All Appropriate Inquiry Standard Required under the Small Business Liability Relief and Brownfields Revitalization Act.*[3]

Based on an evaluation of the information derived from these interviews, the convener determined and recommended to EPA that is was feasible to proceed with the negotiated rulemaking process. The feasibility determination was based on a high level of stakeholder interest in participating in the process, the degree to which interests and issues among the stakeholders were interrelated, the possibility of engaging a balanced committee of representatives and the likelihood

3 Podziba, S., *Convening Assessment Report on the Feasibility of a Negotiated Rulemaking Process to Develop the All Appropriate Inquiry Standard Required Under the Small Business Liability Relief and Brownfields Revitalization Act (Public Law No. 107–118)*, Brookline, 2002, 31.

of success in achieving consensus on the AAI standards within the available time frame and existing resources.

The assessment led to the identification of nine categories of key stakeholders, which are those groups that will be greatly affected or have a strong role in implementing the new standards. The convener recommended that EPA invite representatives from each of the following categories to participate in the negotiated rulemaking: other federal agencies, state government, local government, tribal government, developers (residential, commercial, industrial, for profit, not-for-profit), bankers and lenders, environmentalists, environmental justice community and environmental professionals.

In addition, three groups – environmental attorneys, real estate brokers and environmental insurance professionals – were identified as interested parties with great depth of knowledge relevant to the implementation of the standard. However, these parties typically represent multiple stakeholders, for example, environmental attorneys and insurance companies include developers, environmental professionals and state and local governments among their clients at any given time. Thus, the convener suggested that these parties serve as resource participants, given their ability to analyze the impacts of various options across multiple stakeholders rather than negotiators because of their expected difficulties in developing cohesive negotiating strategies. In addition to the categories of stakeholder, the convener also recommended the organizational representatives for each category of stakeholder. Each organization then identified its primary negotiator and an alternate.

The assessment outlined key concerns within each category of stakeholder. For example, local government officials viewed potential liability for new owners at brownfields sites as a barrier to increased redevelopment of brownfields sites and supported the Brownfields Law as a means to removing a barrier to redevelopment. However, with sites located within their communities, they also wanted to be sure that the AAI standards protected against contamination leaching into soils and groundwater and its potential for impacting human health.

Developers expressed a strong interest in a standard that would be clear, predictable, consistently enforced, reasonably inexpensive, and not too time consuming, and which, when complied with, would provide liability protection without reopeners. Clarity was crucial for developers, who feared that a lack of clarity could result in the loss of a credible liability defense.

Environmental groups were primarily concerned that the standard require rigorous investigation of sites. They wanted historical searches to include title search, spills database, enforcement actions, prior investigations, and visible contaminated areas. They want the standard to trigger sampling when historical searches identify past contamination.

The interests of the environmental justice community were similar to those of the environmental groups. However, as the communities where many brownfields sites are located, the environmental justice community raised an additional concern of public notification of contamination and proposed clean-up plans. One commented on the fears within a community when "people in protective moon suits" arrive to clean-up sites that people have been living near for decades.

The assessment report also identified key issues across stakeholder groups. For example, many stakeholders asked about the need for and length of a 'shelf life' for an AAI assessment report. In other words, how long would an assessment be considered useful to adequately characterize environmental conditions at a property and establish a liability defense. Some thought the shelf life of an assessment should be six months, others one year, and still others, longer. This is especially relevant for sites with groundwater contamination and/or migrating plumes.

Another cross-cutting issue was the scope of the standard. A key question raised by representatives of numerous stakeholder groups related to the scope of the standard was the following: will the standard cover only the Phase I Assessment or provide direction for Phase I and Phase II assessments? Some interviewees supported the former and others the latter.

In addition, some raised the question of whether or not the standard would include requirements for clean-up when contamination is found and suggested that the standard identify triggers for Phase II assessments. Those supporting a limited scope stated that historically, there has been little agreement on what a Phase II assessment should consist of given the unique aspects of each site.

## 6 Participation

For the negotiated rulemaking process to yield a proposed regulation that will be considered legitimate by the regulated community and the public and not subject to challenge after promulgation, the reg neg advisory committee must consist of representatives of all key stakeholder groups. The sponsoring federal agency acts to ensure legitimate membership on the advisory committee.

The convener recommends categories of stakeholders and organizations that may represent them, and the government agency takes steps to ensure the proposed composition of the advisory committee is sufficiently exhaustive. It informs the public of its proposed committee members and provides opportunities for the public to recommend additional categories of stakeholders and participants.

For the AAI Reg Neg, EPA published a Federal Register Notice of Intent to Establish a Negotiated Rulemaking Advisory Committee and asked for comment on the proposed lists of categories of stakeholders and advisory committee members. This served as a check on committee composition and ensured that any stakeholders not identified by the Agency or through the convening process would have an opportunity to nominate additional reg neg committee members. EPA carefully monitored the composition of the Committee to ensure balanced representation from affected and interested stakeholder groups, as required under FACA.

### *6.1 The EPA team*

EPA, as a member of the All Appropriate Inquiry Negotiated Rulemaking Advisory Committee (AAI Negotiated Rulemaking Committee), represented its interests as the Agency responsible for promulgation, implementation, and enforcement of the regulation. The EPA team included the Office of Brownfields Clean-Up and Redevelopment, Office of General Counsel, Office of Site Remediation Enforcement, Office of Site Remediation and Technology Innovation, and the Conflict Prevention and Resolution Center.

The negotiated rulemaking process also enjoyed support from EPA senior management, as illustrated by occasional visits from the Deputy Assistant Administrator and the Office Director for the Brownfields Program. Both thanked the AAI Negotiated Rulemaking Advisory committee members for their commitment and hard work.

The negotiated rulemaking process demanded a great deal of effort from the EPA team, which included a negotiator, a regulatory analyst, a legal advisor, senior staff, administrators and technical and process experts. The regulatory analyst and the negotiator had multiple tasks and responsibilities to perform. In the weeks between committee meetings, EPA staff drafted and revised regulatory language, checked in internally with EPA senior management work group members and technical experts, met with representatives from other federal agencies to learn how proposals under discussion would impact them, reviewed and commented on meeting summaries and meeting agendas, participated in conference calls, responded to outside information requests from the public, responded to concerns raised by members of the public, responded to media requests and managed committee logistics such as travel reimbursement, FACA compliance and *Federal Register* notices.

The effort by all members of this team, and especially EPA staff who drafted and distributed revised regulatory text to reflect committee discussions during and following each committee meeting, significantly contributed to the success of the negotiated rulemaking process. In addition, the internal coordination throughout the process contributed to a relatively smooth ratification process within the Agency for the terms of the standard.

Six meetings were very limited given the complexity of the issues. If the EPA regulatory analyst had not been able to quickly translate committee decisions into draft regulatory language to facilitate committee discussions, the six meetings might not have been sufficient.

## 6.2 Stakeholder committee members

Each organizational member participating in the negotiated rulemaking process was represented by a principal negotiator and an alternate. Committee members understood that its work could become the proposed federal standard for AAI, and this motivated committee members' commitment. The AAI Reg Neg committee members, by stakeholder category, were as follows:

**State Government**

Illinois Environmental Protection Agency (Association of State and Territorial Solid Waste Management Officials (ASTSWMO))

Maryland Department of the Environment (ASTSWMO))

**Local Government**

The U. S. Conference of Mayors
International Municipal Lawyers Association
National Association of Local Government Environmental Professionals

**Tribal Government**

Gila River Indian Community, Department of Environmental Quality

**Developers**

National Association of Home Builders (Residential)
National Association of Development Organizations (Rural Development)
Real Estate Roundtable (Commercial)
International Council of Shopping Centers (Commercial)
National Association of Industrial and Office Parks (Commercial)
Trust for Public Land (Not-for-Profit)
National Brownfields Association (Not-for-Profit)

**Bankers/Lenders**

Environmental Bankers Association
Mortgage Bankers Association of America

**Environmentalists**

Environmental Defense
U. S. Public Interest Research Group

**Environmental Justice**

Center for Public Environmental Oversight
Partnership for Sustainable Brownfields Redevelopment
West Harlem Environmental Action

**Environmental Professionals**

American Society of Civil Engineers
Association of Soil and Foundation Engineers
National Ground Water Association
Wasatch Environmental

### *6.3 Resource participants*

The category of resource participants was uniquely created for the AAI Negotiated Rulemaking. These organizations contributed a great deal of useful information to the negotiations, but did not represent unique or distinct stakeholders. Some of the members of these organizations represented the range of stakeholders. As a result, these organizations could not develop unified negotiating positions on key issues because their members as well as their members' clients held differing views.

Resource participants spoke at meetings, but could not dissent from proposals. This model was effective in efficiently bringing important information to the Committee that could immediately be incorporated into committee discussions and decisions.

The resource participants by stakeholder category were as follows:

- Real Estate Brokers
- Environmental Insurance Professionals
- Environmental Attorneys (through the Section of Environment, Energy, and Resources of the American Bar Association)

### 6.4 *The federal partners work group*

EPA staff decided it was best to convene other federal agency officials during the negotiations of the proposed rule. Knowing that several federal agencies would have significant interest in the AAI Rule, EPA decided to invite staff from several potentially affected federal agencies to form a work group to review the progress and outcomes of the AAI Negotiated Rulemaking Committee throughout the negotiations. This allowed federal agency staff to provide input and comment to the AAI Negotiated Rulemaking Committee. EPA officials relayed federal agency concerns to the negotiated rulemaking committee for its full consideration during the negotiation process. Federal agency staff also benefited from the discussions held by the negotiating committee.

Members of the federal agency work group included staff from the following agencies: U.S. Department of Agriculture, Forest Service; Department of Interior, Bureau of Land Management; Department of Housing and Urban Development, Federal Housing Agency; General Services Agency; Department of Justice; Department of Transportation, Federal Highways Administration; and the Coast Guard and the Federal Deposit Insurance Corporation (FDIC).

Most of these agencies purchase, own, sell, or manage real estate on behalf of the federal government. In their capacity as landowners and land managers, these agencies may be held liable for any environmental contamination on their properties. In addition, when these agencies purchase property for use or management by the federal government they need to ensure compliance with the requirements of the AAI rule, prior to purchasing the property. Given that these agencies need to comply with EPA's final regulation, their interest in the negotiations was significant and their willingness to participate in the regulatory development process was high. The knowledge and experiences of federal agencies involved in property acquisition decisions added additional insights to the regulatory development process that were shared with the AAI Reg Neg Committee and ultimately benefited the proposed rule.

The Department of Justice (DOJ) does not purchase property directly for the federal government's use. However, DOJ represents all other federal agencies in lawsuits and court actions brought against them or filed on behalf of a federal agency, including environmental liability suits. The FDIC also does not purchase real estate directly, but sets standards governing banking practices that affect lending decisions on properties purchased by private entities. The knowledge and experience brought to the process by these government officials also provided value insights and benefits to the negotiations.

The issues related to the proposed AAI rule that were most important to the federal agency work group members included: who could perform or oversee the conduct of the property investigation (e.g. the definition of an environmental professional), when the investigation needed to be performed and its shelf life, and the type and extent of any documentation requirements. The interests and concerns of the federal agency officials were not dissimilar to the interests and concerns of various members of the AAI Negotiated Rulemaking Committee, who themselves represented parties involved in various real estate property transactions.

In addition, EPA officials negotiated the content of the proposed regulation with the Office of Management and Budget (OMB). All proposed and final rulemakings developed by federal agencies are subject to OMB review and approval prior to publication in the *Federal Register*. In addition, OMB provides an opportunity for other interested agencies to review and comment on the content of regulations prior to OMB approving the rulemakings for publications.

## 7 The negotiations

The AAI Reg Neg Committee negotiations occurred between April and November 2003 and included six face-to-face multiple day meetings held in Washington, D. C., a series of work group conference calls between meetings, outreach and consultation with constituencies, and consideration of intensive public input throughout the process.

Each negotiating session followed a formal agenda and was open to the public. Each day of each meeting included time set aside for public comment during which members of the public addressed the AAI Negotiated Rulemaking Committee to offer recommendations, ask questions, and comment on issues under discussion.

After clarifying the scope of issues subject to negotiations, committee members 'workshopped' each issue to identify embedded sub-issues and gain an understanding of concerns and level of importance for each committee member. They deliberated respectfully and creatively in an effort to reach agreements on all issues necessary for an effective standard that met the requirements of the Brownfields Amendments for AAI. Early agreements were considered tentative agreements as nothing was considered agreed upon until all was agreed. In addition, because the multitude of issues to be discussed had to somehow be sequenced, discussions of later issues sometimes required changes to earlier agreements to assure consistency across the rule.

The negotiating process was an iterative discussion of the ten criteria spelled out in the Brownfields Amendments. Each issue was intensively discussed until agreements in concept were reached. As conceptual agreements emerged during negotiations, the EPA drafting team developed draft regulatory text for review by the Committee. The draft text was reviewed and revised over the course of multiple meetings until it reflected tentative agreement. The public policy mediator assisted throughout these deliberations by providing and maintaining the Committee's focus on the issues, from initial concepts through to decision making. When tentative agreement was reached on all issues, the Committee reviewed all of its tentative agreements and made some additional revisions to address new concerns raised by some of its members. Finally, tentative agreements were confirmed as final consensus and the negotiations concluded.

The mediation team drafted meeting summaries after each meeting, which were reviewed, revised and approved by the Committee. The summaries served as records of agreements and identified key discussion points of outstanding issues.

The negotiated rulemaking process allowed for continued review of committee proceedings by constituents of the organizations represented on the AAI Negotiated Rulemaking Committee and the general public. Full consideration was given to all input offered by the public during its deliberations.

Throughout the process, work groups were formed to discuss issues that required more time than could be made available during meetings of the full Committee. Work groups were composed of the AAI Negotiated Rulemaking Committee members most interested in the subject under discussion and resource participants who could provide expertise. All were conducted through facilitated conference calls. Work groups were initiated for issues including definition of environmental professional, objectives and performance goals, potential use of a tiered approach for the standard, and interview requirements. Work groups has no decision-making authority; rather, their proposals were presented to the full Committee for consideration.

In addition, the mediation team maintained ongoing contact with AAI Negotiated Rulemaking Committee members on an as-needed basis to build consensus on controversial issues. Such discussions often led to the development of proposals that were presented to the Committee.

In addition to the 25 members and resource participants of the AAI Negotiated Rulemaking Committee and their organizational constituents, members of the public at large were actively engaged throughout the negotiations. In some instances, committee members surveyed their constituents to obtain additional information on questions and issues of concern. The Committee received and reviewed scores of public comments in the form of emails and letters and heard numerous public comments on issues such as the definition of environmental professional, EPA accreditation of environmental professional certifying agencies, identifying past occupants (including interviews with neighbours) and how to conduct database research of institutional controls.

The negotiations included a preliminary meeting and negotiations on substantive issues. After 13.5 meeting days (108 hours), the Committee completed all of its work at an intense final meeting. Some new issues were raised and the Committee, committed to its success, worked hard to find ways to accommodate all issues raised by all members. All committee members agreed to support the proposed standard they had jointly developed.

## *7.1 The preliminary meeting*

Negotiated rulemaking committees begin deliberations with several preliminary activities. The two-and-a-half day AAI Committee preliminary meeting included a welcome from the EPA deputy administrator; an overview of EPA's goals for the standards; committee member introductions including statements about their goals, concerns and thoughts about AAI requirements; an overview of the negotiated rulemaking process; discussion of ground rules; determination of the scope of issues to be negotiated; informational needs; logistics; public comment; and the initial discussion of substantive issues.

Every negotiating rulemaking process includes the development of ground rules, which serve to clarify expectations and prevent procedural conflicts. They are a set of self-policing agreements among committee members, which in essence, layout guidelines for good faith negotiations. There is no enforcement or formal sanction for breaking a ground rule although the social cohesion developed within the group often contributes to mutual respect among the negotiators that helps to maintain compliance with these early mutual agreements.

The AAI Negotiated Rulemaking Committee ground rules created a common set of understandings concerning governance of their negotiations. Members outlined their mission, goals, deadline, responsibilities of negotiators and mediators, decision-making rule, status of the agreement and member commitments that accrue when final consensus is reached.

Some of the particularly interesting elements of the AAI Negotiated Rulemaking Committee ground rules were the statement of the committee's mission, its decision rule or definition of consensus, and the commitments resulting from agreements reached.

The mission statement clarified the key objectives underlying the AAI standard. It read, in part,

> The Committee will work together as a team to develop all appropriate inquiry standards and practices that are protective of public safety, public health, and the environment and promote productive use of properties subject to the Brownfields Law.

A mission statement that articulates the need to balance among the varied interests of the stakeholders can serve as a helpful reminder that parties must engage in joint problem solving during negotiations. For the AAI Negotiated

Rulemaking Committee, the mission balanced protection of the environment and public health with the goal of increasing land revitalization and community economic development. Since committee members approached these objectives differently, the mission statement continually served as a reminder of the need to account for all the interests reflected among committee members.

Another key element of the procedural ground rules was the decision rule. The AAI Negotiated Rulemaking Committee agreed to operate by consensus of all members. Agreements were considered reached when there was no dissent by any member. In addition, they agreed that once final consensus was achieved, committee members could not thereafter withdraw from the consensus.

Critical to the good faith negotiations was the shared understanding of the arrangements and commitments that flowed from reaching final consensus on all issues. It reflects government and stakeholder motivation in initiating and participating in negotiated rulemaking. This ground rule for the AAI Reg Neg was stated as follows:

> The goal of the AAI Committee is to develop a proposed regulation that reflects a final consensus of the Committee. [. . .] If the AAI Committee reaches a final consensus on all issues, the Agency will use this consensus-based language in its proposed regulations, and AAI Committee members will refrain from commenting negatively on the consensus-based regulatory language.

The purpose of initiating a reg neg is to frontload potential conflict among stakeholders and to create a forum for the disparate interests of stakeholders to be integrated into a clear, concise, enforceable regulation. If the Committee is able to achieve final consensus on all issues, the initiating agency commits to use the agreement as the basis of its NPRM. The negotiators agree not to comment negatively on any aspect of the NPRM so long as it reflects their agreement.

This means that if a Committee member agreed to a section of the standard he or she did not wholeheartedly support but as a trade-off for agreements reached on critical issues, they cannot then use the comment period to further their interests in another forum. In entering into this ground rule, stakeholder negotiators agree to respect the totality of the agreement rather than only its most favoured parts. This ground rule makes clear that all contributed to, benefited from, and are bound to the agreement negotiated.

The Agency benefits from this frontloading process as it expects that most future comments will relate to issues that have already been raised by committee members. Thus, it is expected that no new issues are likely to arise during the comment period and therefore, its response to comments should require less external politicking and limit staff effort required for responses to comments following the labour and time-intensive reg neg process.

### *7.2 Substantive deliberations*

Substantive deliberations begin with a determination of the scope of the negotiations. Typically, the initiating federal agency identifies the issues to be negotiated in a federal register notice. This list is then refined and agreed to by the negotiators prior to initiating in-depth substantive negotiations. The AAI list of issues began as the list of ten criteria for environmental assessments specified in the Brownfields Amendments. They are as follows:

(I) The results of an inquiry by an environmental professional.
(II) Interviews with past and present owners, operators, and occupants of the facility for the purpose of gathering information regarding the potential for contamination at the facility.
(III) Reviews of historical sources, such as chain of title documents, aerial photographs, building department records, and land-use records, to determine previous uses and occupancies of the real property since the property was first developed.
(IV) Searches for recorded environmental clean-up liens against the facility that are filed under Federal, state, or local law.
(V) Reviews of Federal, state, and local government records, waste disposal records, underground storage tank records, and hazardous waste handling, generation, treatment, disposal, and spill records, concerning contamination at or near the facility.
(VI) Visual inspections of the facility and of adjoining properties.
(VII) Specialized knowledge or experience on the part of the defendant. [Defendant or owner cannot hide information not uncovered by environmental professional].
(VIII) The relationship of the purchase price to the value of the property, if the property was not contaminated.
(IX) Commonly known or reasonably ascertainable information about the property.
(X) The degree of obviousness of the presence or likely presence of contamination at the property, and the ability to detect the contamination by appropriate investigation.

In addition to the ten criteria, the AAI committee also identified additional issues, such as how to reduce potential disruptions to the real estate market during the transition to the federal standard and how to ensure that the standard for conducting all appropriate inquiry would be sufficiently comprehensive, without being over burdensome, to facilitate compliance with additional statutory requirements that require landowners to stop any continuing release; prevent any threatened future release; prevent or limit any human, environmental, or natural resource exposure to any previously released hazardous substance; and comply with any land-use restrictions.

After it reached agreement on the scope of the negotiations, the AAI Negotiated Rulemaking Committee 'workshopped' each issue. This is the effort to identify sub-issues and uncover key stakeholder concerns and level of importance for each major issue.

Multiple sub-issues were embedded within each criterion. For example, for the first criterion regarding the environmental professional, committee members identified sub-issues of ensuring the quality, integrity and objectivity of an investigation without imposing significantly burdensome costs; the need to define inquiry; the specific qualifications and level of experience to be required of an environmental professional; the role of an environmental professional and identification of the parts of the assessment that must be performed by an environmental professional; and the significance of any signature or seal placed on a final report by an environmental professional.

For the criterion related to historical sources, they identified sub-issues such as the appropriate shelf life of an assessment, the number and type of documents to be searched and reviewed; how far back in time a search should extend; and how to document searches.

After workshopping the issues, some resolved quickly and others required multiple consultation discussions, work groups between meetings to develop proposals, and negotiations and review over several months.

When verbal agreements in concept were reached, the EPA drafting team translated them into draft regulatory language. These drafts were distributed to the AAI Committee and the public prior to the next negotiating session for review and discussion with their constituents. Over the course of the next meetings, the draft language was reviewed and revised until consensus was reached on the issue as reflected in the regulatory language. Such interim consensus on a particular issue was considered a tentative agreement to allow for reopening issues that were impacted by agreements reached on issues discussed later in the negotiations. In addition, because a consensus agreement must cover all issues of the complete standard, nothing was agreed until everything was agreed. Once a tentative agreement on an issue was reached, it was not part of a future meeting agenda unless it was affected by another issue or until the final review of all issues.

The series of tentative agreements reduced the agenda for each meeting and provided the time needed to negotiate more difficult issues. When agreements in concept were not reached after intensive discussions of an issue, the EPA drafting team prepared text for the various options under discussion and/or left spaces on the emerging draft document to indicate those issues that required further discussion.

The momentum generated by reaching tentative agreements helped provide focus and momentum to resolve the most difficult issues, which remained unresolved until the very last meeting. After tentative agreements were reached on all issues, the Committee reviewed each one to ensure consistency across the entire proposed regulatory text.

The regulatory negotiations also provided a means for integrating expert information and public concern into the deliberations. In the AAI Reg Neg, the interested public provided comments at committee meetings, submitted written comments, and, in some cases, were invited as expert panelists to brief the

Committee or participate on work groups. For example, ASTM International voluntary consensus standard experts provided presentations on particular provisions for the Committee. See Figure 7.1 for the AAI Reg Neg Process Map, a graphic presentation of the component parts of the negotiated rulemaking process.

Throughout reg neg process, stakeholders collectively grappled with complicated, divisive issues to clarify potential regulatory ambiguities. Most of the issues were resolved through amicable discussion, clarification of issues, and discussions of details, often of expected exceptions to the usual case. For example, the Brownfields Amendment criteria require a visual inspection of the property being assesssed. The key issues discussed included what should be inspected, visual inspections of adjoining properties and how to create a limited provision to allow for the liability defense when an on-site visual inspection is impossible due to physical limitations, remote location or other inability to gain access to the subject property.

There was general agreement that the standard should allow for an exemption from the on-site visual inspection requirement in limited circumstances. The standard would require that a good faith effort be taken to gain access to the subject property, that any exemption be confined to extenuating circumstances beyond 'mere refusal' for access to the site and that the regulation require

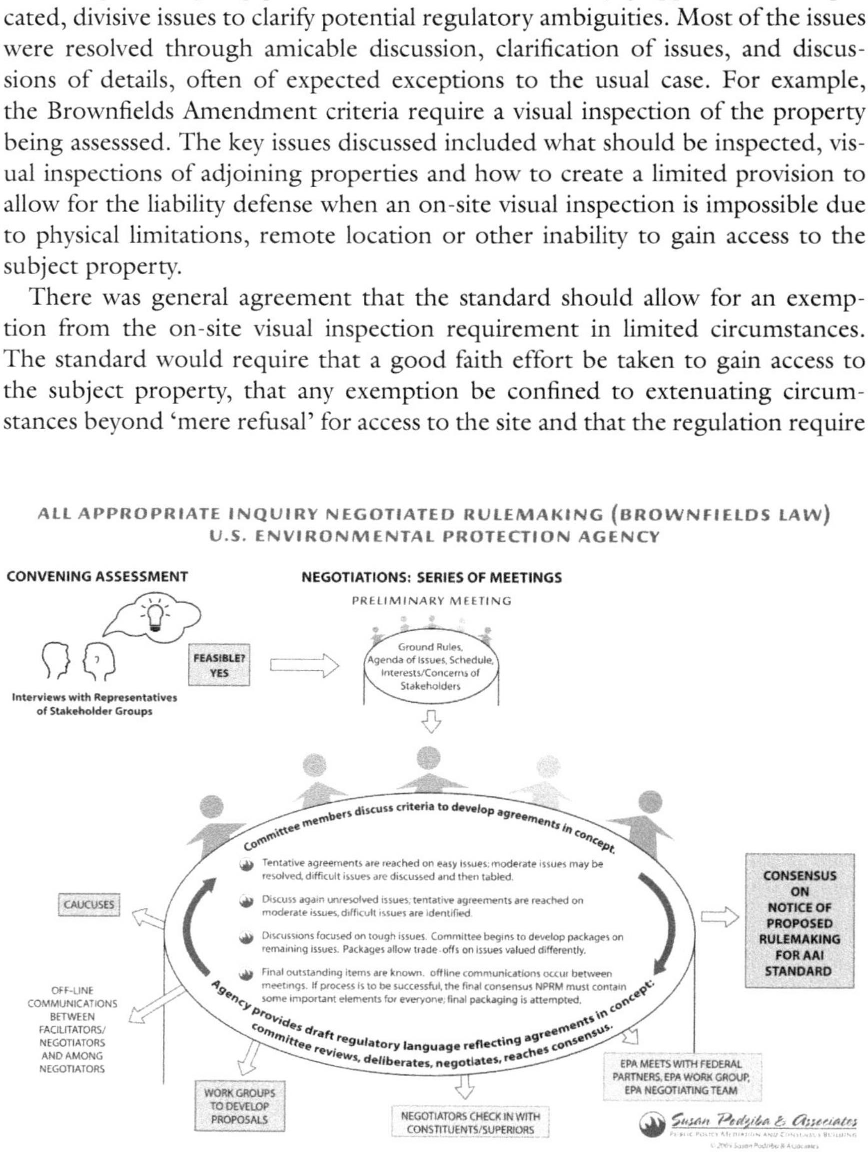


*Figure 7.1* Process Map of the All Appropriate Inquiries Negotiated Rulemaking

documentation of efforts taken to gain access for an on-site inspection and how information obtained through other criteria compensate for the lack of an on-site visual inspection.

The decisions regarding the on-site visual inspection requirement of the AAI standard illustrates the impact of Committee deliberations. Committee members discussed extensively the merits and difficulties associated with requiring visual inspections of properties to be conducted on-site (i.e. within the property boundaries). This issue was relevant for requirements to conduct a visual inspection of the subject property as well as adjoining properties. As early as the convening interviews, municipal representatives asserted that in extraordinary situations, they cannot gain access to properties prior to taking title or acquiring the property, particularly in circumstances such as bankruptcy and tax diligence where properties may be bought through public auction. They were concerned that without building flexibility into the visual inspection requirement (i.e. allowing for visual inspections from surrounding properties or public right-of-ways), these properties would continue to lie fallow because municipalities would not risk incurring CERCLA liability to develop them.

On the other hand, other committee members, especially those from state government and public interest organizations, were wary of providing exceptions to the visual on-site inspection requirement that might result in contaminated properties being acquired and targeted for redevelopment prior to obtaining adequate information to support proper clean-up and protection of public health. Absent a clear indication of the actual physical conditions of a property prior to acquisition, purchasers may not fully understand the financial implications associated with the clean-up and redevelopment of a contaminated property. Committee members raised concerns about the possibility of purchasers acquiring properties without the advantage of an environmental professional observing property conditions by physically walking the property. EPA, in particular, was concerned that liability protections for prospective purchasers could be claimed without a purchaser having sufficient information about the physical conditions of the property.

The Committee worked diligently to develop language that both accounted for extraordinary situations and provided sufficient levels of protection for human health and the environment. Ultimately, given that AAI is a first step in establishing a basis for seeking liability protection, the AAI Negotiated Rulemaking Committee developed a solution that established standards for the collection of information prior to property acquisition without imposing significant burdens upon prospective property owners prior to obtaining ownership of a property.

The Committee agreed to link the visual inspection to the objectives outlined in an earlier section of the standard that outlined performance objectives Concerning inspection of adjoining properties, EPA stated that potential buyers and environmental professionals can request access to adjacent properties, but owners are not required to provide such access. Therefore, the standard allows for visual inspection of adjoining properties from points adjacent to property lines.

Another interesting discussion occurred for the criterion of interviews with past and present owners, operators, and occupants to establish historic uses.

Committee members agreed that the collection of information regarding the types of business operations that occurred at the property from persons familiar with the property is essential to determining potential environmental issues at a property. A key issue related to the collection of such information was how to to obtain such information when a property is abandoned and information from current owners or tenants is not available. This issue led to a discussion of how to clarify the definition of 'abandoned properties'.

Committee members decided to include in the regulation a definition of 'abandoned properties' and to link the interview requirements to objectives and performance factors to emphasize the need to collect specific types of information during the conduct of the AAI investigations, regardless of its specific source (i.e. information not obtainable through interviews should be sought from other sources). In addition, committee members discussed the merits of including a requirement to indentify and interviewi neighbours to gain commonly known information in cases where a property is abandoned. There was a great deal of discussion regarding whether or not neighbours should be contacted for such properties. Some urged that neighbours would likely know what types of businesses were located on a nearby property and what types of general activities took place on the site. Some environmental professionals opposed the requirement of going door-to-door to consult with neighbours.

Ultimately, it was agreed that if past owners or operators of the property were not known or not reachable for interviews, neighbours could be interviewed in their place. Environmental professionals would need to document efforts made to conduct interviews with current owners and tenants. This issue revealed an unexpected alignment of interests that carried through much of the negotations. For issues that reduced risk and required increased regulatory stringencies, banking industry representatives and the environmental justice advocates worked together to ensure that the properties would not create financial risks for bankers and health risks to the community.

The discussisons regarding the need to obtain information during interviews also provided clarity and justification for tailoring the regulation around a set of objectives and performance standards. Committee members recognized that requiring the collection of certain essential information was much more important than dictating the manner in which it is collected. Therefore, the Committee established a clear set of objectives, or the need to collect certain types of information, for example, current and past uses, types of hazardous substances managed, current and past corrective actions to address environmental contamination, institutional controls at the property and engineering controls in place at the property. Much of the rest of the regulation then prescribes methods for obtaining the necessary information established in the objectives, for example, through interviews, inspections, historic sources, databases and government records.

The Committee also establish performance standards for the conduct of the AAI investigation that placed parameters around the general procedures for obtaining the necessary information and the extent of efforts necessary to meet the objectives. The Committee negotiated performance standards that established that information gathered to support the objectives of the AAI information should be publicly available, obtainable from its source within reasonable time and cost constraints and such information must be practicably reviewed. In addition, it was established that collected information should be reviewed and evaluated for its thoroughness and reliability.

The establishment of objectives and performance standards was a break through for the AAI Negotiated Rulemaking Committee and eased many aspects of their subsequent negotiations. The need to caveat specific information collection requirements or establish rigid procedures for each form of information collection was alleviated by the fact that objectives and performance standards established the types of information that needed to be obtained without dictating a specific method of collection for each type of information.

Tailoring the regulation around a set of clear objectives and performance standards did lead however, later in the negotions, to a particularly thorny issue. Late in the negotiations the AAI Reg Neg Committee had extensive negotiations concerning what to do if required information, could not be found or obtained. Their ensuing question was: Could an AAI investigation be deemed complete (or would a prospective purchaser be in compliance with the regulation) if there were 'data gaps?' A committee member representing environmental interests was particularly concerned that an AAI investigation had to result in the collection of all required information. Lengthy, and somewhat contentious, discussions amongst the committee members over how to deal with an inability to obtain essential information, as defined in the regulation's objectives, came close to unraveling much of the progress made by the Committee. However, committee members were successful in negotiating a solution. Data gaps judged to be 'significant' by the environmental professional (i.e. situations where the lack of certain information affected the environmental professional's ability to draw conclusions regarding the environmental conditions of the property) must be documented and the significance of the data gaps must be documented in a final report.

The most difficult issue to resolve, and the final outstanding issue was the definition of the environmental professional, which would determine who would be able to conduct environmental assessments.

The financial component of this issue loomed large regarding the market share of different companies and the cost of the assessment. However, for EPA and many other stakeholders, the critical interest was the actual expertise required to conduct an AAI assessment. AAI is essentially research to evaluate a property for potential environmental contamination based on current and historical uses of the site and its surroundings.

The definition of environmental professional came down to who was best suited, or who should be trusted to conduct the AAI assessment. A coalition of parties representing professional engineers and geologists felt strongly that environmental professionals needed to hold a degree in geology or hydrology, or had to be a licensed professional engineer or licensed professional geologist to be able to accurately conduct an environmental assessment. Many other negotiators opposed this requirement because the AAI assessment does not include hyrologic or geologic study but rather was centred on researching and collecting available information to answer the questions of whether or not current and historic uses of a property suggested the likelihood of environmental contamination at the property, which might then trigger the need for a phase two, or more comprehensive environmental assessment. The phase two assessment more typically requires expertise in geology, hydrology, and chemical engineering.

Of the stakeholder negotiators with experience conducting phase one assessments, many focused on the need to establish a definition of environmental professional that focused on an individual's level of expertise or number of years of experience in conducting phase I site assessments. Many pointed out the need for strong research skills and spoke of employees with history degrees as among those most effective in conducting phase I assessments.

The Committee discussed numerous issues embedded within the definition of environmental professional (EP) including: the possibility of an EP supervising or overseeing the conduct of the work such that others can perform AAI tasks; requiring that only persons meeting the definition of EP be allowed to participate in an AAI investigation, experience requirements; educational requirements; a possible grandfathering clause for those with a certain level of prior experience in conducting phase I investigations without having a required degree; and reliance on state licensing laws.

To further these discussions, between meetings, work groups held conference calls in an effort to develop consensus proposals, and EPA collated and distributed the numerous public comments it received on this issue. The two primary issues raised in the public comments, which provided feedback on proposals offered during prior negotiating sessions, concerned a proposal to require certifications from private certifying organizations within the definition of 'EP' and whether or not to exclude from the definition of 'EP' individuals with experience performing environmental assessments, who do not have science degrees.

EPA continually reiterated that it could not agree to a definition of 'environmental professional' that would require the Agency to develop a process for reviewing and approving private certifying programs. To do so would require a lengthy and ongoing mechanism for determining which programs were acceptable as well as ensuring that there were no changes, over time, in the requirements of approved programs.

Ultimately, to reach agreement on the final issue and therefore, final consensus on all issues, the AAI Negotiated Rulemaking Committee agreed to require the equivalent of: three years of full-time relevant experience for individuals with a professional engineer or geologist license; three years of full-time relevant experience for an individual licensed or certified to perform environmental site assessments by the federal government or a state, tribe or U.S. territory; and five years of full-time relevant experience for individuals with a baccalaureate or higher degree in a relevant discipline of engineering, environmental science or earth science. Individuals who do not have any of the aforementioned licenses, certifications, or degrees, would be required to have a baccalaureate degree and the equivalent of ten years of full-time relevant experience prior to the date of promulgation of the all appropriate inquiry regulation. In addition, EPs conducting AAI are expected to determine the applicability of any relevant state professional licensing requirements. EP are also expected to remain current in their fields through participation in continuing education or other activities, and they should be able to demonstrate such efforts.

Although this resolved issues of the definition of EP, the coalition of engineers demanded, as part of this agreement, an addition to another section of the standard: results of an inquiry by an EP (statement by the EP). This required, as part of the report, a declarative statement by the EP that he or she meets the requirements of the definition of EP, has the qualifications necessary to assess the subject property and has developed and performed the AAI in conformance with the requirements of the all appropriate inquiry regulation.

This was very reluctantly agreed to by all other negotiators. The momentum of the group was that its hard work should not fail as a result of this demand. And so it was the final element required for closure on the only outstanding issue.

## *7.3 Reaching final consensus*

With no dissent on turning all their prior tentative agreements into a final consensus agreement, the AAI negotiators reached final consensus on all issues subject to negotiations. In accordance with the AAI Negotiated Rulemaking Committee's ground rules, EPA published a proposed rule based upon and including the consensus language, and the committee members did not provide formal negative comments on the consensus language presented in the Notice of Proposed Rulemaking.

Final consensus was reached at 12:08 p.m. EST on November 14, 2003, on all issues of the proposed all appropriate inquiry regulation. EPA published the NPRM in the *Federal Register* on August 26, 2004. The public comment period commenced with that publication and continued until October 24, 2005. EPA published the final rule in the *Federal Register* on November 1, 2005, and its effective date was November 1, 2006.

AAI Negotiated Rulemaking Committee members had the intrinsic wisdom, knowledge, and expertise needed to prepare enforceable and cost-effective standards to conduct AAI with limited unintended consequences. In sponsoring the AAI Reg Neg, EPA called into public service people from across the United States with the greatest expertise on AAI and brownfields redevelopment. The power of negotiated rulemaking is found in the deliberations of such people. No one person can know everything needed to develop complex rules; not even with support from a team of consultants. But 25 passionate people with differing perspectives can meld their ideas to become sufficiently unified to develop effective national standards.

## 8. The post-reg neg process

### *8.1 Internal negotiations with EPA offices*

Every proposed and final rulemaking published by EPA goes through a formal regulatory development process. All interested EPA program offices are invited to participate on a work group established for the purposed of developing a single rulemaking. The process is rigid with required steps and procedures and was not designed or ever modified to accommodate negotiated rulemakings.

Members of the EPA internal rulemaking work group, unlike the members of the AAI Negotiated Rulemaking Committee and the members of the other federal agencies work group, did not have interests aligned with those who would be directly affected by the proposed and final rulemakings. Some members of the EPA work group were most interested in the ease of enforcement and compliance with the standard, others were merely interested in the cost-benefit analysis required for the internal rulemaking process, and still other members focused on the effect of the standard on the states, tribes, and environmental communities. As a result, much of the internal EPA negotiations regarding the proposed rule centred not on the technical aspects of investigative steps of the proposed rule, but on the potential costs and impacts of the consensus product that resulted from reg neg. Several members of the internal EPA work group were convinced that the Agency did not need to accept the consensus agreement of the AAI Negotiated Rulemaking Committee as the proposed rule, but that the internal work group could consider it as just one of many options. It became the job of the Designated Federal Official to be a champion for proposed rule developed and accepted by the AAI Negotiated Rulemaking Committee.

After many months of internal negotiations over potential alternatives for a proposed rule and the consideration of costs and impacts of such alternatives, the EPA work group accepted the product of the negotiated rulemaking as the preferred option for the proposed rule. That the AAI Negotiated Rulemaking Committee reached consensus on a proposed rule provided critical leverage for the Designated Federal Official's (DFO) success in moving it forward. Upon completion of the internal EPA negotiations, the rulemaking package – the proposed rule and cost-benefit analysis – was sent to the OMB for review and approval. OMB, as part of its review of the proposed rule, sent the package to other federal agencies for their review and approval. Given that EPA staff had involved other affected federal agency representatives in the rulemaking development process and had solicited their input and comments during the duration of the negotiated rulemaking process, this aspect of the review process went very smoothly.

### *8.2 Working with ASTM international*

Prior to Congress directing EPA to develop standards and practices for conducting AAI, and in response to the 1986 amendments to CERCLA when Congress required that parties conduct AAI prior to claiming the innocent landowner defense, an industry standard was developed and adopted by ASTM International, an international standards developing organization.

In the absence of federal regulations or standards establishing procedures to comply with the statutorily imposed requirement to conduct 'AAI' to qualify as an 'innocent landowner', ASTM International's environmental standards committee ('E50') established a task group to develop and eventually update a standard practice. Until EPA developed and finalized the federal regulation for AAI in 2005, the ASTM E1527–2000 Phase I Environmental Site Assessment Standard remained the generally accepted industry standard for the conduct of AAI, and became the interim standard during the EPA AAI rulemaking.

Given that both the customary business standard and the congressionally imposed interim standard for the conduct of AAI was the ASTM developed standard practice, EPA determined that any effort to develop a federal regulation should be coordinated with ASTM International. ASTM's members were familiar with the development and use of the interim standard and could lend their experience and expertise to EPA's efforts to establish a federal regulation. The chair of the ASTM task group was appointed as a member of the AAI Negotiated Rulemaking Committee.

Due to the general acceptance of and the regulated community's familiarity with the ASTM Phase I Environmental Site Assessment Standard, EPA decided to coordinate the federal regulation with the development of a revised or updated ASTM standard to increase industry acceptance and general regulatory compliance.

During the negotiated rulemaking process, committee members representing EPA and ASTM kept the AAI Negotiated Rulemaking Committee informed of the ASTM task group's discussions and relayed the results of the Committee's discussions and negotiations to the ASTM task group members. However, significant negotiations with ASTM did not commence until the completion of the AAI Negotiated Rulemaking Committee negotiations and EPA's publication of the proposed rule.

Upon publication of the NPRM in the *Federal Register*, EPA accepted public comment on the proposed rule for 90 days. During the public comment period, EPA worked with the ASTM task group to gather additional input and insight related to the provisions of the proposed rule. Patricia Overmeyer served as the Designated Federal Official for the development of the AAI standards was also a member of the ASTM task group that was responsible for updating the E1527 Phase I Site Assessment Standard. EPA was concurrently accepting and reviewing formal public comments received in response to the proposed rule and working with ASTM members on an update to its Phase I Environmental Site Assessment Standard.

The liveliest and most intense negotiations with ASTM members centred on the same issues that were of greatest interest and concern to the AAI Negotiated Rulemaking Committee and the Federal Work Group. These were: setting qualifications for who could conduct or oversee the conduct of the investigations (i.e. the definition of 'EP'), when the investigation must be completed (how soon prior to the closing of a property transaction) and the shelf life of a completed all appropriate inquiry investigation. In addition, ASTM members showed significant interest in the signature requirement for the final report.

ASTM members willingly worked with EPA to ensure that its updated standard would be compliant with the statutory criteria for AAI. The result of ASTM task group and committee negotiations resulted in a revised ASTM Phase I Environmental Site Assessment Standard that EPA considered compliant with the statutory criteria and the final federal regulation developed through the negotiated rulemaking process. In its final rule for AAI (70 FR 66070), EPA referenced the ASTM standard and noted that its use would demonstrate compliance with the federal regulation for AAI.

EPA and ASTM successfully built upon the proposed rule negotiated by the AAI Negotiated Rulemaking Committee, took into account public comments received on the proposed rule, and negotiated a consensus solution that updated the previous ASTM Phase I Environmental Site Assessment Standard and remained compliant with the statutory requirements set forth by Congress. The result was a final federal regulation and an updated ASTM industry standard that could work for all stakeholders and be compliant with statutory requirements

## 9. Post-enactment

The publication of the final rule setting federal regulations for the conduct of AAI provided a necessary degree of certainty to purchasers of contaminated properties and lenders financing such property transactions. Raising the level of certainty regarding the type and level of due diligence necessary to qualify for certain liability protections under CERCLA increases the likelihood that brownfields properties will be purchased. Prospective purchasers can acquire properties knowing they would not be held responsible for previous contamination at a property if they comply with the AAI Rule prior to purchasing a property and follow other statutorily imposed 'due care requirements' following property acquisition. The most important impact of the level of certainty provided by the final regulation probably is related to the degree to which lenders are willing to finance brownfields property transactions. Knowing that prospective property owners would not be held liable for past contamination reduces some of the risk associated with loans on potentially contaminated properties. The greater availability of financing for the purchase of brownfields properties increases the potential demand for such properties and additionally, increases the potential for such properties to be cleaned up and redeveloped. This is not to say that all brownfields properties became more attractive investments as a result of the final rule. Other factors such as location, available labour and proximity to suppliers and other markets significantly affect all real estate market transactions. However, certainty regarding environmental liabilities significantly reduces some of the risk of real estate investments, therefore making financing for such investments more easily obtainable.

Another significant impact of the final rule was to further establish the ASTM E1527 Phase I Environmental Site Assessment Standard as the accepted industry standard for the conduct of property due diligence. General market familiarity with the ASTM standard and its acceptance as the customary business standard greatly increases the potential for compliance with the federal regulation. Overall compliance with the federal regulation further affects the stability of the commercial real estate market by alleviating questions regarding the level of due diligence conducted and potential liability for prior contamination at a property. Clarity regarding required practices and familiarity with the requirements limit the level of uncertainty associated with transactions of potentially contaminated commercial property. Any reduction in uncertainty affecting transactions of brownfields properties increases the potential for community revitalization and sustainable growth.

## Conclusion

Negotiated rulemaking offers the opportunity for federal agencies and relevant stakeholders to work together to develop technically accurate, implementable and enforceable regulations that meet their intended public policy goals within the context of resource and political constraints. In addition, as a result of in-depth deliberations, the regulated communities and the public better understand and respect the government's role in working to balance the interests of a multitude of stakeholders as it seeks to develop, implement, and enforce regulations under complex, real-world conditions. Government officials also come to better understand the interests and perspectives of stakeholders, including the regulated community, and the public. Finally, anecdotal evidence suggests that compliance with regulations developed through negotiated rulemakings may occur more quickly and with less government involvement.

Developing regulations through negotiated rulemakings provides for the integration for technical expertise to government agency regulation and fosters education and compliance with new standards among the regulated community. Although the time commitment for committee members is substantial, members of AAI Negotiated Rulemaking Committee found great benefit in participating.

For the AAI negotiated rulemaking, every expertise required for developing the standards resided within the collective wisdom and experience of the committee members and the public that participated on panels and work groups and provided public comment. This expertise, combined with the hard work of harmonizing perspectives and interests, resulted in a rule that is more likely to achieve its public policy goals with limited unintended consequences than those produced with stakeholder involvement restricted to a formal comment period.

As Congress stated in the NRA, Section 561,

> Adversarial rulemaking deprives the affected parties and the public of the benefits of face-to-face negotiations and cooperation in developing and reaching agreement on a rule. It also deprives them of the benefits of shared information, knowledge, expertise, and technical abilities possessed by the affected parties.

AAI Negotiated Rulemaking Committee members gained from the opportunity to articulate regulatory needs, areas of uncertainty, and the impact that different regulatory options would have on their industries and the public. The AAI process resulted in a standard that balances the goals of brownfields redevelopment and community revitalization with protection of public health and the environment and is rooted in the complex real-world conditions within which the AAI standard must be implemented.

EPA benefited from knowledge of industry, community interests, and other government entities. The negotiated rulemaking process enabled EPA to benefit from the knowledge and expertise of the regulated community, that is, those who will implement the standard in their daily professional lives. In addition, representatives from groups that advocate on behalf of the public, and especially those representing specific community organizations, raised concerns and shared their understandings of likely impacts of the AAI standard on the public health and sustainability of individual communities. Finally, state, tribal, and local government officials provided information concerning program integration and implementation challenges.

The AAI negotiated rulemaking process significantly contributed to public education concerning the AAI standard. The AAI Negotiated Rulemaking Committee included representatives of trade associations that educate their members about government regulations. In addition, members of the public attended meetings of the Committee, and EPA made all committee documents available to the public on the Internet or through the public docket.

The affected public is, therefore, well versed in the AAI standard and the rationales for each of its elements – an infrastructure of knowledgeable individuals exists for ongoing public education of the AAI standard's requirements. In addition, the committee members and members of the public who followed the negotiated rulemaking process better understand the limitations of public sector decision making and the role government plays in working to accomplish its mission as it balances the interests of a multitude of stakeholders.

# 8 The co-construction of projects with environmental externalities

*Antonia Bousbaine*[1] *and Christopher Bryant*[2]

## Introduction

This chapter focuses on the environment (Figure 8.1) and issues regarding different types of projects and their environmental consequences (potential and actual), and discusses the relationship between, on the one hand, the co-construction of 'projects' as a mediation approach to dealing with the negative consequences of any project before a project is determined and put in place and, on the other hand, environmental mediation once the project is operational. When dealing with the natural 'environment', we are of course basically dealing with the values of human society associated with the environment.

'Projects' can involve many things including government policies, programs and initiatives as well as projects initiated by other actors. Our focus is on projects that involve the development of infrastructure of different types and buildings as well as territorial development plans. The latter point reflects the idea that effective development plans, especially strategic development plans and planning processes, under the best of circumstances already involve the discussion of potential conflicts relating to the environment, and a strategic planning process with real community involvement would have already initiated discussion between actors with potentially conflicting values regarding environmental impacts. Such processes are generally ongoing and so when new 'projects' appear on the scene, a process is already in place to involve the different segments of the population and pertinent collective actors[3] in discussions about new projects.

In the following two sections, we first discuss the nature of co-construction and second how co-construction can contribute to avoiding environmental conflicts.

1 Antonia Bousbaine, professor of geography CFW, Wallonie-Bruxelles, 20/12 Avenue de Général du Gaulle, 59880 Saint Saulve, France; and doctoral candidate in the Laplec Laboratory in the University of Liege. Tel: 00–33–626661088; email address: dayasol23@yahoo.fr

2 Christopher Bryant, full professor (1990–2014), adjunct professor (2014-present), Department of Geography, University of Montreal, CP 6128 Succursale Centre-ville, Montréal (Québec), H3C 3J7; and Adjunct Professor (2012-présent), School of Environmental Design and Rural Development, University of Guelph, Guelph (Ontario), N1G 2W1. Tel: 519–846–1361; email address: christopher.robin.bryant@gmail.com

3 Collective actor is a commonly used term to refer to governments at any level, agencies, organizations, associations or any other type of grouping of people that acts as a unit

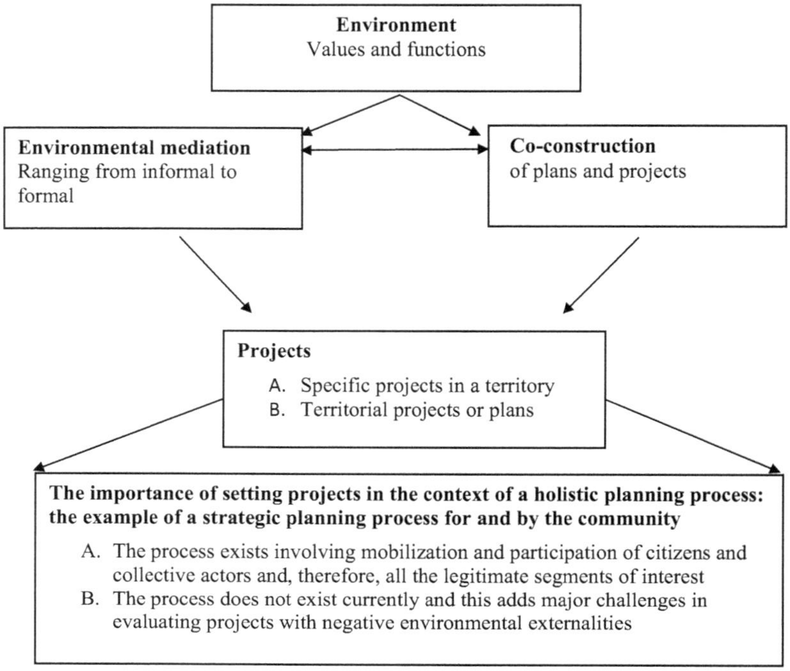


*Figure 8.1* Projects with potential environmentally negative externalities: the roles of environmental mediation and co-construction

In the final section, we discuss differences between North America (especially Canada) and Europe (especially France and Belgium); several examples of different 'projects' are provided to reinforce our arguments.

## 1 What is 'environmental mediation?'

Increasingly, the term 'mediation' is used in all domains – i.e., not just environmental mediation. Many conceptualizations exist including that of Thouzard,[4] who notes that conciliation refers both to negotiation when mediation is used in a more limited sense as well as when it is associated with a more complete meaning as expressed by anthropologist Leroy[5] and Bonafé-Schmitt[6]; while all these authors sought to refine the definition, the main dimensions remain the linkage between mediation and conciliation.

4 Thouzard, H., *La médiation et la résolution des conflits*, PUF, Paris, 1977, 424.
5 Le Roy, É., "La médiation mode d'emploi" (1995) 29 *Droit et Société* 39.
6 Bonafé-Schmitt, J.-P., *La médiation: une justice douce*, Syros-Alternatives, Paris, 1992, 279.

For some it is a special response mode to manage differences in point of view.[7] For others, it is about appeasing conflicting views, with mediation becoming a "form of conflict management".[8] Given these very initial elements, how does mediation work in what domain and how well. What results can we expect? And if there are results, how were they achieved? To what extent does mediation become an alternative to having to live with divergent views among stakeholders?

Despite different opinions, mediation has become a domain in which the intervention of a third party is fundamental. French law defines judiciary mediation as

> [Translation] Mediation (. . .) means any structured process, whatever the name by which two or more parties attempt to reach an agreement for an amicable settlement of their dispute with the assistance of a third party mediator chosen by them or designated, with their agreement, by the judge hearing the case.[9]

In terms of mediation, the distinction is often made between 'formal' conflict resolution which refers to a rights-based process that focuses on claims and the information that supports the claim, whereas 'informal' conflict resolution refers to a situation where there are generally two parties and both discuss their issues with a third-party person who is neutral and independent – e.g., a mediator.[10]

We note the existence of many forms of conflict resolution which are not always highlighted in official texts. Indeed, depending on the situation mediation can be used in different ways involving different numbers of actors but always aiming at an 'amicable' or non-adjudicative outcome.

Environmental mediation takes as its point of departure a conflict (actual or potential) between different parties, each of which advances its own interests; the intervention of a third party who is neutral is not always able to resolve the conflict, and in some cases, as we shall see next, legal authorities become involved. Without dealing with real failures, we will discuss examples where this mediation at least had the merit of exposing real environmental issues.

7 Faget, J., "L'impensé de la médiation: contre-culture ou soft power" (2008) 72 *Empan* 74.

8 Cadoret, A., "La médiation, un outil pour une gestion durable des conflits d'usage" *ASRDLF& ERSA congress*, Paris, 2007, 14.

9 "La médiation (. . .) s'entend de tout processus structuré, quelle qu'en soit la dénomination, par lequel deux ou plusieurs parties tentent de parvenir à un accord en vue de la résolution amiable de leurs différends, avec l'aide d'un tiers le médiateur, choisi par elles ou désigné, avec leur accord, par le juge saisi du litige" (Ordonnance n°2011–1540 du 16/11/2011). "Mediation (. . .) means any structured process, regardless of denomination, by which two or more parties attempt to reach agreement for the friendly resolution of their disputes with the assistance of a third party, a mediator, chosen by them or appointed, with their agreement, by the judge hearing the case" (translation: Ordonnance n°2011–1540 of the 16/11/2011).

10 Douglas, W. and M.A. Bush, 2007. *Conflict Resolution: Formal and Informal Processes*. Access: www.scribd.com/doc/5392007/Conflict-Resolution-Informal-and-Formal-Processes.

Environmental issues play an increasingly important role in society and 'environment' is more and more present in political discourse. The damage suffered by the environment has become a central issue in many international conferences, from the United Nations Conference in 1972 onwards. The environment has thus become a subject of controversy,[11] and even defining it accurately is no easy matter. Nonetheless it has become a major 'issue for society', related to providing a better-quality living environment.[12] All actors thus concerned can participate in debates; it is when potential conflicts arise that some form of 'environmental mediation' becomes important, with the ultimate goal of preserving the best living conditions for both present and future generations. However, in Europe this concept has not reached the level and importance it has in North America, where the concept was initiated and developed.

In terms of the 'co-construction of projects' which, as we will see, can be closely related to mediation or facilitation, the most relevant aspect is a shared vision of all components, understood and analyzed by all stakeholders with a legitimate interest in a 'project' (Figure 8.1). Co-construction implies a willingness to collaborate and achieve success for a project that satisfies all stakeholders. Co-construction respects the diversity of views and perceptions, and involves adopting a comprehensive common language for all actors likely to be affected by a project's implementation. If it appears in the process of any co-construction that nothing draws the actors together to arrive at a mutual agreement, it may eventually lead to some form of tribunal. In the best conditions, co-construction can avoid mediation although the presence of a mediator can be helpful. In fact, from the beginning of any co-construction process nothing prevents the integration of a mediator or a facilitator who would be responsible for ensuring productive discussions and respect for views that initially can be quite divergent. What is important is to ensure the different stakeholders are fully aware of the benefits of a co-construction process. In many cases, a 'leader' can be appointed for each stakeholder, collective actor or segment of legitimate interest; frequently, this is someone who has a very good understanding of the local people and their aspirations. This person would be responsible for reporting the results of discussions between the actors and as-needed support the requests of different actors and segments of the population. Many examples have shown that this can be a major factor leading to success in implementation of a co-constructed project.

The concept of mediation has its roots in the United States in the 1970s, although the culture of mediation had its origins in the pacifist thinking of

11 Cadoret, A., "La médiation, un outil pour une gestion durable des conflits d'usage" *ASRDLF& ERSA congress*, Paris, 2007, 14.

12 Le Louarn, P., "Introduction générale" in A. Gouzien and P. Le Louarn, eds., *Environnement et politique: Constructions juridico-politiques et usages sociaux*, PUR, Rennes, 1996, 9; Charlier, B., *La défense de l'environnement: entre espace et territoire: géographie des conflits environnementaux, déclenchés en France depuis 1974*, Ph.D. thesis in geography, Université de Pau, 1999, 753; Lecourt, A., *Les conflits d'aménagement: analyse théorique et pratique à partir du cas breton*, Ph.D. thesis in Geography, Université de Rennes 2, 2003, 355.

Mennonites and Quakers who had migrated to the United States, with their custom of resolving conflicts through 'mediation' between members of the community itself. The well-known lawyers John Haynes and James Coogler were the initiators of the conceptualization of mediation in the United States, particularly in the family domain. This concept crossed the Quebec border in the late 1970s and was then transmitted to Europe in the late 1980s.[13]

The domains of application became expanded over the years both in North America and Europe. The increasing awareness of environmental impacts since the 1992 Rio Earth Summit put the concept of environmental mediation into the limelight. Mediation is essentially a less expensive way to find a conflict solution, because recourse to legal proceedings is lengthy and are characteristically very expensive for all stakeholders. In the countries across the Atlantic it has found its place, but in Europe while many authors have studied its relevance and the conditions of implementation, and its success, their conclusions remain mixed. Advances are being made, but various examples still underline its limitations. On the other hand, many researchers agree that they see environmental mediation as a process of conflict management in an innovative manner[14]; other observers see it as a real management tool since nothing is defined in advance and individuals with differing views can confront each other. With a mediator who is neutral and maintains distance from the different opinions, the stakeholders and interests involved can exchange opinions and agree, with the help of a mediator, on a 'compromise' that does not harm any of the stakeholders.

The individual is thus at the heart of eventual solutions. The mediator facilitates exchanges and discussions; the mediator does not assume the role of a judge, but ensures the smooth functioning of the process without taking sides. Thus, the mediator does not know the final outcome of the mediation; discussions may be unsuccessful initially and then take a turn in favour of common interests.

Each party present advances its own positions but the mediator ensures that everyone's perspectives start out on an equal footing; indeed, one does not talk about winners and losers but rather a co- constructed project in which each party is at the same level in terms of their respective interests. Mediation allows people to have access to a broad participatory democracy with its principal objective being

13 Castel, R., "L'expert mandaté et l'expert instituant" in J.-G. Vaillancourt, M. Séguin, L. Maheu and L. Cotnoir. *Situations d'expertise et socialisation des savoirs*, Les Presses de l'Université de Montréal : C.R.E.S.A.L., Saint-Étienne, 1985; Jetté, C., B. Levesque, L. Mager and Y. Vaillancourt, *Économie sociale et transformation de l'État-providence dans le domaine de la santé et du bien-être: une recension des écrits (1990–2000)*, PUQ, Sainte-Foy, 2000, 202; Vaillancourt, Y., F. Aubry and C. Jettée, *L'économie sociale dans les services à domicile*, Presses de l'Université du Québec, Québec, 2003, 341; and Vaillancourt, Y., F. Aubry, M. Kearney, L. Thériault and L. Tremblay, "The Contribution of the Social Economy Towards Healthy Social Policy Reforms in Canada: A Quebec Viewpoint" in R. Dennis, ed., *Social Determinants of Health: Canadian Perspectives*, Canadian Scholars' Press Inc., Toronto, 2004, 311–329.

14 Gaddi, D., "Les effets indésirables du processus d'assimilation de la médiation au droit" (2012) 170 *Informations sociales* 28.

the transformation of society and 'living well' together.[15] Thus, there is definitely a significant convergence between co-construction and environmental mediation in a more informal setting. This is certainly the case with strategic development planning processes by the community in which projects and actions are central.

Some authors suggest that the 'parity of participation'[16] is the central part of any mediation particularly when dealing with environmental issues. The environment has become the concern of practically everyone, without distinction of social class and through environmental mediation, the different population segments are on an equal footing and can communicate without any *a priori*; the legitimate interests of each individual are properly identified and considered. The mediator, an impartial and independent person, helps and listens to each person; ideally, all exchanges should be respectful and constructive and placed into the territorial context.

Although environmental mediation aims to involve all segments of the population, we note that at the beginning of the process, some participants can be out of touch with some of the technical realities regarding environmental information (e.g. waste recycling). In such circumstances, mediators must fully assume their role by bringing together the explanatory elements necessary to achieve full equity and progress of the discussions.

Listening and understanding by all parties involved are necessary from the start of a mediation process. Examples have often shown that actions that are relatively informal, in the sense that they simply involve an agreement between the parties that does not require the involvement of a lawyer, can lead to very pertinent results in terms of the development of a 'viable' solution for all parties, especially when it comes to co-constructed projects.

## 2 What do we mean by co-construction?

Co-construction implies that two or more parties can decide that they wish to discuss and come to an agreement on a policy, a program or a project or initiative in which each party has an interest and particular perspectives, and the ultimate output needs to have the support of each party in order to be successful. They do not need a mediator, although the discussion (or discussions if it is determined that several small groups of collective actors can discuss the issues and then share the results of their group discussions in order to arrive at a consensus) obviously needs to be chaired effectively. This is different to mediation in the sense that the co-construction process does not necessarily need to have an independent party to manage the discussions.

Through some examples, we note certain conditions of this co-construction process. Figure 8.1 is a conceptual diagram that presents the different dimensions

15 Faget, J., "L'impensé de la médiation: contre-culture ou soft power" (2012) 72 *Empan* 74.
16 For example, Fraser, N., *Qu'est-ce que la justice sociale? Reconnaissance et redistribution*, La Découverte, Paris, 2005, 178.

and challenges of co-construction. Above all else, the stakeholders in the development of a project must have a real desire for a successful project. This requires that each participant must fully understand their own interests and understand the interests of others involved. Co-construction can also be applied to public environmental policies as well as the development of programs aimed at managing development while respecting the environment. In the strategic planning of territorial development and policies, political bodies need to address citizen participation and their interests well in advance of the presentation of projects; and strategic planning of development can itself be a co-constructed project with participation of citizens and collective actors (see the example of Haliburton County in section 5). Any co-constructed project must from the start attempt to take account of all facets of the project and be prepared to introduce new perspectives as they emerge. This can take several weeks and even months, even resulting in a reorientation of the project. The most complicated task is to agree over the long term on the development of projects that meet the environmental standards and values of population in the territory.

It is undeniable that in recent years the sustainable development concept has become increasingly recognized in the development of territorial planning policies. Since the Rio Earth Summit, the principle of citizen participation has been widely emphasized even if it has not always been effectively pursued. As an example, we can note that the 1992 Act in France, reinforced by the 1995 Act, the Barnier Act,[17] deals with environmental protection and public participation in land-use planning and water management. Of especial importance is the Aarhus Convention,[18] which stresses that everyone has the right to be informed, to be involved in decisions and pursue legal remedies,[19] ratified in 2002 by the French state, and including several other European States. These various legal instruments have in effect promoted public participation in decision making related to environmental management. This gives considerable weight to citizens in, for example, species protection and waste management or whatever else affects the common good of society environmentally. While this is certainly positive, it also means that often the concept of environmental mediation is becoming more and more difficult given the difficulties of finding a solution that satisfies all interested parties. It would also be more than interesting to know what percentage of the population is actually aware of their rights, as well as the rules and regulations that concern the environment.

In many cases the policies (which is one type of project; others include government programs and specific initiatives) put in place can be supported by a co-construction process involving the various segments of the population, particularly when the project is likely to give rise to environmental impacts. It is also

17 *Loi relative au renforcement de la protection de l'environnement*, loi n°95–101 du 2/02/1995.

18 UNECE, *Convention on Access to Information, Public Participation in Decision-making and Access to Justice in Environmental Matters*, 1998.

19 *La Convention d'Aarhus, pilier de la démocratie environnementale*. Access: www.toutsurlenvironnement.fr/Aarhus/la-convention-daarhus-pilier-de-la-democratie-environnementale.

important to reflect on the type of 'governance' required, and what role the average citizen can play in project implementation. Our reflection is based primarily on a very specific type of area: the countryside. We argue that co-construction (of projects and development plans) can avoid formal environmental mediation processes where there is an independent third party to manage the process. Furthermore, this co-construction process converges with environmental mediation as co-construction which is itself a type of environmental mediation when environmental issues are being dealt with or generated. Such a process is likely to involve the different segments of legitimate interest and collective actors right from the outset of discussions about different projects including any overall development plan. Participation and mobilization of citizens is paramount.

In the countryside, many functions coexist and overlap, and these are the same areas where most conflicts are observed.[20] Hence, developing co-constructed projects on different scales (e.g. wind farms and new airports on the one hand and co-habitation involving agricultural activities and non-farm rural residential development on the other) can be valuable for bringing together the government and citizens including farmers. Some projects have been referred to as polluters by their neighbours – which, not surprisingly, lead to the emergence of conflicts. While solutions are often difficult to envisage when there are numerous actors involved, the co-construction of some projects has produced interesting results and satisfied a wide range of actors.

A unique characteristic of co-constructed projects in rural areas is the fact that they are initiated by citizens. Indeed, as shown by Beuret and Trehet,[21] through the analysis of co-constructed projects in rural areas in Brittany, of the 86 projects identified, 70% of the discussions were initiated by people outside the political sphere. By contrast, public policy representatives are not always inclusive of citizens. This has caused real blockages, reflecting a rejection of state control, which for some is synonymous with authority and a lack of understanding of the rural areas in which they live. This can be explained by the fact that representatives of public actors at regional and central state levels rarely come from the same places where the affected populations live and work.

Co-construction could thus become an effective tool for managing environmental mediation when no other solution appears possible. Co-constructing projects can substantially reduce or even avoid conflicts at the very beginning by involving all the actors who actually have some common interests. This process favours the creation and strengthening of relationships between participants during the development and implementation of a project.

Often environmental perceptions differ fundamentally between various actors. Farmers perceive their space as their tool (the land resource); however, the arrival

20 Caron, A. and A. Torre, "Les conflits d'usage dans les espaces ruraux: Une analyse économique" in P. Perrier-Cornet, ed., *À qui appartient l'espace rural?*, Éditions de l'Aube, La Tour d'Aigues, 2002, 1.

21 Beuret, J.-E. and C. Trehet, "Pour la gestion concertée de l'espace rural: appuyer des médiations territoriales", 2001, 43 *Courrier de l'Environnement de l'INRA* 25.

of neo-rural populations in these areas is often due to a variety of reasons including their values regarding landscape amenities and attractive land prices. These populations rarely consider the work of farmers or that of developers wishing to install business parks or shopping centres, projects which are generally far removed from the values of the non-farm residents of these areas.

In such situations, only a co-constructed project may lead to situations of acceptance of each other – a 'living together' environment – and giving raise to little if any negative environmental impact. In our review of numerous examples discussed by researchers, it appears that co-construction is primarily based on dialogue, a mutual respect for each other and, especially, the capacity to listen to others. Of course, the actors have to understand the different dimensions of a project and its potential consequences in order to contribute to the construction of a definite project that is environmentally friendly and acceptable to all.

In many rural areas, it is not always easy to achieve co-constructed projects. A mediator can sometimes be the architect of a co-construction process, so he or she takes on a significant role. The main difficulty is primarily linked to previous policies prevailing in these spaces. Indeed, environmental policies implemented by state entities have often been poorly perceived and understood by the farmers as the principal 'managers' of these areas. Indeed, several decades ago in many Western countries, farmer had been persuaded to adopt the 'productivist' mode of production, now synonymous with negative environmental externalities – including water pollution, soil erosion and loss of biodiversity. The number of scientific articles and texts that have researched and discussed these negative externalities is substantial.[22]

As an example, water management remains a domain where farmers are often seen at the front of the stage. However, other users frequently have a negative perception of the agricultural world, which they accuse of being a 'polluter'. The productivist practices employed by farmers have become increasingly questioned thus destabilizing agriculture in many parts of the developed world, as farmers are asked to modify their work practices once again to adopt different ones promoting a greater respect of the environment.

Nevertheless, some projects eventually materialize. This is where the mediator becomes important, as a person who is very attentive and capable of presenting the arguments that each party can understand. Where there has already been a process of co-construction of a vision and a strategic development plan for a municipality or region, most of the legitimate interests segments have already participated in discussions and a new project can be more easily integrated because of this collaborative approach.

22 Epule, T.E., C.R. Bryant, C. Akkari and O. Daouda, "Can Organic Fertilizers Set the Pace for a Greener Arable Agricultural Revolution in Africa? Analysis, Synthesis and Way Forward" (2015) 47(1) *Land Use Policy* 179–187; Zak, D.P.M., *Reducing Negative Environmental Externalities from Agricultural Production: Methods, Models and Policies*, Ph.D. thesis (Environment & Resources) at the University of Wisconsin-Madison, 2010, 163; *Agroecology: Resilient and Productive*. Access: www.panna.org/agroecology-farming-solutions/agroecology-resilient-productive.

In co-constructed projects, the legitimacy of each actor must be recognized by all participants so that each can fully participate in developing the project. In addition, each actor must acquire a profound knowledge of the project in all its details.[23] Co-construction can be established early on with the support of a resource person (a mediator), designated impartially, who assumes the role of facilitator and guarantor of the respect of the 'rules' of the discussion. In this case, the initial objective is to build a shared vision of the present and future situation and its challenges.[24]

Over the years, environmental impacts, as well as citizens' and collective actors' interests, have taken increasing importance in development plans and territorial development programs, projects or actions. This can be explained by the fact that in France, as in many other countries, there are many laws that support environmental conservation. Moreover, the inclusion of citizens is perceived as central for achieving 'participatory democracy'. With this in mind, political authorities should no longer 'impose' projects without consulting the public in advance – although many still do. Consultation can take a variety of forms including public surveys (e.g. through the Études d'Incidences Environnementales (EIE) or Environmental Impacts Studies), that are open to all actors who have the right to express their opinion and be involved in processes based on the mobilization of the appropriate collective actors and population segments. EIE allows all citizens to have access to potentially all data available related to a project development that could have impacts on the environment. By being fully informed, the public can make its views known and challenge, if necessary, the negative impacts that could result from a particular project. When all stakeholders are involved in the co-construction process, they can contribute to modifying projects and influencing the various actors.

The particular case of the installation of a wind turbine farm often gives rise to significant concerns by residents living nearby. Opposition committees are often organized to challenge these projects which are habitually large in scale, covering a relatively large area and, therefore, involving many actors. Although the desire to involve as many people in the acceptance of such a project is quite appropriate, people participating in this co-construction do not necessarily all focus on the same issues and agree to the project's final development. This is when some form of mediation could be very useful. In addition to these potential human health impacts, animals can also be affected (e.g. lack of milk productivity, aggression and hostility) and there are also impacts on the landscape which in many cases is the main impetus for the organization of defense committees in many developed countries.

23 Ibid.

24 Guiheneuf, P.-Y., "Encourager la participation: quelle formation des animateurs et des acteurs locaux à la médiation environnementale" Communication to the colloquium *Recherche de réflexion et d'échanges sur les pratiques éducatives? L'éducation à l'environnement pour un développement durable : informer, former ou éduquer*, IUFM, Université de Montpellier, 2007.

However, some surveys conducted by researchers show that the majority of non-farm residents agree with the development of these renewable energies but at the same time the NIMBY perspective (Not in My Back Yard) is also present. Thus, one of the major concerns is focused on the destruction of the landscape by the installation of wind turbine farms – e.g. in the Department of Aude, one of the windiest regions of France and where since 1990 many such projects have been developed.[25]

In this territory, there are multiple functions of the land and, as a result, there are people whose attachment to the land diverge and for whom the living environment does not possess the same values. This has the effect of giving rise to environmental conflicts between them. The developers or promoters of these projects have a definite financial interest and they receive subsidies and other types of aid, while for the other actors, the issue is basically one of defending the territory where they live. Thus, co-construction appears necessary even though it is not an easy task, especially as the state often seems to play a double game, on the one hand wanting to preserve the environment and on the other hand supporting the installation of wind turbine farms. Many environmental impacts are often excluded in the discussions about wind turbine farms (such as impacts on heritage landscapes), which helps explain the increasing number and importance of committees contesting such projects even though these wind turbine farms are much better for the environment than hydro, fossil fuel or nuclear energy. One potential solution is to consider locating such wind turbine farms elsewhere where some environmental impacts related to conserving heritage landscapes (and other impacts) are not an issue. When co-construction of a project is needed, the actors involved often criticize state bodies and the lack of texts which clearly define the conditions for implementation of these wind turbine farms and how the views of other actors who live in the same territory should be taken into consideration.

Other examples of large-scale projects include dams with their role in water management. For such a project, co-construction is also a favourable avenue to increase the probability of realizing the project, so long as all the elements such as the whole range of facts and of legitimate interests are discussed and everyone interested is given access to the discussions. Nevertheless, in macro-scale projects it becomes increasingly utopian to believe in the success of such a co-constructed project. Even if the parties start from a real and profound desire to make the project successful, it is often difficult to find ways to bring the different actors to agree and converge on an acceptable project. The multiplicity of actors and institutional levels may constitute an obstacle to effective co-construction.

The greater the number of actors involved and the more their aspirations are contradictory, the more complex it will be to consider all the issues and achieve a viable project. In these circumstances, only a facilitator or mediator who has a

25 Valette, E., "Intégration environnementale de l'éolien et régulation locale des conflits: l'action des collectivités territoriales dans l'Aude (France)" (2005) 6(3) *VertigO – la revue électronique en sciences de l'environnement*, 1–10.

certain charisma can provide the key to success. On the other hand, some projects can proceed very successfully and informally, and success will be even stronger particularly when the people involved know the territory first-hand (as residents) and are able to defend it.

When co-construction is relatively informal, it can become akin to an environmental mediation since the establishment and progress of negotiations between the different parties are realized with the approval and involvement of the people present. Generally, in such cases, a single person acts as the mediator. This has been the case in British Columbia, where conflicts often emerged in the agricultural land reserves between neo-ruralites and long-term farmers. The agricultural land reserves were created following the provincial legislation to protect agricultural land.[26] Sorting out and resolving the conflicts was mostly facilitated by a single civil servant from the provincial Ministry of Agriculture in the different farmland reserves who would work informally with the non-farm residents and farmers with the result that it was not necessary for the provincial cabinet to become involved. Other examples demonstrate that a project that has the potential to be developed can fail without the appropriate co-construction on the part of various actors implicated. This generally results in the project being implemented, but without the agreement of all actors.

For instance, in 2014 in Wallonia, in the context of an informal process, a farmers' committee was organized which joined up with the neo-rural population to protest against and block the implementation of a business park in their living space. Initially, a constructive result seemed unlikely and, in January 2014, a letter from the inter-communal body, which handles the management and installation of Economic Activity Parks (EAP), announced the expropriation of farmland for this project. Consultation between different population segments helped block this project. The farmers defended their primary tool, farmland, while the neo-ruralites who rallied to help the farmers also managed to preserve their surrounding landscape and avoid negative environmental impacts. This case is very interesting because, while the initiative was taken by a farmer who went knocking on doors to warn neo-ruralites, he was also able to convince the mayor of the municipalities involved (Pont-à-Celles and Courcelles) to take the lead and support the approach of this farmer.[27] Thus, in this example, a project was cancelled on the basis of the legitimate interests of certain actors, a situation not unfamiliar to some found in the environmental mediation domain.

Other examples of co-construction, such as the development of holistic strategic development plans for and by the community, can provide the means to reduce potential future conflicts as they can provide various segments of legitimate

26 Caldwell, W., S. Hilts and B. Wilton, eds., *Farmland Preservation – Land for Future Generations*, Centre for Land and Water Stewardship, University of Guelph, Guelph, 2007, 61–86.

27 Bousbaine, A.-D. and C.R. Bryant, "La cohabitation des populations agricoles et non agricoles face aux nouvelles dynamiques économiques des espaces périurbains" International Conference *L'agriculture périurbaine: impacts du fait urbain, stratégies et jeux d'acteurs*, Oum El Bouaghi, 2015.

interests with experience in working together, regardless of the diversity of values. Among the most difficult projects are those that are parachuted by the central government and its ministries for the 'good of society'. How to involve citizens in such a project? How can the approach of the state be changed, especially when there is a strategic development plan that has already been constructed by the citizens?

Frequently, projects have been developed by political actors and professionals (including consultants) without citizens having either the opportunity or even the right to review and provide advice including constructive criticism. Thus, in such cases, the interests of some actors inevitably prevail at the expense of others. However, some processes involve the community both its individual citizens and collective actors. This is sometimes done at the beginning of the development of a strategic plan with its various projects where attempts are made to integrate some form of co-construction. Often, the initial project (plan) becomes modified in terms of the environmental impacts that are brought to light. Consultation meetings and real listening are essential in the face of the frequent multiple interests present.

## 3 The purpose and context of any co-construction process in order to avoid conflict related to environmental issues

Although co-construction is recognized as a helpful process for resolving some environmental conflicts, achieving co-construction requires that certain parameters be met. Some authors highlight the differences between 'bottom-up' and 'top-down' management.[28] Often, the key elements of success or failure are related to the actors involved, the size of the project and the scale of its implementation, as well as whether the project is bottom up or top down in conception. In summary, the key to any successful co-construction builds on the existing dynamics in a well-defined territory or space and takes into account the project's objective and the actors with legitimate interests in such a project.

Indeed, many examples show that when projects are based on a local or bottom-up approach such as co-construction which emphasizes the consultation of local committees or associations, without putting state institutions directly up front, frequently the result leads to a resolution of the conflicts and the project's implementation (see section 5). In this situation, the consultation initiative seeks to bring together local stakeholders to reach an agreement and ultimately lead to the acceptance of the project. This seems perfectly logical: those who live in their territory are arguably best able to define the project.

Dialogue and consultation as early as possible are essential in conflict resolution, especially when a project is based in a region, such as a department (France) or country (e.g. Canada, the United Kingdom). Trying to impose a point of view

28 Beuret, J.-E. and C. Trehet, "Pour la gestion concertée de l'espace rural: appuyer des médiations territoriales", 2001, 43 *Courrier de l'Environnement de l'INRA* 25.

does not usually give good results: instead, it generally accentuates differences and the interested parties frequently end up in court. It is best to understand the interests of everyone and bring together the most reluctant actors to identify the issues associated with any project. This is often the situation when a new project is set up in an area where there are already tensions between populations. This could be the case where farmers in rural areas and supported by a strong committee, would decide to reject new measures imposed on water management.

It is essential to convince the actors of the merits of the project (e.g. to reduce water pollution in a rural area). This allows projects to be better understood by the multiple actors in the same territory. This also means that special efforts must be made to ensure that any technical data that are being used to define and explain the benefits of a project must be made comprehensible to all considering that not all stakeholders are 'experts'. This should facilitate the appropriation of a given project as can the constructive suggestions made by the whole range of interested actors. This explains why in Environmental Impact Studies (or Assessments), any reports produced by the project developer must be understandable by everyone involved.

In addition, a key to success of any positive co-construction is to be found in the strategies that can help avoid or minimize potential conflicts. This may require substantial analysis which may require several months of work and consultations. In many respects, these strategies are made for and by the community, which from the beginning of the project should be properly consulted and involved in all later stages as well. The voluntary nature of these consultations is a condition that can lead to a viable co-constructed project. The state can take on a role at the outset of the development of a project (depending of course on the scale of the project) provided that it takes into account the dynamics that already exist in the territory; *a priori* this is not a simple situation to manage but some co-constructed projects have been achieved with the help of associations or committees that fiercely defend their environment.

While an initial project itself can be top down or bottom up in its conception, it is not uncommon to see bottom-up management develop, where either the local actors are the initiators of the project,[29] and/or where local organizations which possess a profound understanding of the territory can in fact participate in the management of a project even if the project's conception was initially top down. This form of management is yet another way to reduce conflict; indeed, it suggests ways to develop local projects by taking into account the need to address environmental issues. Local (or regional) organizations that are specific to the municipality or region, including non-municipal organizations, have a solid footing in the territory and their involvement in local project co-construction is more feasible. Thus, a mediation process can be initiated involving the different actors in the territory with the mediation being facilitated by the involvement of one or more local stakeholders.

29 Ibid.

It is also possible that such a project may extend to another level and become an inter-departmental (in France) or an inter-municipal project. We noted that in projects that have been co-constructed informally by several actors, success is almost immediate; this has been the case in Herve in eastern Belgium. Here, a non-profit organization (NPO), Land of Herve – Future (Pays de Herve – Futur),[30] a movement initiated by a group of concerned citizens, has managed to create a synergy between the 11 towns that make up the Herve region. This association, a textbook case in Wallonia, decided to replant old varieties of fruit trees with tall stems and become engaged in the conservation of biodiversity and the survival of bees, particularly for the pollination of fruits but also to preserve the very special landscape in this part of Wallonia. Through consultations and discussions, this NPO completed numerous projects that were aligned with the interest of local stakeholders. The NPO's work was also widely supported by the Walloon Minister for Local Authorities. Working groups exist and are the pillars of successful co-constructed projects. This NPO unifies actors around development projects so that development is more balanced and sustainable. It has also put into place a long-term development reflection with a forward-looking approach and involving the different actors who have agreed to be part of the process.

In Brittany, France, a similar action was established informally to reconstitute the old farmland landscape, the *bocage*, which had disappeared under the new policies of the Common Agricultural Policy of the European Union. It is only through consultation and co-constructing projects with a common purpose that some projects are able to fully succeed. Other examples exist both in Europe and North America.

Nevertheless, we cannot forget that there are some projects where there is incompatibility in co-construction between actors and any attempt to bring together the actors appears to be a waste of time. This is especially the case when a project is parachuted into an area where environmental preservation committees have a significant weight, including leaders who have strong capacities for dialogue and rallying other actors. There may well be a real desire for consultation after the initial resistance encountered. However, in many situations where some observers see these projects as having been 'imposed', the project is rejected from the outset and subsequently cancelled by its initiators.

## 4 Examples: convergence/divergence: North America/Europe

In North America and in Europe, environmental mediation is still struggling to succeed. Everything depends on the mindset of the actors involved and the nature of territorial governance. It is very difficult to compare continents, such as Europe and North America, which diverge so much in terms of their state structure and administrative divisions. France is divided into regions, departments and

30 ASBL (Association Sans But Lucratif) Pays de Herve – Futur. Access: www.paysdehervefutur.be.

municipalities (and the regional structures are undergoing transformation again since 2014) whereas in a country like Belgium three major regions exist: Wallonia, Brussels and Flanders, each governed by its own government. Although in relation to environmental issues, European Union countries must comply with European directives, significant differences remain.

In North America, and more specifically Canada, many environmental issues have been placed up front, which resulted in a significant increase of the awareness of the need to preserve the environment and the impacts of major planning projects. The concept of environmental mediation appeared in the Province of Quebec during the 1980s.[31] Environmental mediation developed as an alternative to the 'public hearing' process introduced by the BAPE (Bureau d'Audience Publique sur l'Environnement or the Office of Public Hearings on the Environment), which for over 30 years already represents a considerable achievement in terms of public involvement in environmental issues.[32] While some authors[33] during the 1990s criticized certain aspects of the BAPE, progress in the field of participatory democracy has been real. Nevertheless, the BAPE process contains some imperfections regarding public participation in the development of projects with environmental impacts.[34] Nonetheless, Quebec serves as a benchmark for public hearings, and the number of projects assessed by the BAPE continues to grow since its inception in 1978.

The target population frequently includes individuals with the least means and resources to participate. This observation is linked with the costs incurred in a consultation – developers, on the one hand, are being paid for their participation, but for the majority, it is public or personal funds that covers their expenses. Similarly during public inquiries, experts and lawyers are paid, but not the citizens. Séguin also highlights the 'real lack of independence' of the BAPE, suggesting that the BAPE often seems to follow the requirements of the government to move a project along, although this appears to have improved considerably within the last ten years.[35] Finally, Séguin also stresses the point that the BAPE is neither present at the beginning of the process of selection of alternatives, nor at the end of the process in decision making by policy makers. In short, there appears to be a limited integration of the population's concerns into the final outcome. Although the public is invited to attend the consultation hearings and the public has the feeling of contributing to the decision-making process, in many cases this is only an illusion. Indeed, it appears to Séguin that these consultations

31 BAPE, *La médiation en environnement: une nouvelle approche au BAPE*, Gouvernment of Quebec, Quebec, 1994, 65. Access: www.bape.gouv.qc.ca/sections/documentation/Mediation_environnement.pdf

32 Dziedzicki, J.-M. and L. Meuret, "Médiation(s) environnementale(s): quelles pratiques et quelles perspectives en France?", 2000, 1 *Séance* 17.

33 For example: Séguin, M., "La médiation environnementale" in J.-G. Vaillancourt, M. Séguin, L. Maheu and L. Cotnoir, eds., *La gestion écologique des déchets*, Les presses de l'université de Montréal, Montréal, 1999, 153.

34 Ibid.

35 Ibid.

exist to make decisions more acceptable and credible, yet there are decisions that have already been endorsed upstream by the political powers. Several projects have also been cancelled due to population's participation in the BAPE process and its involvement in and dedication to the protection of their territory (for example the Parc éolien (wind farm) of Saint-Valentin). One might pose the question of whether some of these cancelled projects might have been able to be implemented had there been a real co-construction process from the start.

Mediation is a tool that allows a better understanding between the different parties. We can therefore question the relevance of the BAPE, and the real involvement of the people. Other authors[36] have seen the BAPE as an instrument that has evolved since its creation, allowing citizen involvement in projects with environmental impacts. The BAPE does provide a mediation service before the public consultation process begins, therefore, the success of this depends on whether the public (the different segments of interest) and collective actors have complete trust in the BAPE's independence in such a process. Simard and Gauthier do in fact also converge with Séguin's salient points, recognizing that the institutionalization of public debate on environment and development via the BAPE is a useful but nonetheless limited experience. Public debates are organized, but they do not have the effect of rebalancing decision-making power. Indeed, government decisions usually reflect a precedence of the interests of private actors who initiate project over those of citizens. These authors also emphasize that in many situations citizen participation in public debate is confined to a project at the local level. Nonetheless, citizen participation continues to grow in importance in Canada, and from this perspective, the two continents, North America and Europe, converge. However, flaws still exist, and the examples presented next highlight them. Co-constructed development projects incorporating a wide range of actors and segments of interest remain limited, and project proponents frequently submit projects without any real direct involvement of communities who would be directly affected by the projects.

Thus, we still witness a top-down approach, which in the vast majority of cases excludes local opinions. In Canada, this has, however, diminished as the culture of participatory democracy has become more anchored in today's cultures; but in most projects, economic interests are clearly winning. The approaches used have been seriously challenged, representing a potential turning point for the BAPE, with perhaps some impact on Europe. Furthermore, it is also interesting to note that in Ontario the companies that are subscribing to the Large Renewable Procurement I Request for Proposals regarding large energy projects are obliged to run public meetings even before the project is approved.[37]

36 For example, Gauthier, M. and L. Simard, "Le bureau d'audiences publiques sur l'environnement du Québec: genèse et développement d'un instrument voué à la participation publique", 2001, 17(1) *Télescope* 39.

37 Independent Electricity System Operator, *Large Renewable Procurement*, 2013. Access: www.ieso.ca/Pages/Participate/Generation-Procurement/Large-Renewable-Procurement/default.aspx.

In Europe, the road ahead in the domain of environmental mediation and especially public involvement is still a long one. Nonetheless, in France there is the National Public Debate Commission (Commission Nationale de Débat Public), and in Canada, the BAPE is a major reference point as well as examples in other European countries which all have the potential to lead to greater community involvement in the construction and implementation of projects. However, to date the results are mixed.[38] Certainly, participatory democracy remains a response for elected officials faced with the loss of confidence of civil society as a way of regaining some legitimacy, but in reality, this participation is limited. Dziedzicki[39] based his research on a comparative study of several European countries (Germany, Switzerland, Belgium and France) and Quebec. The image of environmental mediation is still relatively limited, although in Switzerland, Wallonia (Belgium), Germany and Quebec it has become much more developed and institutionalized. France is trying to position itself in relation to what has been achieved in Canada, but is still on the sidelines. It was not until 1992 that the concept of 'local democracy' appears for the first time in the Orientation Act (Acte d'orientation) of February 6, 1992; but in reality, people just have a right to information and consultation.[40] There is little question of co-construction of local projects.

In Europe, the involvement of the population is not as well entrenched as in the United States. It must be recognized that in Canada, people are much more involved in consultation and discussions upstream of projects. This trend can be observed in relation to certain projects which have generated much resistance, such as the extraction of shale gas. This particular type of project also caused an outcry in France. But how many citizens are aware of the rights they have to put a stop to such projects (in the absence of course of legislation that itself eliminates such projects, as in France). In Wallonia, findings are similar, and Walloons apparently do not have the spirit of 'challenge'. To confirm this, one only has to investigate the implementation of the project involving the creation of the Brussels-Charleroi airport which involved some 1,245 hectares of largely prime agricultural land. Bousbaine personally met with the expropriated farmers, who were unaware of their rights. As some pointed out, "We don't dispute a Government decision" – a remark that is largely convergent with what the French researcher Dziedzicki highlighted in his comparative study of several European countries.[41]

38 Dziedzicki, J.-M., "La gestion des conflits d'aménagement entre participation du public et médiation", 2003, 23(1) *Annuaire 2003 des collectivités locales* 635; Dziedzicki, J.-M. and L. Meuret, "Médiation(s) environnementale(s): quelles pratiques et quelles perspectives en France?", 2000, 1 *Séance* 17.

39 Ibid.

40 Bilek, A., D. Carassus and D. Gardey, "La gestion démocratique des politiques de développement durable: une analyse comparative à l'échelle internationale dans le cas de la gestion des déchets" in *3ème Dialogue Euroméditerranéen de Management Public, "Développement Durable et Action Publique*, Université Paul CézanneAix-Marseille III, Tunis, 2010. Access : http://www.med-eu.org/documents/MED3/BILEK-CARASSUS-GARDEY.pdf

41 See note 38.

Finally, many projects are implemented either with or against the approval of the local population; although the notion of environmental mediation exists, it remains limited, even though it is much less expensive that recourse to the courts. Given that environmental impacts constitute an important parameter and are central to the spirit of sustainable development, governments ought to respect the rights of citizens to contribute to the development of projects that directly or indirectly affect their living environment – but this is unfortunately frequently not the case. In relation to this, our findings suggest that co-constructed projects have become closer to citizens' concerns, and while the implementation of certain projects remains difficult, it is only through the involvement of people that co-construction can become effective. These include wind farm projects or EAP projects. The involvement of strong leaders remains a significant condition in realizing such co-construction, but also requires the strong support of political authorities.

Furthermore, the examples discussed by many authors in Canada show that the involvement of citizens is much more developed than in Europe. Over the last ten years, the BAPE in Quebec has provided a forum where citizens can intervene more effectively by broadening the scope of a project on a larger scale thus yielding better results. However, this participation in a formal process raises the question of the mobilization of the population without which participation can be very biased.

In Europe and, particularly, Wallonia, the examples in recent years demonstrate the will to reach agreement on projects; the NPO Space Environment (Espace Environnement)[42] has worked towards the successful implementation of mediation without actually talking about co-constructed projects. A contact was made during July 2015, with one of the officials (Mrs Fontenoy), who spoke about the various projects that this NPO has been involved in. Here is one example:

### *Installation of a wind farm in Courcelles*

*Context*: The Municipality of Courcelles contacted the Maison de l'Environnement[43] to mediate the public briefing as part of the process for obtaining a single permit for a wind farm project, initiated by the company Ventis. The company has its own 'mediator' but the town, anxious to ensure an acceptable dialogue about the project, asked for discussions to be moderated by an independent body and hence proposed to use the services of the Maison de l'Environnement.

*Approach and findings*: Despite the short notice and the proponent's reluctance, a meeting was organized between the company and the town. The applicant accepted the mediation proposal for the Maison de l'Environnement to act as a neutral third party to promote a climate of dialogue and trust conducive to

42 Espace Environment. Access: www.espace-environnement.be.

43 Espace Environnement. *La maison de l'Environnement*. Access: www.espace-environnement.be/maison-de-environnement/.

fruitful exchanges. Its role also involved introducing each speaker and their functions, providing an outline of the procedure and timing for each participant's involvement in the discussions and preparing a report to ensure the transmission of the best possible information to people who were unable to attend the meeting. An information paper outlining the procedure, the contact persons and useful links was provided by the Maison de l'Environnement while the applicant produced a document outlining the project.

*Analysis*: At the meeting, about 70 people participated and shared their comments and questions during the question-and-answer session that followed the presentations by Ventis and the designated office for the Environmental Impact Study.

The mediator, by reformulating the questions, re-focusing some digressions and synthesizing the elements highlighted in the debates established a constructive dialogue between participants. After the meeting, both those living close to the proposed project, the representatives of the community colleges and the applicant were satisfied with the meeting in terms of its structure, the issues raised and the components identified. A report was prepared by the Maison de l'Environnement and sent to the town in charge of preparing the official minutes. This note-taking contributed to strengthening the climate of confidence among local residents. In addition, several questions focused on the project and the Municipality of Courcelles committed itself, after the meeting, to organize an information session on the subject, outside the context of the specific wind farm project. This proposal was also well received in another municipality where other projects were in the pipeline. Indeed, during 2013, two projects were initiated one by Electrabel, the other by EDF Luminus. For the latter project, the mediating of the preliminary public information meeting was managed by the Maison de l'Environnement on November 5 with 65 people present.

In Wallonia in recent years, the involvement of local populations has become much more important than in France; the small size of this territory (30,528 km$^2$) – or 18 times less than the area of France – tends to facilitate taking citizen perspectives into account. Setting up co-construction of projects still remains to be undertaken, but efforts are being made in this direction.

The French examples tend to highlight the lack of involvement of the population, although laws exist (Grenelle 1 and 2), which stipulate public consultation, with implementation at the municipal level; nonetheless, we must recognize that the actions remain mostly limited to information provision and citizens are rarely involved in decision making. Participatory democracy can be seen as an organizational learning process, recognizing and involving all stakeholders, who can explore the more viable and acceptable solutions for all the actors concerned; this appears simple on paper but is much more complicated in reality.[44]

44 Callon, M., P. Lascourmes and Y. Barthes, *Agir dans l'incertain: Essai sur la démocratie technique*, Éditions Le Seuil, Paris, 2001, 358.

In France, some municipalities have managed to involve local communities in environmental mediation, although it is not clearly identified as such. For example, in the City of Strasbourg, consultation of the people at the neighbourhood level is well developed, allowing city council to take into consideration the advisory opinions gathered by the neighbourhood committees. Governments therefore have full knowledge of these claims, and it is really up to these government bodies to integrate these claims or not to integrate them in achieving this or that project. Finally, these same bodies have to decide whether they want to deal with a co-constructed project or conversely whether such and such a project will have to be dealt with by the courts, if no mediation is possible.

In England as in Ireland, certain examples can be noted such as the People's Panel, involving 5,000 citizens from different socio-professional and geographic milieus, and of different ages which enabled the Cabinet Office to take note of their advice in the elaboration of public policies, between 1998 and 2002. This panel provided support to public authorities in the reorientation of their policies while at the same time integrating changes that reflected the advice of citizens. This is similar to Ireland where citizens are directly consulted. This also has involved a type of co-construction of projects, which yields good results in practice.

Finally, it is important for any initiative or specific project to be placed into a broader context involving development planning for the community or territory. While there are several types of planning that exist, the one most pertinent to providing for community involvement which can have a permanent impact on the co-construction of specific initiatives or projects is strategic planning for development for and by the 'community'. Such a strategic planning process is in itself a 'project', and its key characteristic are that of an active involvement of the citizens and collective actors right from the start of the process. This approach to strategic planning in Canada has progressively become more and more important since the late 1980s. Under the best circumstances, citizen participation involves active mobilization of each segment of the population, including teenagers, retirees, handicapped people and the unemployed, as well, of course, as business entrepreneurs and managers and both female and male employees, all of whom can be mobilized using the appropriate means of communication with each group. One of the best examples that has been in process for almost 20 years is that of Haliburton County in Eastern Ontario.[45] Not only did citizens and collective actors define a vision for the territory, but different working groups were established to identify and put into place different initiatives, including an environmental conservation group. Citizens took responsibility for managing

45 Bryant, C.R., "Community-based Strategic Planning, Mobilisation and Action at the Edge of the Urban Field: The Case of Haliburton County" in I. Bowler, C.R. Bryant and A. Firmino, eds., *Progress in Research on Sustainable Rural Systems*, Universidade Nova de Lisboa, Centro de Estudos de Geografia e Planeamento Regional, Lisbon, 1999, 211; County of Haliburton, *Strategic Planning*, 2015. Access: https://haliburtoncounty.ca/services/planning-and-gis/strategic-plan/

different initiatives through the different working groups. This example is still flagged as an example where citizens constructed a strategic planning process and became involved in managing initiatives and the whole process contributed to putting in place an official land-use plan for the county several years later. It is a perfect example of what a co-construction process can achieve – a holistic planning process that places all initiatives into context, environmental conservation taking on a major role in the development and implementation of any specific project as appropriate and an active (and proud) involvement of citizens through effective mobilization and communication processes.

## Conclusion

Both environmental mediation and co-construction have multiple facets and can be linked to each other in several circumstances. Co-construction of a 'project' has been recognized as a cheaper way to understand and work with the differences that arise from project proposals, whether it is a small or large project. Although the concept of environmental mediation was born in North America from the 1970s onwards, Europe has been attempting to integrate the same concept. The BAPE in Quebec constitutes a reference point in Europe, particularly in France.

Environmental issues have become increasingly important in developed societies since the 1992 Rio Earth Summit, and citizen participation has become one of the fundamental principles of sustainable development. The discourse promoting citizen involvement continues to occupy an increasingly significant place within societies, but there is still much left to achieve. However, the co-construction of any project almost becomes a guarantee of success, and involves frequently a simple form of mediation, with the 'mediator' needing to be impartial, fair and capable of listening to all stakeholders. This co-construction with an informal form of environmental mediation is encountered more frequently in Canada than in Europe, where governments are still cautious about this approach. To implement co-construction, both at the level of any land development project (infrastructure, business parks, wind farms, etc.), and for community driven strategic development plans, certain conditions are required.

These conditions are not easy to establish, because differences in perspectives can also increase. It is important both to have a 'real' willingness to listen and take into consideration the legitimate interests of each party, and at the same time broadening the dialogue to include a maximum number of actors, regardless of social background and educational level. It is likely to be all the more acceptable if a bottom-up approach is emphasized rather than the top-down approach. The examples presented demonstrated that informal bottom-up initiatives at co-construction can provide more relevant results than when projects are 'parachuted' into a territory whose specificities are often poorly understood by those initiating the projects.

A number of studies by French researchers have highlighted the serious lack of consultation and involvement of citizens in project development. The citizen is simply 'informed' but has little or no part in project development, despite legislation in several countries that emphasizes the role of citizens. Economic interests frequently dominate over environmental considerations, leading inevitably to conflicts, which despite mediation often end up in court.

Efforts need to be made to emphasize the relevance of co-constructed projects that avoid many setbacks to the different parties involved and which can also logically lead to ongoing long-term project monitoring. There is still a long way to go to achieve co-construction in the broad sense; as long as this situation prevails, environmental mediation seems the only solution for citizens to be heard and defend their legitimate interests. Alternatively, integrating projects into a long-term strategic development planning process by and for the community is an important way of dealing with new projects as they emerge, for these processes are flexible and do not stop at a particular point in time. It is noteworthy, however, that conditions may well be changing for the future of public participation in environmental evaluation.[46]

46 For example, *Secrétariat International Francophone pour l'Évaluation Environnementale* (SIFÉE), 2015. Access: www.sifee.org/

# 9 Mediating potential environmental conflict with a social learning model

## Six case studies from the State of Santa Catarina, Brazil

*Anne Browning-Aiken,*[1] *José Antonio Silvestre Fernandes Neto*[2] *and Daniel José da Silva*[3]

## Introduction

This chapter examines how environmental conflict mediation in Brazil offers a model and a process for identifying different kinds of environmental conflicts, a system for constructively managing those conflicts and an opportunity to transform conflict into productive learning experiences. While Brazil initiated a legal Mediation and Conciliation process[4] to be used in courtrooms in the 1990s, GTHIDRO or *Grupo Transdisciplinar de Pesquisas em Governança de Bens Comuns*, a transdisciplinary group of researchers at the Federal University of Santa Catarina, created another form of mediation used outside the courtroom to address potential problems in local (community and state) governance of natural resources, which the research group call 'socio-ecological learning'. They have incorporated a dynamic and complex program or model of participatory 'cycles of learning' that brings six southern Brazilian community committees in the state of Santa Catarina to a common understanding of socio-ecological processes, laws and potential for collective action.[5]

1 Ph.D. in anthropology (University of Arizona)., School of Anthropology, English Department Writing Program, and Udall Center for Studies in Public Policy, Fulbright Scholar 2010. Email address: browning@u.arizona.edu.
2 Ph.D. in environmental engineering (Federal University of the State of Santa Catarina – UFSC). Researcher of Health, Public Policy and Governance. Oswaldo Cruz Foundation (www.fiocruz.br). Email address: antonio.silvestre@fiocruz.br
3 Ph.D. in production engineering (Federal University of the State of Santa Catarina – UFSC). Senior Researcher of Common Goods Governance. Federal University of Santa Catarina (www.ufsc.br).
Email address: daniel.silva@ufsc.br
4 Almeida, T. and A. Braga Neto, "Brazil and the Alternative Methods for Conflict Resolution" 2007.
5 Browning-Aiken, A., M.C.C. da Silva, J.A.S. Fernandes Neto and D. da Silva, "Assessing the Role of Socio-ecological Learning in Participatory Governance: Building Resilience in Six Brazilian River Basin Committees" (2014) 30 *Desenvolvimento e Meio Ambiente* 59.

By 'socio-ecological learning' we are using the model proposed by Pahl-Wostl and Hare[6] that "embeds social learning in the socio-ecologic system where the outcomes of the participatory management process are of a technical and relational nature", or, more simply "learning together to manage together".[7] The research group recognizes that individual responses to environmental conflicts such as pollution and overuse of natural resources depend upon individual perceptions of the problem.[8] In this model for mediation GTHIDRO distinguishes between social learning processes and outcomes, and between individual and social learning. Social learning is much more than just public participation or pro-environmental behaviours. With Reed et al.,[9] GTHIDRO argues that to be considered 'social learning', a process must

(1) demonstrate that a change in understanding has taken place in the individuals involved;
(2) demonstrate that this change goes beyond the individual and becomes situated within wider social units or communities of practice;
(3) occur through social interactions and processes between actors within a social network.

The group agrees with Reed et al.

> that a clearer picture of what is meant by social learning can enhance our ability to critically evaluate outcomes and better understand the processes through which social learning occurs. In this way, it may be possible to better facilitate the desired outcomes of social learning processes.[10]

GTHIDRO also recognizes that the success of this form of environmental conflict mediation depends upon the supportive role of facilitators, participant commitment, and a clear organizational structure and process.[11]

This chapter is divided into seven sections. We begin with the geographic context and strategic reasons for selecting the six Brazilian basin committees within the state of Santa Catarina. Second, we describe the methodology used in this

6 Pahl-Wostl, C. and M. Hare, "Processes of Social Learning in Integrated Resources Management" (2004) 14 *Journal of Community and Applied Social Psychology* 193.

7 Mostert, E., M. Craps and C. Pahl-Wostl, "Social Learning: The Key to Integrated Water Resources Management?" (2008) 33 *Water International* 293.

8 Sairinen, R., "Environmental Conflict Mediation" in F. Vanclay and A. Maria Esteves, eds., *New Directions in Social Impact Assessment: Conceptual and Methodological Advances*, Edward Elgar Publishing, Northampton, 2011, 273.

9 Reed, M.S., A.C. Evely, G. Cundill, I. Fazey, J. Glass, A. Laing, J. Newig, B. Parrish, C. Prell, C. Raymond and L.C. Stringer, "What Is Social Learning?" (2010) 15(4) *Ecology and Society* r1. Access: www.ecologyandsociety.org/vol15/iss4/resp1/.

10 Ibid.

11 Maiello, A., "The Organizational View of Public Participation: A Narrative Analysis" (2014) 27 *Systemic Practice and Action Research* 499.

six-basin study and the nature of the data sources. Third, we explain the conceptual model PEDS (Planejamento Estratégico do Desenvolvimento Sustentável or Strategic Planning for Sustainable Development), which GTHIDRO has developed as a mediation model based on social learning and which occurs throughout the development of the river basin committees. Fourth, we present examples of the social learning process in six basins. Fifth, we examine the results of the research group and the Committee evaluations. Finally, we discuss what can be learned from the results of our research and suggest that the PEDS models a form of environmental conflict mediation that might be particularly applicable elsewhere in communities facing water or another potential environmental crises.

## 1 Geographic context

The state of Santa Catarina has a history of meteorological extremes from rains that result in floods and heavy run-off to dryness following the wet period. In addition to the loss of human lives, there are major economic losses since the state is the fifth largest food producer in Brazil (ham, chicken, apples, rice, mussels, and oysters). In 2004 alone, the state experienced wet weather-related damages amounting to more than 1 million reis and draught damages up to 128 million reis.[12] Thus agricultural success is very dependent upon a good climate information system and good agricultural practices regarding water.[13] In addition, approximately 22.7% of the population has no water treatment for potable water, a figure higher than the national level.[14] Generally speaking, the basins near the coast tend to have more rice cultivation, while the basins in the higher elevations are devoted to animal and agricultural farming. GTHIDRO focuses on the sub-hydrologic basins linked to the large Guarani Aquifer, which underlies parts of Argentina, Brazil, Paraguay and Uruguay.

A sub-basin complex links the Rio Tubarão (towns of Orleans and Braço do Norte) to the Rio Araranguá (towns of Ermos, Turvo, Araranguá, among others.), Rio Tijucas (town of same name), Rio Canoas (town of Urubici) and Fragosos Basin (town of Concórdia).

## 2 Methodology

Social learning as an essential process in environmental conflict mediation described in this chapter received a strong impetus with the enactment of the Brazilian National Water Resources Management Act of 1997, which included both water policy and an integrated water management system with tools or guidelines for designing water management plans. At the core of this policy and management system lay the explicit emphasis on stakeholder participation in this planning and management process. This chapter reflects the experiences of the authors in

12 Instituto de Planejamento e Economia agrícola de Santa Catarina, *Levantamento agropecuário da Santa Catarina – 2002–2003: dados preliminares: fevereiro de 2005*, Florianopolis, 2005, 255.

13 Projeto Tecnologias Sociais para a Gestão da Água, *Dossiês das Tecnologias, versão Preliminar*, 2007. Access: http://v1.tsga.ufsc.br/images/pdf/dossie_completo.pdf.

14 Ibid, 70.

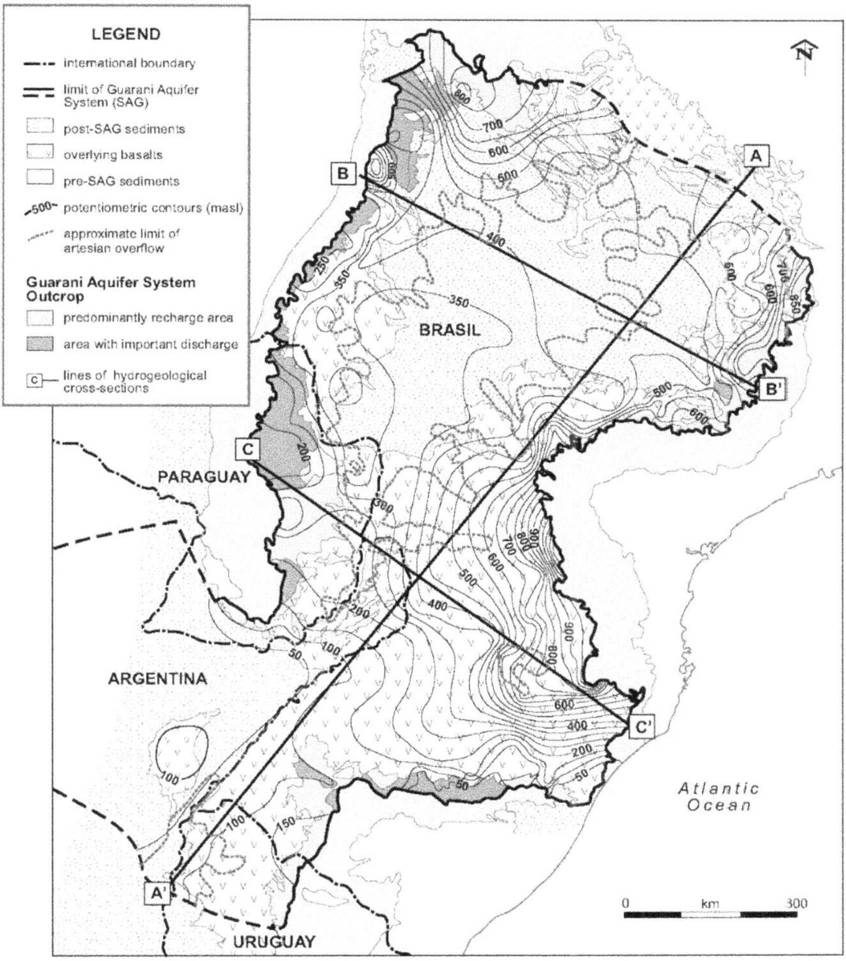


*Figure 9.1* Guarani Aquifer[15]

developing an effective system of social participation in watershed governance through cycles of learning with existing or potential watershed councils, municipal, state and federal water and land-use agencies, and with local schools. Information about these cycles of learning is thus based on their personal experiences with basin communities in planning and coordinating a series of projects focused on water quality issues and environmental conservation of watersheds. The data and materials were recorded in ten *relatórios* or reports from these projects, masters

15 Foster, S., Hirata, R., Vidal, A., Schmidt, G., and Hector Garduño. Sustainable Groundwater Management: Concepts and Tools Sustainable Groundwater Management Lessons from Practice, Case Profile Collection Number 9, World Bank, Nov. 2009. Access: http://siteresources.worldbank.org/INTWAT/Resources/GWMATE_English_CP_09.pdf.

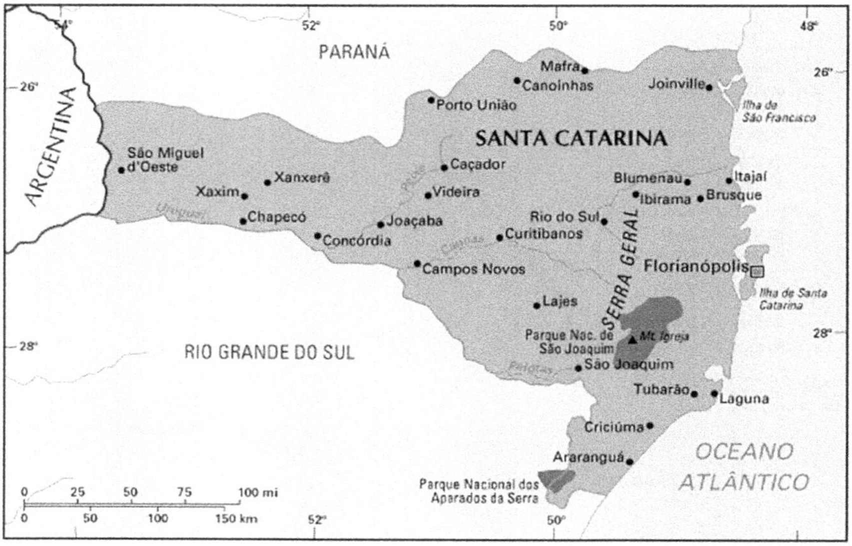


*Figure 9.2* Major towns within Santa Catarina, Brazil[16]

and Ph.D. theses written by UFSC students participating in the projects and educational materials developed for watershed committees and local schools.

The Strategic Planning Model for Sustainable Development, entitled PEDS (Figure 9.3), lays out the steps for getting diverse sectors of the population to work together, to understand what kinds of knowledge are required for watershed governance, to formulate a strategic watershed plan, and to evaluate and adapt the plan continuously. We examine the effectiveness of this model for mediation in terms of the project's series of self-evaluations and other experiences in social learning for watershed governance in Brazil and elsewhere. This Strategic Planning Model for Sustainable Development was developed by GTHIDRO based on the constructivist method of Piaget and Paulo Freire and on the concept of love as the valorization of the subjective perspective of each person in a social group[17] Similar to the conceptual model developed by

16 Justino Vieira, Hamilton. *Projeto Tecnologias Sociais para a Gestão da Água, Dossiês das Tecnologias, versão Preliminar*, 2007. Access: http://v1.tsga.ufsc.br/images/pdf/dossie_completo.pdf. Access: www.wpmap.org/wp-content/uploads/2012/06/santa-catarina.gif.

17 Da Silva, D., *Uma abordagem cognitiva ao Planejamento Estratégico do Desenvolvimento Sustentável*, Florianópolis, Ph.D. thesis in production engineering – Universidade Federal de Santa Catarina, 1998, 240.

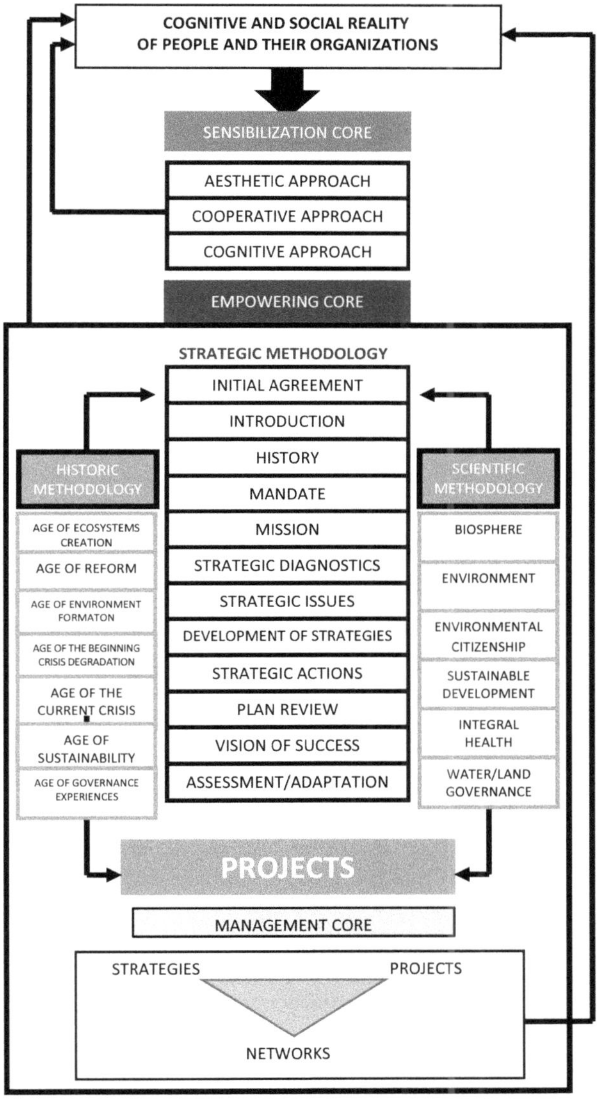


*Figure 9.3* PEDS Model: Strategic Planning for Sustainable Development[18]

18 Da Silva, D., *Uma abordagem cognitiva ao Planejamento Estratégico do Desenvolvimento Sustentável*, Florianópolis, Ph.D. thesis in production engineering – Universidade Federal de Santa Catarina, 1998, 240 and Fernandes Neto, J.A.S., *Modelo Urubici de Governança da Água e do Território: uma tecnologia social a serviço do desenvolvimento sustentável local*, Florianópolis, Ph.D. thesis in environmental engineering – Universidade Federal de Santa Catarina, 2010, 235.

*Figure 9.4* *Urubici* model of governance: triad of premises[20]

Pahl-Wostl and Hare (2004)[19] this framework embeds the process of social learning in the context of governance structure and natural environment. It emphasizes that in the process of resource management, social involvement (e.g. the generation of social capital, the development of new social practices) is as important as content management (e.g. the development and communication of knowledge about the state of a water resource and the use of models to predict the effects of measures to achieve a good ecological state of a river). The outcomes of the management process are not only technical qualities such as an improved state of the environment but also relational qualities such as an improved capability of the actors to solve conflicts and come to cooperative agreements.

Basin communities use the PEDS model as a cumulative and reiterative process for establishing and evaluating the effective governance of a river basin. Social learning is a key part of this process, and takes several forms, as we will indicate in the following description of the model framework. With Pahl-Wostl et al. and Mostert et al., we point out that using social learning within this framework offers basin stakeholders a process for working together 1) to understand each other's value systems for natural resource decision making, 2) to develop trust, 3) to jointly define the nature of the problem they are trying to address, 4) to engage in fact-finding, 5) to develop and assess different strategies for addressing problems and 6) to carry out a plan and assess its success in achieving their goals.[21] The entire model for mediation in natural resource governance is premised on a triad of a community's previous experiences with resource or development projects, the willingness of the community participants to learn from each other and to understand and apply the science and laws necessary to carry out a project, and the ultimate goal of creating and implementing a local management plan for the natural resource.

19 Pahl-Wostl, C. and M. Hare, "Processes of Social Learning in Integrated Resources Management" (2004) 14 *Journal of Community and Applied Social Psychology*, 193.

20 Fernandes Neto, J.A.S., *Modelo Urubici de Governança da Água e do Território: uma tecnologia social a serviço do desenvolvimento sustentável local*, Florianópolis, Ph.D. thesis in environmental engineering – Universidade Federal de Santa Catarina, 2010, 235.

21 Mostert, E., M. Craps and C. Pahl-Wostl, "Social Learning: The Key to Integrated Water Resources Management?" (2008) 33 *Water International* 293.

## 3 Social learning in six river basin communities in Santa Catarina, Brazil

### *3.1 Santo Amaro and Águas Mornas (Cubatão River Basin) sensibilization, initial agreement and science pedagogy in the schools: "Social Management of the Water in the Rio Cubatão-Sul, S.C., August 2010-June 2011"*

This project established an executive basin committee with the express purpose of constructing a basin management plan that would include three basic elements: an environmental education network throughout the schools, a system for managing hydrologic data, and monitoring program for water quality. In order to arrive at an Initial Agreement for doing this collaborative work, the group, led by a local coordinator and facilitated by Professor Daniel da Silva used a mediation technique that demonstrated how everyone came to the table with differing perspectives on how the environment could be visualized and interpreted. Everyone was asked to draw a flower in a vase from a real model and then to draw it again without looking at the actual object or first drawing. In addition to proving that the cognitive and social reality of each person was different, this exercise demonstrated how each individual had different skills in drawing or verbalizing his or her thoughts. These different perspectives and skills were to be valued and respected as part of their process of working together. The participants were further sensitized to the actual environment they were working in by going on a field trip to the basin to discuss the aesthetic dimensions of the region, the water cycle in the basin (cognitive dimension), and the nature of cooperation required to address the issues the Committee was interested in.

In 2011, the Committee had begun to discuss the establishment of an environmental education network during a national conference on Social Management of Brazilian River Basins in the town of Santo Amaro. UFSC students, under the direction of da Silva, had already been teaching basic concepts in the local schools such as ecology, biosphere, and the water cycle, the history of environmental degradation, and environmental stewardship with the cooperation of science teachers. Each of these classes used several dynamic or concrete ways to physically, conceptually and emotionally instruct the students. For example, the concept of water scarcity was demonstrated by placing three gymnastic mats on the floor, representing bodies of water and then playing musical chairs. Each time the music stopped, one of the mats was withdrawn so that more and more students ended up on one mat.

### *3.2 Concórdia (Jacutinga Basin): establishing the cognitive and social reality of participants*

In order to inventory the kinds of previous experiences with natural resource projects, determine what kinds of concepts were learned in those earlier processes and evaluate the strengths and weaknesses of those concepts, the UFSC

Environmental Psychology Lab gave a questionnaire to 225 participants of the Tecnologias Sociais para a Gestão da Água (TSGA) projects. This first step was used in June 2009 in the cities of Concórdia, Urubici, Turvo, Orleans and Braço do Norte, all in the state of Santa Catarina. Invited participants were selected from the Agricultural Research Center and Rural Extension of Santa Catarina (Empresa de Pesquisa Agropecuária e Extensão Rural de Santa Catarina or EPAGRI); educators from the elementary to the technical and superior levels; municipal health, security and agricultural offices; environmental police; city aldermen; rural agricultural producers; rural agricultural unions; professional associations; public school directors; members of rural agricultural cooperatives; and others considered to be important community representatives. Of the total 225, 7% (15 participants) were from Concórdia and 40% (91 participants) had taken the questionnaire for an earlier TSGA project in 2007. This group was used for a comparative study with those new participants.[22] The first part of this questionnaire asked participants to write five words or expressions that they associate with the word *water*. The words *saúde* (health), *limpeza* (cleanness or cleanliness), *poluição* (pollution), *higiene* (hygiene), *indispensável* (indispensable), *nascente* (source or spring), *potabilidade* (potability), *alimento* (food), *qualidade* (quality) and *preservação* (preservation) were repeated the most frequently (eight times or more) in all cities. *Saúde* was repeated with the greatest frequency.[23]

The second question asked respondents to relate water to the concept of quality in five words or expressions. The testers interpreted the frequency *of despoluída, limpa, incolor, potabilidade* and *preservação* to mean that the value of water was determined by its quality, which, in turn, was associated with its use and maintenance of health and life. Preservation of this resource was essential to maintain this use value. The third question asked for five associations with polluted water, and the words *mal, calamidade and alternativas* ('bad', 'catastrophe' and 'other options') occurred most frequently.[24]

A fourth question asked for five associations between water use and water exploration, with results suggesting that the words *adequate, food, drink, knowledge, contamination, loss, building consciousness, economize, expenses, irrigation, necessity* and *rational* formed a word core.[25]

The configuration of the word choices was not the same for each city, but the results were brought back to the participants in a working group for further discussion to identify what perspectives the group had about their own water, how they valued it, and what they saw were the challenges of maintaining basin water quality for their particular uses. This strategy helped the participants to recognize both the diversity and complexity in their experiences and expectations. For this reason, we consider it a form of mediation.

22 *Relatório 7*, 43. Document available through the author Da Silva.

23 *Relatório parcial 7*, 540. Document available through the author Da Silva.

24 *Relatório 7*, 57.

25 Ibid, 5.

In Concórdia, the results of the working group led to the organization of a Field Day for Pig Raising and the Environment by the Regional Committee of the Suinoculture Association of the Upper Uruguai Basin Towns. Approximately 1,000 participants rotated through exhibits where they received information about best practices for suinoculture.[26] Demonstrations for treating residues (biodigestores) from pig raising and reusing the residue for fertilizer and water for additional pigs were also constructed on private farms.

### *3.3 Braço do Norte (Tubarão Basin): applying environmental education and demonstrations*

Studies of Santa Catarina indicate the state has one of the highest indices of environmental pollution in Brazil, which represents an imbalance between economic development (7% of the national Produto Interno Bruto (PIB)) and natural resource use (water). One of the primary agricultural activities, pig raising, principally family farming with less than 50 hectares, generates the amount of waste drainage or pollution equivalent to 25 million inhabitants (5.7 thousand farm animals). Close confinement of the animals, poor management practices, and lack of wastewater treatment have resulted in serious damage of the watershed.[27] Other types of pollution, such as mining of sand and untreated domestic sewage, were also present.[28] In order to help the town of Braço do Norte address these problems and to form an Initial Agreement, in 2008 the GTHIDRO team and the town designed a pilot project entitled Management of Residual Suinoculture Waste with a Focus on the Efficient and Integrated Use of Water. A key part of this project was the environmental education of the participants. Within ten months, 42 people, including the *Brazilian* Agricultural Research Corporation's (EMBRAPA), the Santa Catarina Information Center for Environmental Resources and Hydrometeorology, Farming and Animal Research, and Rural Extension Company of Santa Catarina (CIRAM – EPAGRI), rural producers, municipal officials and commercial leaders, environmental advocates and non-governmental organizations (NGOs), were trained in the water laws, the relationship between different types of economic production and their impacts on the basin ecosystem, and technology for pig sanitation.

The group initially used a mediation tool, called 'Three Moments' (a shortened version of the Cognitive and Social Reality Questionnaire) to establish the key water problems the community faced, explore the nature of the problem, and discuss the activities necessary to address these problems.[29] During this time, pilot

26 Ibid, 23, Dia de Campo da Suinocultura e Meio Ambiente.

27 *Tecnologias Sociais para a Gestao da Água*. Access: http://tsga.ufsc.br/.

28 Comitê do Região Tubarão e Complexo Lagunar, *Diagnóstico dos Recursos Hídricos e Organização dos Agentes da Bacia do Rio Tubarão e Complexo Lagunar*, Volume 2G, 5.

29 Projeto Tecnologias Sociais para a Gestão da Água, *2° relatório parcial texto principal*, 2007, 94.

projects were also established as demonstration spots within private farms. One of these demonstration plots included the storage and treatment of pig waste on the farm of Sr. Valdir Wiggers.[30] At this demonstration site the sewage residue from pig production was first sent to a decantation pond with aeration to remove solids and sediments. The next step was to create and deploy a biodigestor or pond for treatment with an aquatic plant (lemnas aquaticas or duckweed) to remove bacteria. Then finally this material was sent to a holding pond from which the treated material could be pumped and combined with compost for fertilized irrigation.[31] The biogas produced an average concentration of 70% methane and 30% $CO_2$, which was converted to electricity and used to run small heaters in the winter.[32] The group of 42 people from Braço do Norte became a community of learners with the GTHIDRO team by helping to construct the materials at the demonstration site.

The idea of producing thematic maps emerged as a result of the town's Initial Agreement and the participants' discussions about the nature of their earlier experiences with development projects. The Tecnologias Sociais para a Gestão da Água (TSGA) team offered to teach the group how to read different kinds of maps and use the geographic information systems (GIS) *ARCExplorer, Spring* and *Google Earth*. First, the Urubici group learned how to collect specific data about soil types, vegetation cover, geohydrology, landscape landmarks, etc., and to organize them into data banks. Much of the data was available online in the form of satellite images or digitalized maps, but the group also divided itself into thematic groups to compare the maps with what they actually discovered in the field at specific geographic coordinates. Then, with the help of the Geographic Information Systems (GIS), they created thematic maps on geology, hydrology, ecology, sanitation and permanent preservation areas. These themes were selected because the community realized the information was essential to any kind of watershed planning. In this sense, creating thematic maps was a means of empowering the community. Next, they constructed two maps of the water demand: one for sanitation purposes and the other for educational tourism.

The thematic groups also went into the town and surrounding areas to match geographic locations with landmarks or evidence of the particular themes. They photographed the sites they visited so they could be linked with the maps' coordinates. This geographic exercise came as a surprise to many participants, even after living in the area for many years. During the field trips participants were heard saying,

30 Ibid, 30.

31 Projeto Tecnologias Sociais para a Gestão da Água, *Dossiês das Tecnologias, versão Preliminar*, 2007. Access: http://v1.tsga.ufsc.br/images/pdf/dossie_completo.pdf.

32 Projeto Tecnologias Sociais para a Gestão da Água, *2° relatório parcial texto principal*, 2007, 30.

"For us it has always been like this. These mountains and rivers have always been here".

"I never thought that Water Rock actually gave us water from the Guarani Aquifer!"

"Cathedral Rock is our natural patrimony, so we need to take care of it".

"In the old times, people would look at the Araucaria as a wood resource to be cut and sold".

"There's trash on the top of the mountain that's going to flow down the mountain to us!"

These observations led the group to recognize that the land supporting the Araucaria trees should be preserved and that the community should encourage tourism as an economic venture.

Each group's maps and photos drew increased interest among the townspeople. The groups acted as mediators for the community. As the groups discussed their findings, they began to discover links between the different themes and realize the complexity of the interactions between the socio-economic dynamics and the ecosystem. They knew this kind of information was essential to establishing any kind of strategic planning. These presentations gained the group municipal support, represented by the elected prefect and the chief of police, as well as requests for membership from NGOs not previously involved in the group's work. The entire community was also convinced that they needed to construct a sustainable development plan that would include the construction of a conservation area around the recharge area and other waterfalls associated with the Guarani Aquifer, a water and sanitation plan, an educational program of environmental tourism and a conservation plan for the preserving the remaining araucarias. The community also realized that the resources in their area could be considered common goods for which they were all responsible. The products of their work can be seen in the touist guide, a placard along with a farm house as part of the conservation area, and the two maps for tourism and water/sanitation.

### 3.4 *Urubici (Canoas Basin): evaluating a community's empowerment for water governance*

Although evaluation is featured in the last part of the model, it is also used at the end of each project activity with four questions or requests: *What are the strong points of the activity? Parts that need improvement? Further suggestions or recommendations? Give one word that synthesizes this activity/experience.* These are all recorded and used during the team's planning sessions prior to moving on to another activity or stage of the model. The final evaluation, made with the basin committee and other participants, occurs at the end of the project. The main purpose is to evaluate the group's sense of empowerment. The team defines 'community empowerment' in terms of the group's increased ability to communicate ideas and values. In order for this to be a significant measurement, the

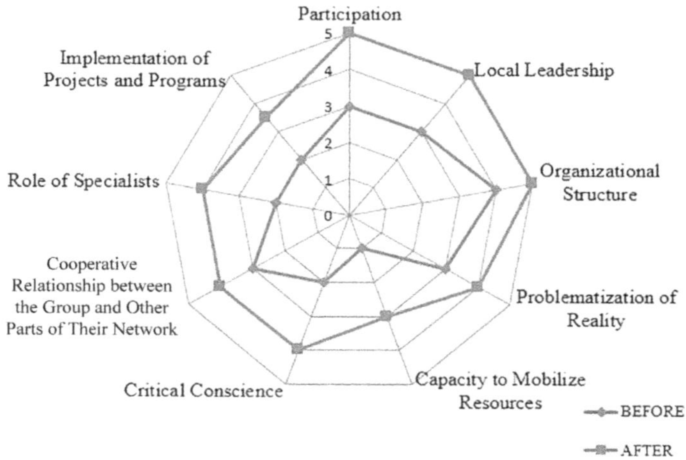


*Figure 9.5* Community Empowerment Evaluation[33]

evaluation also has to occur at the beginning of the project as well during the cognitive and social reality stage. At the conclusion of the project, each individual is asked to respond to nine dimensions of social empowerment as measured by Laverack.[34] Figure 9.5 represents the compiled evaluations for the Urubici group, with whom GTHIDRO had been working for ten years:

In addition to workshop evaluations, Fernandes Neto created and implemented a broader schematic assessment which required a baseline and final evaluation on six specific aspects of social learning within the community governance group. Because of the recent addition of this tool to the mediation model, out of all the basins, only Urubici actually used this method of assessment. Participation of the Urubici community was measured by the willingness of the participants, which included municipal officials and the Regional Council of Tourism, to break up into work groups in order to deal with the complexity of the issues they faced. It also refers to the level of discussions about the issues held during any meeting.

The first arm of the web was *participation*, which is one of the most important aspects in order to build empowerment. Only through participation in small or large groups, each one of the members of a community may be able to define, analyze, and deal with questions which refer to their ensemble.

*Local leadership* was the second arm, which aims to visualize the willingness of community leaders to recognize and deal with complex problems, rather than dismissing items as 'externalities'.

33 Fernandes Neto, J.A.S., *Modelo Urubici de Governança da Água e do Território: uma tecnologia social a serviço do desenvolvimento sustentável local*, Florianópolis, Ph.D. thesis in environmental engineering – Universidade Federal de Santa Catarina, 2010, 235.

34 Laverack, G. and N. Wallerstein, "Measuring Community Empowerment: A Fresh Look at Organizational Domains" (2001) 16(2) *Health Promotion International* 179.

*Organizational structure* refers to the degree of broad representation within the basin committee. This appears to be the Urubici group's strong point, even from the beginning.

*Problematization of reality* means to examine or question what appears to be reality. It is another way to recognize the complexity of watershed governance and to construct or acquire new knowledge about the nature of problems of resource governance. It also requires participants to question and consider whether an issue is either a cause or symptom of larger problems. This was particularly the case with learning about the new laws and about the nature of the area in and around Urubici.

The *capacity to mobilize resources* refers not only to funding for projects but also to the ability to find and use knowledge sources, whether it is local or scientific knowledge. The segment was clearly a problem for the group, but they did make some improvement over the course of time.

The sixth arm, *critical conscience*, requires the group to coalesce from a series of interests to a group aware of the values and knowledge of other members of the group and to use this knowledge to find solutions to problems.

The *cooperative relationship with the group with other parts of their network* is an extension of the critical conscience. In the case of the Urubici group, this meat that the group stopped blaming municipal officials for not solving problems and began working with them as part of a community of learners. This arm showed positive change over time

The eighth arm covered the role or use of *specialists in the process of social learning*, and the group showed about the same progress as the two preceding domains. The final domain covered the degree to which *the group implemented projects and programs.* This remained a challenge for the group because, despite their increased level of maturity and knowledge about resource governance, the group still did not think they could carry out all their projects. There was also some resistance from the larger community about the project to create an *Araucaria angustifolia* conservation area.

This before-and-after evaluation was presented to the group for discussion, and in a sense provided the group with additional social learning about themselves as a group. It also mediated the way for the group to move ahead and find solutions for adapting or implementing unfinished projects. Other projects were not yet ready for evaluation, so we have only this one example of the final part of the model, the final evaluation.

## 4 Discussion

This mediation model for building a community's capacity for local resource governance through various forms of social learning pays far more attention to each process in the model and to the importance of each individual understanding the cumulative nature of the process, learning to work within the group, learning about hydrology, map making, laws, organizational and project design – subjects the individual may have had neither knowledge nor interest in until the group began to meet. The research group itself adjusted the model several times, as the diagrams from the masters and dissertation indicate over time. They too learned by experience to make the model work more smoothly and effectively.

Perhaps the model's greatest achievement is its ability to improve the management core group's capacity to plan and implement projects of their own design, using strategies they have learned and networks they have established in their watershed and state. This capacity is the very key to success in any development projects, for the team or any development agency cannot remain in the community forever. The community itself must be able to manage the resource, which may require several projects, as was the case with Urubici. In addition, much of what is acquired during the social learning process carries over into other ventures and truly enhances a community's capacity to value its human capital and to create a management plan for now and the future.

The success of this model of mediation is also due to the policy and legal support by the Brazilian government. The water, conservation and municipal laws spell out exactly what is expected from each community, they establish guidelines for representation on a water committee and they are integrated with each other so that there are no departmental policy conflicts. The federal and state governments also supply some funding, and they encourage the communities to collaborate with universities and companies that provide funding for the kind of research and outreach that GTHIDRO does. In fact, research indicates that mediation through social learning can help government perform its role more effectively.[35]

Finally, the success of social learning also depends upon the group having a good trained facilitator who knows how to organize meetings effectively and can get individuals to 'own' the projects as if they invented they invented them. A good facilitator is also required for potential conflicts, dominating personalities and eliciting creative thinking of each person within the group.

## Conclusion

Watershed collaboration literature points out how difficult it is to identify objective measures of social learning,[36] especially since the configuration of issues, participants, policies and support is different in each case. However, reviewing the work of GTHIDRO with six water basin communities, where policy and legal support are the same, provides us with a sense of continuity in the use of a mediation model for resource governance built specifically on social learning. While the potential for competition between economic sectors for the various uses of water and energy is always present,[37] Brazilian water laws and government have

35 Klijn, E.H. and J.F.M. Koppenjan, "Public Management and Policy Networks: Foundations of a Network Approach to Governance" (2000) 2 *Public Management Review* 135.

36 Kumler, L.M. and M.C. Lemos, "Managing Waters of the Paraíba do Sul River Basin, Brazil: A Case Study in Institutional Change and Social Learning" (2008) 13(2) *Ecology and Society* 22; Mostert, E., M. Craps and C. Pahl-Wostl, "Social Learning: The Key to Integrated Water Resources Management?" (2008) 33 *Water International* 293.

provided communities and university researchers in the state of Santa Catarina support for cooperation and collaborative planning on water and energy issues. In fact, the concept of community empowerment pervades the PEDS model and is confirmed by workshop evaluations, Fernandes Neto's before-and-after spider web measurements and by the enthusiasm of local water users for their work together.

Mediation is a process that is both time and resource intensive, but working with complex socio-ecological systems, this version of it has the advantage of being integrated and comprehensive,[38] as well as designed to address misunderstandings that reflect a lack of knowledge, a political bias, or a very self-serving narrow perspective. Creating resource governance requires a high learning curve, even change in both group and individual behaviour. Mediation, if used constructively, can do just that.

37 Priscoli, J.D. and A.T. Wolf, *Managing and Transforming Water Conflicts*, Cambridge University Press, New York, 2009, 20.

38 Hooper, B.P. and G.T. McDonald, "Facilitating Integrated Resource and Environmental Management: Australian and Canadian Perspective" (1999) 42(5) *Journal of Environmental Planning & Management* 747; Margerum, R.D. and D. Whitall, "The Challenges and Implications of Collaborative Management on a River Basin Scale" (2004) 47(3) *Journal of Environmental Planning & Management* 409.

# 10 The environmental complaint letters and visits system in China

*Shijun Zhang*[1]

## Introduction

Environmental dispute resolution generally includes settlements through litigation and non-litigation approaches. Among other reasons, the litigation approach, being costly and inefficient, which phenomenon is called 'litigation explosion'. Alternative dispute resolution (ADR) originated in the United States and gradually developed since 1970s. At the same time, similar non-litigation approach for environmental dispute settlement has sprang up in Japan and Taiwan. With the background of China's reform and opening up in 1980s, modern environmental issues emerged and became more serious along with the rapid economic development. Meanwhile, environmental disputes have increasingly built up. However, in the light of the deficiencies in China's environmental legislation, the limited capability of courts in dealing with environmental disputes, and the lack of public trust for courts, litigation has never been the main approach to resolve environmental disputes. It was estimated by a research in 2009 that only 3% of environmental disputes were accepted by courts.[2] Most environmental disputes are settled either by complaining to administrative organs, which essentially is a selective settlement mechanism combining administration and litigation, or through 'complaint letters and visits', a unique Chinese approach for dispute settlement outside of judicial system.

This Article looks back to the development history of China's environmental complaint letters and visits system first. Then this Article analyzes the necessity of environmental complaint letters and visits in environmental disputes resolution. This is not only because that the environmental complaint letters and visits fit in China's traditional culture and current situation. More importantly, it is the most effective and low-cost way in environmental disputes resolution. But with the reform of judicial system in China, especially the environmental protection departments are not willing to involve themselves in environmental disputes resolution, the most recent environment legislation tends to abolish

1 Professor of law, Law School of Shandong University, PRC.

2 All China Environment Federation, *See How to Safeguard One's Right While Facing the Pollution Accident, How Far Can the Environmental Court Go.* Access: www.acef.com.cn/site2/envlaw/news/38066.shtml.

the environmental disputes resolution responsibility for Environmental Protection Department. This Article examines the defects of current environmental complaint letters and visits system, and suggests two major ways to improve the environmental complaint letters and visits system. The first is to set up specialized agency for environmental dispute settlement. The second is to entitle the environmental disputes settlement agency power and means to settle disputes.

## 1 An overview of environmental complaint letters and visits in China

'Complaint letters and visits' came from 'complaint letters and visits from the people', which was originally adopted by the Communist Party of China (CPC). The system with unique Chinese characteristics, is an invention of the CPC, aiming to fulfil the ideological commitment of 'serving the people' in such a way that encourages people to report issues, which will be subsequently investigated and solved by government. The ideological effect is that the party maintains close connections with the people, and achieves the goal of 'from the masses, to the masses'.[3] As a typical product of China, 'complaint letters and visits' arose from a particular Chinese social and political environment. The system, historically derived from national leaders' instructions and working habits, was initially designed to enhance the relationship between the party and the people from top to bottom and to seek better understanding and more support for the new regime.[4] With respect to legislation, *Decisions on Handling People's Letters and Meeting People*, a regulation promulgated by the National Administration Council in 1951, is considered the starting point of China's modern system of complaint letters and visits.

In the early stage, complaint letters and visits were not related with environmental disputes but mainly with political matters. It is concluded by a scholar that the system of complaint letters and visits has gone through four primary stages.[5] The first stage, the preliminary formation stage of the system, was from the founding of the People's Republic of China to 1957, during which the National Administration Council promulgated *Decisions on Handling People's Letters and Meeting People* on June 7, 1951. This is generally considered the starting point of the formal establishment of the system.[6] During the second stage from 1957 to 1978, complaint letters and visits were mostly the result of mass mobilization, a considerable amount of which was related to political participation. The third

3 Bofeng, C., "Vexatious Suits, Complaint Letters and Visits and Chinese Legal Tradition--Issues Concerning Vexatious Suits During the Transforming Period of Law [J]" (2004) 2 *Peking University Law Journal* 226.

4 Yujie, N., "The Historical Review and Current Situation of Complaint Letters and Visits in China" (2010) 11 *Chinese Administration Management* 36.

5 Jianbing, C., *Research on the Complaint Letters and Visits System [D]*, Thesis of Master Degree of East China University of Politics and Law, 2006, 14.

6 Jianbing, C., *Research on the Complaint Letters and Visits System [D]*, Thesis of Master Degree of East China University of Politics and Law, Shanghai, 2006, 13.

stage was from the Third Consultation Session of the Eleventh Central Committee of the CPC in 1978 to the Twelfth National Congress of the CPC in 1982. The main task of the system in this stage was to solve a large amount of historical issues and restore justice to those falsely charged cases. Since 1982, which is the fourth stage, the primary function of the complaint letters and visits system, with the political task in the third stage having been mostly completed, has transformed into disputes settlement and rights relief. The last stage is a legalization process of the complaint letters and visits system, during which many pertinent laws and regulations have been published, such as *Work Rules on Receiving Visits of the Complaint Letters and Visits Department of the Supreme People's Court* (promulgated on June 20, 1980), *Work Rules on Charging, Appeal and Procuratorial Work of the Supreme People's Procuratorate* (promulgated on December 10, 1986), and *Regulation on Complaint Letters and Visits* (promulgated by State Council on October 28, 1995). After the promulgation of *Regulation on Complaint Letters and Visits*, central government departments, many provincial and municipal governments also successively published regulations, complaint letters and visits working rules and interim provisions.

Meanwhile, as Chinese society and economy have been growing rapidly and public awareness of environmental protection has been enhanced, environmental problems have become an increasing concern, leading to substantial rise about environmental disputes and environmental complaint letters and visits. According to the statistical data released by *China Environment Yearbook*, the number of environmental complaint letters and visits started to surge in the mid-1990s. In 1995, the total national amount of environmental complaint letters and visits were 58,678, while the number reached 608,245 in 2005. In order to improve the environmental complaint letters and visits system and deal with environmental disputes, the State Environmental Protection Administration (SEPA), which based on the 1995 *Regulation on Complaint Letters and Visits*, enacted *Measures for Environmental Complaint Letters and Visits* in 1997.This indicated that the Chinese government began to consider bringing the environmental complaint letters and visits into the legalization process and Chinese environmental complaint letters and visits system was initially established.

With the deepening of reformation, the accelerating transformation of economy and society, and the adjustment of social interest structure, together with numerous new circumstances and problems caused by those complaint letters and visits from the public, the State Council of PRC, faced an extremely difficult situation and published the revised *Regulation on Complaint Letters and Visits* in 2005 to deal with complaint letters and visits. Subsequently, the SEPA revised the 1997 *Measures for Environmental Complaint Letters and Visits* in 2006. The revision of the two regulations promoted the further improvement of the Chinese complaint letters and visits system and the environmental complaint letters and visits system.

According to more than 60 years of experience of complaint letters and visits and relevant laws since the founding of the PRC, complaint letters and visits system is becoming a mechanism that official offices deal with complaint letters and visits, which based on the policies of CPC and of the state, for example, taking administrative or economic measures, going through consultation or mediation, conducting political and ideological education to take care of various issues.[7] Whereas environmental complaint letters and visits is of particular significance in settling environmental disputes in Chinese society. One Chinese scholar similarly asserted that public participation is primarily conducted in three forms: complaint letters and visits, proposals in the People's Congress and Political Consultative Conference and administrative arbitration by Environmental Protection Bureau. Above all, environmental complaint letters and visits is the soundest system in the process of institutionalization of citizens' environmental participation.[8]

## 2 Why environmental complaint letters and visits is the main approach for environmental dispute settlement in China?

As stated earlier, people in China seldom resort to lawsuits in the event of environmental disputes, the number of which accepted by courts is merely around 3% of the total amount.[9] In the current process of legal modernization, the legal institutional arrangements of both litigation and non-litigation offer multiple choices for remedies and environmental dispute settlement, but why do people prefer complaint letters and visits – the non-litigation remedy? This preference to complaint letters and visits has its historical and cultural reasons and relates to realistic predicaments of environmental litigation in China. Moreover, when it comes to right relief in contemporary China, complaint letters and visits are given a special meaning and institutional value.

### *2.1 Environmental complaint letters and visits correspond with the need of traditional Chinese legal culture*

The self-sufficient natural economy had been the dominant economic production mode of Chinese agricultural society during over 5,000 years feudal history of ancient China. By virtue of the characteristics of natural economy, which were self-sufficient, underdeveloped technology and lack of convenient and low-cost transportation, people confined themselves in limited space, isolated from each other and kept insular and conservative views; thus, people in traditional society barely went to Kwana (governmental office in Feudal China) to solve their disputes.

7 Yanwei, Y., *Jurisprudential Analysis of the Complaint Letters and Visits System [D]*, Thesis of Master Degree of China University of Political Science and Law, Beijing, 2004, 5.

8 Xufeng, Z., "The Role of Environmental Citizen Society in Environmental Governance [J]" (2008) 10 *China Social Sciences Documentation* 122.

9 All China Environment Federation, *See How to Safeguard One's Right While Facing the Pollution Accident, How Far Can the Environmental Court Go*. Access: www.acef.com.cn/site2/envlaw/news/38066.shtml.

Confucius, the representative of Chinese traditional culture, demonstrated such 'detesting lawsuit' sentiment: "When hearing cases, I, too, intend to keep them from happening again".[10] Therefore, it is safe to say that Confucius was very supportive of this non-lawsuit attitude, which could also be shown in one of the classic works of Confucianism *Chou I*. For example,

> When things are not going well, it is better for a person to face it with forbearance. In case that a lawsuit is involved, he shall maintain a peaceful mind, as the result will not be auspicious even if the problem is solved by the lawsuit. Therefore, instead of resorting to lawsuits to settle disputes, relying on prestigious men to mediate between two sides.[11]

Against this background, disputes were usually not resolved by feudal officials, but clansmen or other private organizations (i.e. guilds).[12]

### 2.2 *The realistic predicament for environmental litigation in China*

The judicial solution to environmental disputes is rather authoritative. However, environmental litigation is confronted with severe difficulties, mainly in presenting evidences and examination and approval. Either the identification of causality between pollution and damage, or the calculation of the amount of damages is extremely complex and professional. At present, China has an enormous insufficiency in appraisal institutions for environmental pollution. Owing to a lack of uniform technique standards and methods, sometimes appraisal institutions come out disparate or even opposite results about one case, which makes the courts in a dilemma. Difficulties in case-filing and high cost constitute the third reason for environmental litigation dilemma. Pollution victims cannot afford the expensive litigation cost and appraisal fees. Moreover, implicit local protectionism makes environmental litigation more difficult, because local fiscal levy depends on polluting enterprises and the courts' expenditure comes from finance as well. More than half of the environmental lawsuits end up with pollution victims being the losing party who should have been compensated.[13] In China, pollution victims tend to be vulnerable, especially low-income groups. Since they cannot afford the high litigation costs, they have to give up lawsuits, resulting in complaint letters and visits becoming primary solution for environmental disputes.

10 *Analects of Confucius*, Book XII: Yen-Yuan.

11 *Zhou Yi*.

12 Reference to relevant views: Zhi Ping, L., *Seeking the Harmony in Natural Order*, Chinese Edition, 2002, 199; Li, S., *Rule of Law and Its Local Resources*, Chinese Edition, 1996, 32; Jinfan, Z., *The Tradition and Modern Transition of Chinese Law (the Second Edition)*, Law Press China, 2005, 270.

13 Shijun, Z., "The Analysis of the Administrative Resolutions of Environmental Disputes" (2003), 18(6) *The Rule of Law Forum* 60.

### 2.3 *The advantages of environmental complaint letters and visits in environmental dispute resolution mechanism*

China has a large number of environmental disputes, but the lawsuit-detesting culture together with the predicament in practice pushes the public to stay away from courts and turn to non-litigation approach, administrative organs in particular. Environmental complaint letters and visits, as one type of complaint letters and visits, has its comparative edge to lawsuits by providing a more convenient remedy approach for victims in environmental disputes. To begin with, environmental complaint letters and visits have relatively low cost. Official offices do not charge any fees but give complaint makers a certain amount of subsidies. Thus victims are more willing to choose environmental complaint letters and visits with low-cost and flexible procedure rather than costly and time-consuming lawsuits with complex procedure. Second, environmental complaint letters and visits need low evidence requirements. Complaint makers[14] need only to submit the basic facts relevant to damages suffered from environmental pollution. Neither accurate evidences proving that enterprises have been emitting pollutants nor judicial authentication materials concerning personal or property damages are required. Specific conditions about the pollution caused by enterprises are investigated by official institutions that deal with environmental complaint letters and visits, generally by environmental protection authorities at all levels through administrative process. Damages are not necessarily based on judicial authentication conclusions, but dispute settlement process or environmental administrative organs that provide consultation mechanism for both sides in environmental disputes. Comparing with the evidence rules in civil actions, environmental complaint letters and visits greatly alleviate the injured party's burden of proof and offer timely and efficient remedies. In addition, environmental complaint letters and visits system could temporarily make the complaint makers emotionormal (emotion normal). It provides a channel for them to actively report environmental protection conditions and propose suggestions about environmental management or complain about environmental disputes, and thereby pacify their moods and ease the situation. Unlike lawsuits where cases are heard by judges, the reception staff at the official offices could sit down and have a conversation with complaint makers, during which circumstances they are listened to and answered to their questions. The existence of the environmental complaint letter and visits system restrains complaint makers from taking a more aggressive way to seek reliefs and protect their interests, and thereby contributes to maintaining the stability of social order.

Official offices that deal with environmental complaint letters and visits are generally set up inside the environmental administrative organs at all levels. They

14 According to the 2006 *Measures for Environmental Complaint Letters and Visits* enacted by the State Environmental Protection Administration, the complaint maker refers to citizens, legal persons and other organizations that propose suggestions and opinions or make complaints about the conditions of environmental protection to environmental protection administrative departments at all levels in such forms as letter, email, fax, telephone or visits.

have the responsibility of environmental supervision by entitling to organize, coordinate and dispose matters involving environmental complaint letters and visits on behalf of the corresponding environmental administrative organs.[15]. According to the environmental management system established by *Environmental Protection Law of PRC*, environmental protection authorities at all levels are the administrative departments in charge of the overall supervision of environmental protection in their administrative districts. As they are familiar with local environmental conditions, environmental problems and the status of enterprise pollution, they have a full understanding of environmental laws, regulations and policies, and are equipped with environmental technologies, environmental supervision methods and environmental information, together with the huge advantages in fact-finding and evidence collection benefited from their authority and expertise, environmental protection authorities at all levels can offset the deficiency in the concerning parties' lack of ability to present evidences, and, with the help of environmental experts, accurately determine the facts, causes, responsibilities and damages of environmental pollution, thus achieve a more reasonable result than it would have gone through a trial. Environmental protection authorities are conferred the powers to monitor environmental hazards, to cope with environmental pollution incidents and disputes, to exert and pursue to related laws, to apply various administrative measures against environmental tortfeasors (including, among others, on-site inspection, survey, sample detection, photograph, taping, evidence collection, supervision of the facilities for the prevention of pollution and examination of the operation record). They may also take compulsory measures against ongoing environmental infringement which include, but is not limited to, administrative and legal means as warnings, fines, revocation of pollutant discharge permits, rectifications with a prescribed time limit, and shutting down and move. In this way, environmental protection authorities can directly deal with environmental pollution, reduce the cost of dispute settlement and relieve the burden of victims. Above all, environmental complaint letters and visits led by environmental protection authorities, in comparison with the courts' procedural functions, have evident advantages in terms of cost and expertise. All this make it the prior choice for environmental dispute settlement.

15 *Measures for Environmental Complaint Letters and Visits*, Article 8: Environmental protection administrative departments at county level shall establish or designate environmental complaint letters and visits office with full-time or part-time staff. Environmental protection administrative departments of provinces, autonomous regions and districted cities shall establish separate environmental complaint letters and visits offices. The environmental complaint letters and visits offices of environmental protection administrative departments at all levels shall, on behalf of their corresponding departments, take charge of the work to organize, coordinate, deal with and supervise complaint letters and visits and other related matters, and ensure the accesses to environmental complaint letters and visits.

## 3 The challenges confronting environmental complaint letters and visits system

For a fairly long time, the environmental complaint letters and visits system has played a major role in settling environmental disputes. According to the provisions of the 2006 *Measures for Environmental Complaint Letters and Visits*, the main bodies of environmental complaint letters and visits activities are environmental protection administrative departments at all levels, and the competent administrative departments of environmental protection at or above the provincial level shall set up independent environmental letters and visits work mechanism in the light of relevant provisions. As stipulated in Article 15 of *Measures for Environmental Complaint Letters and Visits*, after environmental protection departments at all levels accept and hear environmental complaint letters and visits cases, they can organize relevant social groups, legal aid agencies, professionals and community volunteers to participate effectively in counsel, education, negotiation, mediation, hearing and other methods to handle environmental issues which reported by complaint makers legally, timely and reasonably. In accordance with Article 41 of the 1989 *Environmental Protection Act*, administrative authorities usually, in the long-term practice of dealing with environmental complaint letters and visits, use administrative mediation and administrative processing methods to solve the environment disputes after they accept complaints from environmental victims. Before 1992, environmental administrative authorities, for the most part, settled environmental disputes by mediation, in the failure of which, either declared its failure or made administrative decisions. Practice has proven that it was difficult to reach a mediation agreement for the parties through mediating when it comes to serious environmental disputes. If an administrative mediation fails, making administrative punishment decision in time (mainly in the form of administrative decisions or awards), is an effective way. With environmental departments which have professional advantage in the driver's seat, dealing with environmental complaint letters and visits through, among other methods, administrative mediation has played a crucial role in environmental dispute resolution. According to the data of Chinese General Social Survey in 2006 (CGSS2006) conducted by the Department of Sociology of Renmin University of China and the Department of Social Sciences of Hong Kong University Science and Technology, when facing with environmental disputes, most people (59.4%) prefer to choose non-institutionalized methods especially private relief to directly negotiate with polluters (40.5%). When resorting to institutionalized methods, most people (39.5%) hope to solve disputes through governments, which is mainly in the form of complaint letters and visits and complaints. Only 1.1% of the people hope to settle such disputes through litigation. Please see the detailed statistics at Table 10.1.

However, in cases of involvement of administrative measures when dealing with environmental letters and visits and environmental disputes, if any party is not satisfied with the administrative punishment decision and files a lawsuit, environmental protection departments may become defendant. Therefore,

*Table 10.1* Survey of action mode

| *Mechanism of dispute settlement* | | *Action mode* | *Sample number* | *Proportion* |
|---|---|---|---|---|
| Institutionalized dispute solution | Litigation | Filing a suit | 2 | 1.1% |
| | Administrative punishment | Turn to government departments | 73 | 39.5% |
| Non-institutionalized dispute solution | | Negotiate with polluters directly | 75 | 40.5% |
| | | Reflect to the media | 7 | 3.8% |
| | | Others | 28 | 15.1% |

environmental protection departments are not willing to take the responsibility of dealing with environmental disputes or intervening between polluters and victims to avoid troubles. In recent years, during the process of the revisions of environmental laws, Ministry of Environmental Protection has used its advantageous position in drafting amendments to gradually modify and derogate its responsibility to dealing with environmental disputes through administrative methods. Responsibilities of environmental protection departments in the environmental dispute resolution was stipulated in Article 41 of the 1989 *Environmental Protection Act*, which was executed for long time in China:

> The disputes in liability or amount of compensation can be decided by the competent administrative department for environmental protection or other departments in accordance with the law who have environmental supervision and management right, on the basis of the request of the parties; If any party concerned refuses to accept the decision, they may bring a suit in a people's court. The party may also bring a suit in a people's court directly.

The ways for environmental protection departments to deal with environmental disputes mainly include administrative mediation and administrative adjudication. But due to the fact that using administrative adjudication to deal with environmental disputes may make environmental protection departments become the defendant in the lawsuit, environmental protection departments at all levels have tried to avoid the use of administrative decisions. Efforts of environmental protection departments to perform less duties in environmental disputes by trying to influence legislation began on January 31, 1992, in the *Approval of the State Environmental Protection Agency* comments, which was drafted by NPC Law Committee Office. The main content of the Approval is,

> When the parties concerned refuse to accept the compensation decision and bring a suit in a people's court, they shall not take environmental protection departments as defendant of administrative proceeding, but shall file a civil

lawsuit against the original pollution compensation disputes. At the same time, the people's court shall not accept and trial the disputes as administrative cases.

Though the Approval does not conform to the regulations of legal interpretation in *the Law on Legislation of the PRC*, it is considered as legal interpretation for environmental departments to be exempt from administrative means when dealing with environmental disputes. In fact, this Approval has affected the written responsibilities of environmental protection departments in dealing with environmental disputes. The *Environmental Pollution Prevention and Control Law of Solid Wastes* enacted in 1995, the *Act on Air Pollution Prevention and Control* revised in 2000 and the *Water Pollution Prevention and Control Law* revised in 2008 all stipulate that "The disputes in liability or amount of compensation can be mediated by a competent administrative department for environmental protection on the basis of the request of the parties". In the latest revision of *Environmental Protection Law*, effective in 2015, the responsibility of the environmental protection departments in the environmental dispute resolution is completely abolished. With regard to dispute resolution, Article 64 of the new *Environmental Protection Law* stipulates, "Them who cause destruction due to environmental pollution and ecological damage shall assume the tort liability in accordance with the relevant provisions of the tort liability law of the People 's Republic of China".

It has been difficult for environmental complaint letters and visits to play its due role in environmental dispute resolution in the consideration of main responsible departments gradually quitting administrative measures such as mediation and adjudication as well as various defects in the environmental complaint letters and visits system itself.

### *3.1 The complaint letters and visits agency is single mandated with restricted privileges*

According to the *Regulation on Complaint Letters and Visits*, the complaint reporting handling office fulfil the following duties: accepting, assigning and transferring the matters as described in the complaint letters and visits; handling the matters as described in the complaint letters and visits as assigned by the people's governments at and above the same level; coordinating the handling of the important complaint letters and visits; supervising and checking the handling of matters as described in complaint letters and visits. As mentioned earlier, complaint letters and visits agencies are confined to procedural matters like "acceptance, assignation, transference, coordination and supervision". In short, even if the complaint letters and visits agency requires further verification of the situation, it merely 'may' investigate other organizations and persons, and is only entitled in regard to specific matters concerning complaint letters and visits, substantive issues are not explicitly stipulated in the *Regulation on Complaint Letters and Visits*, with 'the three suggestions'.

The complaint letters and visits agencies have no independent authority to solve the environmental dispute problems. Therefore, it is rather cumbersome to completely resolve the problem of people's complaint letters and visits from the legislative perspective.

### *3.2 The lack of operating specifications*

Although the complaint letters and visits have been established as a legal system, it lacks clear internal operating specifications. According to the *Regulation on Complaint Letters and Visits*, the work of complaint letters and visits agencies mainly concentrate on reporting, transferring, delivering and informing complaint makers other solutions, while the only matter directly handled by the agencies is absent of specific process requirement. In practice, complaint letters and visits agencies generally do not directly deal with cases. Most of them act as the 'transit station' of diversion and re-exports. The higher the level of the agency, the more apparent this phenomenon appears. Complaint letters and visits cases are submitted, transferred and sent to relevant offices by complaint letters and visits agencies. Sometimes such a case will be sent back to the office where the complaint maker works, which contributes to retaliation against the complaint maker. Meanwhile, although the *Regulation on Complaint Letters and Visits* sets a deadline for handling concerned matters, it does not provide a notification system informing results involved.

## 4 Key points of improvement of the environmental complaint letters and visits system

Presently, China's complaint letters and visits system is facing predicament, and controversy has been created whether the system should retain or not. This situation is mainly based on the following reasons:

> After the complaint letters and visits system established, it once played an effective and subtle role in easing social contradictions and safeguarding the stability and unity of the whole social life. However, along with the rapid development of China's economy, conflicts of interest intensify further; in the period of the system transition, a lack of rules is leading to phenomenon of corruption and social injustice. All these problems make the function of the complaint letters and visits system to alter. The original function of contact with the masses and reflecting public opinion tends to be weakened, but function of right relief rises to more important position, and the complaint letters and visits system has become main means for a considerable part of the public to fight with the government. The tend of making use of complaint letters and visits system organized politically, and involved in foreign affairs is to be a great threat to the society and the government. The system is doubted by all circles of the society. As a result, to

retain the system of complaint letters and visits or not has become a focus of the current debate.[16]

The environmental complaint letters and visits system faces predicament as well. Analyzed from the external environment, the direction of China's judicial reform is gradually turning to advocate the rule of law. Thus when environmental disputes appear, it would be more attractive to solve them through the court proceedings. Especially, when the environmental protection departments do not want to take the responsibility of solving environmental disputes, it would be more reasonable to turn to the court for environmental pollution victims. From the environmental complaint letters and visits system itself, there are also plenty of disadvantages to the settlement of disputes.

These two aspects do great harm in environmental complaint letters and visits system's handling with the environmental disputes. Advocating the rule of law, does not mean that the environmental disputes must be resolved through legal channels. The court does not have advantages in dealing with environmental disputes, on the contrary, it faces with so many difficulties to deal with the problems. In fact, Chinese courts have been encumbered with the numerous cases. Currently, the method of Court-entrusted Mediation[17] is experimented to settle the disputes in order to reduce the appeal of the court.[18] The problems of the environmental complaint letters and visits system itself can be solved through compensating the institutional drawbacks eventually to achieve a better solution to the environmental disputes. China is still in the stage of industrialization. Although the growth of economic slows down, it remains to be one of the countries who have fastest economic growth in the world. And the conflict caused by environmental disputes will exist in China over a long period of time. Therefore, it is necessary to review the drawbacks in current environmental dispute processing mechanism carefully, improve the environmental complaint letters and visits system, and to find an effective way to resolve disputes. Japan, South Korea, Taiwan of China and other countries and regions, whose economic developed a lot in the region of East Asia, have experienced the period of sharp pollution conflicts caused by rapid economic development. These countries and regions

16 Songjie, H., "On the Path of the Reform of the System of Letters and Visits Under the Background of Social Transformation" [J/OL] *The Rule of Law Forum*. Access: http //bbs.chinaeoUrt.org/index.PhP?showtoPie=39039

17 Court-entrusted mediation means that the court gives the civil case out before or after the case is accepted to a specific organization or individual to host the mediation, also known as 'entrusted mediation' or 'send out mediation. See also Jiaxing, L. and P. Jianfeng, eds., *Civil Procedure Law Course*, Peking University Press, 2008, 178.

18 The formal establishment of the Court-entrusted mediation system began in August 18, 2004, the Provisions of the Supreme People's Court on Several Issues concerning the civil mediation work of the people's court. Thereafter, it was further clarified on March 1, 2007, in Opinions of the Supreme People's Court on making lawsuit mediation further essential in constructing harmonious socialist society.

have similar culture and social background to China, and they are all densely populated areas, so it is worthy for China to learning the environment dispute resolution mechanism from them. Considering the main problems of China's environmental complaint letters and visits system itself and the environmental dispute solution system of these countries and regions, the emphasis should be laid on setting up a specific dispute processing mechanism, and giving rights and authority to these mechanism to settle disputes.

## *4.1 Setting up specific organizations for environmental dispute processing*

### *4.1.1 Environmental public nuisance dispute coordination commission system in Japan*

In order to fill the requirements of pollution controlling and environmental protection, Japanese government issued the *Act of Public Nuisance Dispute Processing* in 1970, in which the provisions of the administrative system of environmental disputes were formulated. Based on the Act established systems of Environmental Public Nuisance Dispute Coordination Commission and Pollution Nuisance Affliction Talk. These two are similar to some extent to environmental complaint letters and visits system in China.

In the administration system, the central government set up the Public Nuisance Dispute Coordination Commission as higher leading bodies, and set up Department of Public Nuisance as a specific agency to deal with pollution complaints in every Prefectural county and city, town, township (including special district) of Japan. There are public nuisance mediators in Department of Public Nuisance. The Public Nuisance Dispute Coordination Commission shall be composed of a chairman and six committee members. They are appointed by Japanese prime minister after the approval of the Congress. In order to ensure the neutrality and independence of the Public Nuisance Dispute Coordination Commission, the role and function for the chairman and committee members within their term of office is protected by law and is not changed easily because of external interference.

### *4.1.2 Environmental dispute resolution commission in South Korea*

South Korea promulgated the '*Environmental Disputes Resolution Act*' (also known as the '*Environmental Pollution Victims Dispute Processing Law*') in 1997, in which entrenched the administrative settlement mechanism of environmental disputes. The Environmental Dispute Resolution Commission, which is established according to the Act, is the main body of administrative settlement mechanism of environmental disputes. The Commission is composed of two levels-the central level and the local level. The central level is appointed by the president of South Korea, and the local level is appointed by regional and district administrations.

### *4.1.3 Environmental dispute resolution agency in Taiwan*

In 1992, Taiwan promulgated the *Act of Public Nuisance Dispute Processing*. The Act provides: Environmental Protection Administration, Direct-controlled municipality and government of county (city) shall set up full-time personnel to handle with the following matters: (1) Dealing with pollution complaints. (2) Necessary investigations, guidance and suggestions for pollution complaint processing. (3) Directing the complainers to ask for mediation or arbitration in accordance with the procedures in the law.

According to *Measures for Environmental Complaint Letters and Visits* of China,[19] the department responsible for environmental letters and visits work is not an independent agency. It is an inner branch of administrative departments of the environmental protection, and has no post and power to deal with environmental disputes independently. In China's administrative management system, an agency without independent human resources, financial resources, or material resources cannot take responsibilities independently. Thus the capacity and final effect would be also greatly reduced in environmental disputes processing. In improving institutional settings of the environmental letters and visits mechanism, Environmental Complaint Letters and Visits Processing Center or Environmental Dispute Coordination Commission or other similar institutions can be considered to set in the Ministry of Environmental Protection, and environmental administrative organs at all levels set up the corresponding Environmental Complaint Letters and Visits Processing Center. Environmental administrative organs at all levels shall be responsible for the environmental disputes within their jurisdiction of the area under the principle of territorial jurisdiction, and environmental disputes crossing administrative areas should be solved by level jurisdiction. The Environmental Complaint Letters and Visits Processing Center should consist of staff working in the environmental administrative organs, judges in the people's court, environment experts, legal experts and people in environmental protection organizations and scientific and educational circles. Besides, representatives of area businesses and the masses and the neighbourhood committee staff are to be involved in the centre.

## *4.2 The power and the way to settle disputes of the environmental complaint letters and visits agency*

In order to fully handling environment disputes, we need not only environmental specialized agencies but also the corresponding power to settle environmental disputes.

Japan's '*Environmental Dispute Resolution Act*' provides for administrative handling of environmental disputes, including disputes nuisance good offices,

19 According to article 8 of *Measures for Environmental Complaint Letters and Visits of China*, only the provincial environmental protection departments, and the larger city divided into districts must set up a separate environmental letters and visits work agency.

mediation, arbitration and alternative dispute ruling and other solutions like administrative litigation lawsuit solution. Japan's pollution adjustment committee is responsible for handling environmental dispute complaints from the public, including ruling the causal relation of environmental disputes and the recognition.

Environmental Dispute Resolution Commission in accordance with South Korea's '*Environmental Dispute Settlement Law*', is engaged in environmental administrative dispute settlement body. The Committee, as a quasi-judicial body, has the power to make unilateral rulings resolution. Once the parties accept mediation of environmental disputes of the Commission's recommendations, environmental administrative system will be the only effective way to solve environmental disputes. South Korea's environmental dispute administrative solutions lie in three ways: pre-conciliation, mediation and arbitration. The first two do not produce legal effect unless the parties voluntarily submit conciliation committee; the latter have the force of law, the parties accept the agreement that will no longer bring a civil action. Early pre-mediation conciliation procedures, such as the parties to resolve the dispute in the early mediation program, we should no longer conduct the conciliation proceedings. Environmental pollution victims can apply directly for the arbitration procedure, but the Commission found that when mediation is more conducive to the settlement of disputes, arbitration proceedings may be terminated and conciliation proceedings begin. We can apply for civil proceedings to resolve when mediation and arbitration cannot solve disputes.

According to the relevant provisions of the Taiwan '*Environmental Dispute Resolution Act*', the committee dealing with public nuisance dispute mediation mainly concentrates on municipalities, counties, and the 'EPA' ruling committee. These two bodies "as the trial court level, are responsible for applying public nuisance dispute mediation and accept the award".[20] Visible, mediation and adjudication of environmental disputes has a statutory approach in Taiwan. Mediation means mediation committee should consult the parties dispute between the parties to mediate, to persuade the parties that can led to the two sides reached a settlement agreement; or at the request of the parties concerned bodies, to investigate the relevant facts of the dispute, and accordingly, make a mediation proposal, if the parties do not file an opposition within the specified time, then this program was established. Made after the establishment of a mediation and the mediation by the court review, it has the same effect with the court decision; the parties shall not sue for the same matter to the court again; the parties may also request the court to enforce a forced mediation.

According to the current China's '*Measures for Environmental Complaint Letters and Visits*', duties and powers of environmental petition mechanism are limited to receiving, forwarding and are assigned to coordinate environmental

20 Chi Yang, C., *Environmental Law Introduction*, China University of Political Science Press, Beijing, 2003, 304.

petitions process, its function is limited to procedural powers, and no independent functions and powers handle the environmental disputes, the result of which is dealing with environmental disputes petitions, it has no legally binding mechanism.[21] Thus, the petition agencies dealing with environmental disputes in effect of natural greatly reduced. In Japan, South Korea, China Taiwan and other environmental disputes mechanisms, they are able to play their dispute settlement functions because these institutions have a variety of means, including dispute settlement good offices, mediation, arbitration and award. South Korea's environmental disputes resolution board has authority to make unilateral decision resolution, which also has legal binding force, thus it will be more efficient in handling environmental disputes.

On the perfection of China's environmental petition mechanism of responsibility and authority, what we can do to explicitly deal with environmental disputes are mediation, adjudication and administrative arbitration (including the existing administrative rulings, decisions, etc.). First, the administrative mediation can take a variety of means like mediation, negotiation, etc. after complying with statutory procedures, conciliation statement has legal effect (given the mediation judicial settlement book like legal effect). If the mediation fails, the complaint handling institution has the right to exercise the power of administrative adjudication. Second, administrative rulings, according to the start of one of the parties the program can apply to start, it is a kind of quasi-judicial procedure. The identification of applicable law facts and solve disputes, there are essential differences between mediation and arbitration, as its specialized knowledge and technical means to ascertain facts based on time, it is different from judicial means, and it can be said to be an administrative trial. The main contents of the ruling include the determination of the cause of damage and the liability of tort, the remedy (mainly the amount of compensation) and the production of administrative adjudication, and the administrative adjudication should be legally binding.

### 4.3 *Chinese local legislation breakthrough in terms of environmental petition*

In fact, as early as the 1990s, many provinces of China has established rules on the development of effective environmental petitions and disputes regulations, through local legislation.[22] In 2014, the Sichuan Provincial Environmental Protection Bureau issued the "*Sichuan Environmental Dispute Mediation Level Management Rule*", based on making full use of existing environmental complaint handling mechanism. It clearly provides for the establishment of an environmental disputes body to exercise its functions:

21 See: *Environmental Petition Approach*, art. 10.

22 Such as: *Henan Environmental Pollution Disputes Interim Measures* (1991), *Hubei Environmental Dispute Mediation Rule* (1992), *Qinghai Environment Damage Compensation Dispute Mediation Rule* (1992), *Shandong Provincial Environmental Pollution Disputes Rule* (1994).

First, establish institutions to ensure professional environmental dispute resolution.

In the establishment of environmental disputes by the environmental protection, the State-owned Assets Supervision and Administration Commission, courts, prosecutors and other departments of the mediation on the basis of external linkage mechanism, and set up by the director in charge of the leadership within the environmental protection system, organs and relevant business department heads as members of provincial, city, professional and county environmental dispute mediation committee, responsible for the environment within the purview of dispute resolution organization and leadership and coordination. The mediation room is set up under the professional mediation committee, composed of authority relevant business departments to deploy professional, coordination, good mediation personnel, is mainly responsible for the investigation, study on the environmental disputes and resolve. The establishment of the township (neighbourhood) organizations, combined with the actual, full use of the township (neighbourhood) people's existing mediation and judicial mediation bodies, to determine the person responsible for the mediation of environmental disputes. In addition, the team building, environmental protection departments at all levels should broaden the channels, absorb the relevant departments and industry experts, lawyers, etc., to enrich the mediation team. On job security, dispute resolution requirements of the environmental budget funds into the sector.

Second, focus conferences to ensure that environmental disputes risk assessment standardized.

Environmental dispute developed risk assessment criteria is established, the requirements of the city (prefecture) and county (city, district), township (neighbourhood) levels are based on the length of time occurred within the jurisdiction of environmental disputes, the number of people involved, the degree of difficulty to resolve, at three risk assessment working days, according to grade I to grade III rating to determine environmental disputes. Events that may lead to environmental disputes, we require timely assessment and that clear the level of risk in one day and defuse the responsible units.

Third, hierarchical management, to ensure that resolve the responsibility to implement concreted.

'*Sichuan Provincial Environmental Dispute Mediation Level Management Rule*', the responsibility of environmental dispute mediation and classification management are divided. Evaluation for grade III environmental disputes organized by the environmental protection departments at or above the county level is clear about the villages and towns (street) to resolve, evaluations for grade II environmental disputes resolve the county (city, district) environmental protection departments coordination responsibilities units evaluations for environmental disputes in grade I are based on the municipal environmental protection departments' coordination responsibilities units to resolve. For the counties (cities, districts), involving multiple departments and municipal level major difficult environmental disputes, the municipal environmental protection department shall report to the people's government or mediation focal point, a clear linkage to defuse the lead and cooperative units to resolve. At the same time, we also implement a classification of environmental disputes dynamic management, for the environmental disputes have been assessed escalation of requirements, we must reassess and clear the level of risk and defuse the responsible units.

# Index

For Product Safety Concerns and Information please contact our EU
representative GPSR@taylorandfrancis.com
Taylor & Francis Verlag GmbH, Kaufingerstraße 24, 80331 München, Germany

www.ingramcontent.com/pod-product-compliance
Ingram Content Group UK Ltd.
Pitfield, Milton Keynes, MK11 3LW, UK
UKHW021302190926
475701UK00009B/584
* 9 7 8 0 3 6 7 8 8 8 7 2 5 *